EVERYDAY
Slow Cooker
& ONE-DISH RECIPES

TASTE OF HOME BOOKS • RDA ENTHUSIAST BRANDS, LLC • MILWAUKEE, WI

© 2022 RDA Enthusiast Brands, LLC.
1610 N. 2nd St., Suite 102, Milwaukee WI 53212-3906
All rights reserved. Taste of Home is a registered
trademark of RDA Enthusiast Brands, LLC.
Visit us at tasteofhome.com for other *Taste of Home*
books and products.

International Standard Book Number:
D 978-1-62145-864-7
U 978-1-62145-865-4

Component Number:
D 119400108H
U 119400110H

ISSN: 1944-6382

Executive Editor: Mark Hagen
Senior Art Director: Raeann Thompson
Senior Editors: Christine Rukavena, Julie Schnittka
Assistant Editor: Sammi DiVito
Senior Designer: Jazmin Delgado
Copy Editor: Cathy Jakicic
Food Editor: Rashanda Cobbins

Cover Photography
Photographer: Mark Derse
Set Stylist: Melissa Franco
Food Stylist: Shannon Norris

Pictured on front cover:
Mexican Street Corn Chowder, p. 65
Pictured on title page:
Cornish Hens with Potatoes, p. 33
Pictured on back cover:
Slow-Cooker Spiral Ham, p. 45
Easy Shrimp Stir-Fry, p. 146
Burger Sliders with Secret Sauce, p. 155

Printed in USA
10 9 8 7 6 5 4 3 2 1

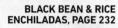

**BLACK BEAN & RICE
ENCHILADAS, PAGE 232**

Contents

Dig in to delicious (& doable) meals—every day!

Enjoy the classics and explore new flavors with the 321 easy, succulent recipes in this collection.

Generations of home cooks have relied on *Taste of Home* for the kind of great recipes Mom and Grandma used to make. And as the *Taste of Home* family gets bigger, our enormous recipe file continues to grow! Yes, you can turn here for classic meatball dishes, slow-cooked ribs and addictive cheesy dips. And you'll also find an irresistibly lightened-up white pizza (p. 183), delectable hoisin shrimp (p. 138), and good-for-you Mediterranean chickpeas (p. 236). Even as tastes evolve, our love for Mom's home cooking remains the same. So go ahead, treat the family to a new favorite tonight!

**CRAWFISH FETTUCCINE
PAGE 143**

HANDY ICONS IN THIS BOOK

🍎 Recipes are lower in calories, fat and/or sodium, as determined by a registered dietitian nutritionist.

❄ These fix-ahead dishes include directions for freezing and reheating.

17

68

Slow-Cook with Confidence

Follow these tips for slow-cooking success every time.

PLAN AHEAD TO PREP AND GO.
In most cases, you can prepare and load ingredients into the slow-cooker insert beforehand and store it in the refrigerator overnight. But an insert can crack if exposed to rapid temperature changes. Let the insert sit out just long enough to reach room temperature before placing in the slow cooker.

USE THAWED INGREDIENTS.
Although throwing frozen chicken breasts into the slow cooker may seem easy, it's not a smart shortcut. Thawing foods in a slow cooker can create the ideal environment for bacteria to grow, so thaw frozen meat and veggies ahead of time. The exception: If using a prepackaged slow-cooker meal kit, follow instructions as written.

LINE THE CROCK FOR EASE OF USE.
Some recipes in this book call for a **foil collar** or **sling**. Here's why:

▸ A **foil collar** prevents scorching of rich, saucy dishes near the slow cooker's heating element. To make a collar, fold two 18-in.-long pieces of foil into strips 4 in. wide. Line the crock's perimeter with the strips; spray with cooking spray.

▸ A **sling** helps you lift layered foods out of the crock without much fuss. To make, fold one or more pieces of heavy-duty foil into strips. Place on bottom and up side of the slow cooker; coat with cooking spray.

TAKE THE TIME TO BROWN.
Give yourself a few extra minutes to brown your meat in a skillet before placing in the slow cooker. Doing so will add rich color and more flavor to the finished dish.

KEEP THE LID CLOSED.
Don't peek! While it's tempting to lift the lid and check on your meal's progress, resist the urge. Every time you open the lid, you'll have to add about 30 minutes to the total cooking time.

ADJUST COOK TIME AS NEEDED.
Live at a high altitude? Slow-cooking will take longer. Add about 30 minutes for each hour of cooking the recipe calls for; legumes will take about twice as long.

Want your food done sooner? Cooking one hour on high is roughly equal to two hours on low, so adjust the recipe to suit your schedule.

Stovetop Suppers Are Super Convenient

Stovetop cooking is quick and easy. In fact, many of the stovetop meals in this book need just one pot, making cleanup a breeze. Haul out your favorite skillet and let's get cooking!

CHOOSE THE RIGHT PAN FOR THE JOB.

The right cookware can simplify meal preparation when cooking on the stovetop. The basic skillets every kitchen needs include a 10- or 12-in. skillet with lid and an 8- or 9-in. saute/omelet pan.

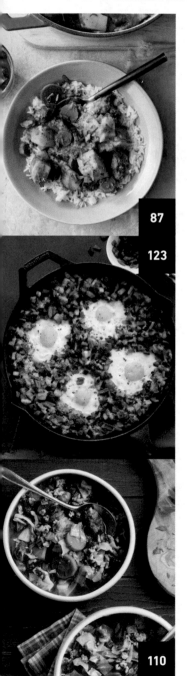

Good quality cookware conducts heat quickly and cooks food evenly. The type of metal and thickness of the pan affect performance. Consider these pros and cons for each of the most common cookware metals:

Copper does conduct heat the best, but it is expensive, tarnishes (and usually requires periodic polishing) and reacts with acidic ingredients, which is why the interior of a copper pan is usually lined with tin or stainless steel.

Aluminum is a good conductor of heat and is less expensive than copper. However, aluminum reacts with acidic ingredients.

Anodized aluminum has the same positive qualities as aluminum, but the surface is electrochemically treated so it will not react to acidic ingredients. The surface is resistant to scratches and is nonstick.

Cast iron conducts heat very well. It is usually heavy. Cast iron also needs regular seasoning to prevent sticking and rusting.

Nonstick is especially preferred for cooking delicate foods, such as eggs, pancakes or thin fish fillets. It won't scorch foods if you're cooking in batches. It can be scratched easily and has maximum temperature limitations.

Stainless steel is durable and retains its new look for years. It isn't a good conductor of heat, which is why it often has an aluminum or copper core or bottom.

MASTER THESE COMMON STOVETOP COOKING TECHNIQUES.

Sauteeing Add a small amount of oil to a hot skillet and heat over medium-high heat. For best results, cut food into uniform pieces before adding. Don't overcrowd in pan. Stir frequently while cooking.

Frying Pour ¼-½ in. oil into a skillet. Heat over medium-high heat until hot. The oil is ready when it shimmers (gives off visible waves of heat). Never leave the pan unattended, and don't overheat the oil or it will smoke. Pat food dry before frying and, if desired, dip in batter or coat it with crumbs. Fry, uncovered, until food is golden brown and cooked through.

Braising Season meat; coat with flour if recipe directs. In Dutch oven, brown meat in oil in batches. To ensure nice browning, do not crowd. Set meat aside; cook vegetables, adding flour if recipe directs. Add broth gradually, stirring to deglaze pan and to keep lumps from forming. Return meat to pan and stir until mixture comes to a boil.

Steaming Place a steamer basket or bamboo steamer in a pan with water. Bring water to a boil (boiling water shouldn't touch the steamer) and place food in the basket; cover and steam. Add more water to pan as necessary, making sure pan does not run dry.

157

Oven Entrees Bake Hands-Free

You can't beat a meal-in-one recipe for convenience and comfort. Review these hints while the oven preheats.

CHOOSE THE RIGHT BAKEWARE.

Metal baking pans Excellent conductors of heat, these create nice browning on rolls, coffee cakes and other baked goods. Metal is a safe, smart choice for under the broiler. It may react with acidic foods such as tomato sauce or cranberries and create a metallic taste or discoloration.

Glass baking dishes Glass provides slower, more even baking for egg dishes, custards and casseroles. It takes longer to heat than metal, but once heated, the dish holds the heat longer. This is undesirable for many desserts, as sugary batters may overbrown in glass. If you wish to bake in a glass dish even though the recipe calls for a metal pan, decrease the oven temperature by 25°.

Other baking dishes Ceramic or stoneware baking dishes generally perform much like glass but are more attractive. They may be safe for higher temperatures than glass; refer to the manufacturer's instructions.

CONFIRM THE OVEN'S TEMPERATURE.

Use an oven thermometer to check. Preheat oven to the desired temperature; place an oven thermometer on the center rack. Close the oven door and leave the oven on at the set temperature. Keep thermometer in the oven for 15 minutes before reading. Adjust the oven temperature accordingly to ensure best baking results.

ADJUST FOR HOT OR COOL SPOTS.

To test your oven for uneven temperatures, try the bread test. Heat the oven to 350° while arranging six to nine slices of white bread on a large cookie sheet. Place in oven for 5-10 minutes; check if the slices are starting to brown or burn. If some slices are noticeably darker or lighter than others, the oven may have hot or cool spots. To adjust for these, rotate pans while baking.

ELIMINATE SPILLS—THE SMART WAY.

Line a rimmed baking sheet with foil and place it on the bottom oven rack directly below the baking dish. Any drips or spills from the recipe will fall onto the foil-lined pan instead of the oven bottom.

We don't recommend lining the bottom of your oven with aluminum foil or other liners, as there's a chance that they could melt and stick to the oven, causing damage.

Want to clean up a drip while it's still hot? Grab your oven mitt, a pair of tongs and a damp dishcloth. Move the cloth with the tongs to help prevent burns.

188

VEGAN CHILI OLE!
PAGE 59

27

45

52

68

Slow Cooker

One of the things we love most about the slow cooker is how it turns affordable cuts of meat, including round steak and pork shoulder, into tender, scrumptious meals. It works wonders with other thrifty choices, such as dried beans and oatmeal, too. And for entertaining ease, nothing beats a set-and-forget recipe served up warm, right out of the crock!

Beef & Ground Beef

OLD-FASHIONED
POOR MAN'S STEAK

OLD-FASHIONED POOR MAN'S STEAK

These flavorful steaks fit into everybody's budget. A special friend shared the recipe, and I think of her each time I make it.
—Susan Wright, Mineral Wells, WV

PREP: 25 min. + chilling • **COOK:** 4 hours
MAKES: 9 servings

- 1 cup crushed saltine crackers (about 30 crackers)
- ⅓ cup water
  Salt and pepper to taste
- 2 lbs. ground beef
- ¼ cup all-purpose flour
- 2 Tbsp. canola oil
- 2 cans (10¾ oz. each) condensed cream of mushroom soup, undiluted
  Hot mashed potatoes or noodles
  Minced fresh parsley, optional

1. In a large bowl, combine the cracker crumbs, water, salt and pepper. Crumble beef over the mixture and mix lightly but thoroughly. Press into an ungreased 9-in. square pan. Cover and refrigerate for at least 3 hours.

2. Cut into 3-in. squares; dredge in flour. In a large skillet, heat oil over medium heat; add beef and cook until browned on both sides, 2-3 minutes on each side.

3. Transfer to a 3-qt. slow cooker with a slotted spatula or spoon. Add the soup.

4. Cover and cook on high 4 hours or until meat is no longer pink, . Serve with mashed potatoes or noodles. If desired, top with minced parsley.

1 serving: 292 cal., 18g fat (6g sat. fat), 68mg chol., 372mg sod., 10g carb. (1g sugars, 1g fiber), 22g pro.

"Delicious home-cooked comfort food! Instead of using the slow cooker, I baked it in the oven at 350° for about an hour."
—JETLUVS2COOK, TASTEOFHOME.COM

TENDER STEAK FAJITAS

MEAL-IN-ONE CASSEROLE

Salsa gives zip to this hearty fix-and-forget-it meal. The vrecipe makes more than my husband and I can eat, so I freeze half of it. We think it tastes even better the second time.
—*Dorothy Pritchett, Wills Point, TX*

- -

PREP: 15 min. • **COOK:** 4 hours
MAKES: 6 servings

- 1   lb. ground beef
- 1   medium onion, chopped
- 1   medium green pepper, chopped
- 1   can (15¼ oz.) whole kernel corn, drained
- 1   can (4 oz.) mushroom stems and pieces, drained
- 1   tsp. salt
- ¼   tsp. pepper
- 1⅓ cups salsa
- 5   cups cooked medium egg noodles
- 1   can (28 oz.) diced tomatoes, undrained
- 1   cup water
- 1   cup shredded cheddar cheese or blend of cheddar, Monterey Jack and American cheese

1. In a large skillet, cook beef and onion over medium heat until meat is no longer pink; drain.
2. Transfer to a 5-qt. slow cooker. Top with the green pepper, corn and mushrooms. Sprinkle with salt and pepper. Pour salsa over mushrooms. Top with noodles. Pour tomatoes and water over all. Sprinkle with the cheese.
3. Cover and cook on low until heated through, about 4 hours.
1 serving: 421 cal., 14g fat (7g sat. fat), 87mg chol., 1240mg sod., 44g carb. (12g sugars, 7g fiber), 25g pro.

TENDER STEAK FAJITAS

Flank steak turns out tender, juicy and flavorful in the slow cooker when I make these tempting fajitas. I like to serve them with a side of Spanish rice.
—*Twila Burkholder, Middleburg, PA*

- -

PREP: 20 min. • **COOK:** 6 hours
MAKES: 6 servings

- 1   beef flank steak (1½ lbs.)
- 1   medium onion, sliced
- 1   cup tomato juice
- 1   jalapeno pepper, seeded and chopped
- 2   garlic cloves, minced
- 1   Tbsp. minced fresh cilantro
- 1   tsp. ground cumin
- 1   tsp. chili powder
- ¼   tsp. salt
- 1   medium green pepper, julienned
- 1   medium sweet red pepper, julienned
- 6   flour tortillas (8 in.), warmed

Optional: Shredded cheddar cheese, sour cream and guacamole

1. Thinly slice steak across the grain into strips; place in a 5-qt. slow cooker. Add the onion, tomato juice, jalapeno, garlic, cilantro, cumin, chili powder and salt. Cover and cook on low for 5 hours.
2. Add green and red peppers. Cover and cook 1 hour longer or until meat and vegetables are tender.
3. Using a slotted spoon, center meat mixture on each tortilla. Sprinkle with cheese if desired. Fold sides of tortilla over filling. Serve with sour cream and guacamole if desired.
Note: Wear disposable gloves when cutting hot peppers; the oils can burn skin. Avoid touching your face.
1 fajita: 340 cal., 12g fat (4g sat. fat), 48mg chol., 549mg sod., 33g carb. (4g sugars, 2g fiber), 25g pro. **Diabetic exchanges:** 3 lean meat, 2 starch, 1 vegetable.

ALL-DAY MEATBALL STEW

TEXAS-STYLE BEEF BRISKET

A friend had success with this recipe, so I tried it. When my husband told me how much he loved it, I knew I'd be making it often.
—*Vivian Warner, Elkhart, KS*

- -

PREP: 25 min. + marinating
COOK: 6½ hours • **MAKES:** 12 servings

- 3   Tbsp. Worcestershire sauce
- 1   Tbsp. chili powder
- 2   garlic cloves, minced
- 1   tsp. celery salt
- 1   tsp. pepper
- 1   tsp. liquid smoke, optional
- 1   fresh beef brisket (6 lbs.)
- ½   cup beef broth
- 2   bay leaves

BARBECUE SAUCE
- 1   medium onion, chopped
- 2   Tbsp. canola oil
- 2   garlic cloves, minced
- 1   cup ketchup
- ½   cup molasses
- ¼   cup cider vinegar
- 2   tsp. chili powder
- ½   tsp. ground mustard

1. In a large bowl or shallow dish, combine Worcestershire sauce, chili powder, garlic, celery salt, pepper and, if desired, liquid smoke. Cut brisket in half; add to bowl and turn to coat. Cover and refrigerate brisket overnight.
2. Transfer beef to a 5- or 6-qt. slow cooker; add broth and bay leaves. Cover and cook on low for 6-8 hours or until meat is tender.
3. For sauce, in a small saucepan, saute onion in oil until tender. Add garlic; cook 1 minute longer. Stir in the remaining ingredients; heat through.
4. Remove brisket from the slow cooker; discard bay leaves. Place 1 cup cooking juices in a measuring cup; skim fat. Add to barbecue sauce. Discard remaining juices.
5. Return brisket to the slow cooker; top with sauce mixture. Cover and cook on high for 30 minutes to allow flavors to blend. Thinly slice beef across the grain; serve with sauce.
6 oz. cooked beef with ¼ cup sauce:
381 cal., 12g fat (4g sat. fat), 96mg chol., 548mg sod., 18g carb. (14g sugars, 1g fiber), 47g pro.

❄

ALL-DAY MEATBALL STEW

Frozen meatballs and other convenient ingredients simplify this homey stew. Each bite boasts lots of fresh veggie flavor and comforting, rich gravy. It cooks all day and smells so good, it's hard to resist!
—*Anita Hoffman, Holland, PA*

- -

PREP: 20 min. • **COOK:** 8½ hours
MAKES: 8 servings (3 qt.)

- 2   pkg. (12 oz. each) frozen fully cooked Italian meatballs
- 5   medium potatoes, peeled and cubed
- 1   lb. fresh baby carrots
- 1   medium onion, halved and sliced
- 1   jar (4½ oz.) sliced mushrooms, drained
- 2   cans (8 oz. each) tomato sauce
- 1   can (10½ oz.) condensed beef broth, undiluted
- ¾   cup water
- ¾   cup dry red wine or beef broth
- ½   tsp. garlic powder
- ¼   tsp. pepper
- 2   Tbsp. all-purpose flour
- ½   cup cold water

1. Place the meatballs, potatoes, carrots, onion and mushrooms in a 5- or 6-qt. slow cooker. In a large bowl, combine the tomato sauce, broth, water, wine, garlic powder and pepper; pour over top. Cover and cook on low until vegetables are tender, 8-10 hours.
2. Combine flour and water until smooth; gradually stir into stew. Cover and cook on high until thickened, about 30 minutes.
Freeze option: Freeze cooled stew in freezer containers. To use, partially thaw in refrigerator overnight. Heat through in a saucepan, stirring occasionally; add broth if necessary.
1½ cups: 384 cal., 20g fat (9g sat. fat), 41mg chol., 1317mg sod., 35g carb. (7g sugars, 5g fiber), 19g pro.

TEXAS-STYLE
BEEF BRISKET

SLOW-COOKER BEEF AU JUS

It's easy to fix this roast, which has lots of onion flavor. Sometimes I also add cubed potatoes and baby carrots to the slow cooker to make a terrific meal with plenty of leftovers.

—*Carol Hille, Grand Junction, CO*

- -

PREP: 20 min. • **COOK:** 6 hours + standing
MAKES: 10 servings

- 1   beef rump roast or bottom round roast (3 lbs.)
- 1   large onion, sliced
- ¾   cup reduced-sodium beef broth
- 1   envelope (1 oz.) au jus gravy mix
- 2   garlic cloves, halved
- ¼   tsp. pepper

1. Cut roast in half. In a large skillet coated with cooking spray, brown the meat on all sides over medium-high heat.
2. Place onion in a 5-qt. slow cooker. Top with meat. Combine the broth, gravy mix, garlic and pepper; pour over meat. Cover and cook on low for 6-7 hours or until meat is tender.
3. Remove meat to a cutting board. Let stand for 10 minutes. Thinly slice meat and return to the slow cooker; serve with cooking juices and onion.
3 oz. cooked beef: 188 cal., 7g fat (2g sat. fat), 82mg chol., 471mg sod., 3g carb. (0 sugars, 0 fiber), 28g pro.

🍎 MUSHROOM STEAK

Usually, I'd make this dish in the oven. But when I knew I wouldn't have time for it to bake one night, I let it simmer all day in the slow cooker and had great results.

—*Sandy Pettinger, Lincoln, NE*

- -

PREP: 20 min. • **COOK:** 7 hours
MAKES: 6 servings

- ⅓   cup all-purpose flour
- ½   tsp. salt
- ½   tsp. pepper, divided
- 1   beef top round steak (2 lbs.), cut into 1½-in. strips
- 2   cups sliced fresh mushrooms
- 1   small onion, cut into thin wedges
- 1   can (10¾ oz.) condensed golden mushroom soup, undiluted
- ¼   cup sherry or beef broth
- ½   tsp. dried oregano
- ¼   tsp. dried thyme
    Hot cooked egg noodles

1. In a large resealable container, combine the flour, salt and ¼ tsp. pepper. Add beef, a few pieces at a time, and shake to coat.
2. In a 3-qt. slow cooker, combine the mushrooms, onion and beef. Combine the soup, sherry, oregano, thyme and remaining pepper; pour over top. Cover and cook on low until the beef is tender, 7-9 hours. Serve with noodles.
¾ cup: 265 cal., 6g fat (2g sat. fat), 87mg chol., 612mg sod., 12g carb. (1g sugars, 1g fiber), 36g pro. **Diabetic exchanges:** 5 lean meat, 1 starch.

"This turned out well. I didn't have 7 hours, so after dipping the meat in flour mixture, I seared it in the skillet. Nice flavor!"
—MARILYNM, TASTEOFHOME.COM

MUSHROOM STEAK

POMEGRANATE
SHORT RIBS

CORNED BEEF & CABBAGE FOR THE WINE LOVER

With its rich, elegant flavor and lovely appearance, you'd never guess how easy it is to prepare this traditional St. Patrick's Day favorite. Thanks to the slow cooker, it comes together effortlessly.
—*Susan Cepeda, Miami Lakes, FL*

PREP: 25 min. • **COOK:** 8 hours
MAKES: 6 servings

- ¾ lb. fingerling potatoes, cut in half
- 2 cups fresh baby carrots
- 2 medium onions, cut into wedges
- 4 garlic cloves, minced
- 1½ cups white wine or beef broth
- 1 corned beef brisket with spice packet (3 to 3½ lbs.)
- ½ cup stone-ground mustard
- 1 small head cabbage, cut into thin wedges
- 1 can (14 oz.) sauerkraut, rinsed and well drained

1. In a 6- or 7-qt. slow cooker, combine the potatoes, carrots, onions and garlic. Pour wine over vegetables. Cut brisket in half. Spread with mustard; place over vegetables (discard spice packet from corned beef or save for another use).
2. Cover and cook on low until meat and vegetables are tender, 8-10 hours, adding cabbage and sauerkraut during the last hour of cooking. Serve beef with vegetables.
5 oz. cooked beef with 1½ cups vegetables: 592 cal., 32g fat (10g sat. fat), 156mg chol., 2712mg sod., 32g carb. (13g sugars, 8g fiber), 35g pro.

TEST KITCHEN TIP
Use what you have on hand for this simple recipe. Cut-up regular carrots and chopped red potatoes will work just fine.

POMEGRANATE SHORT RIBS

I like drizzling the pomegranate molasses sauce on top of simple roasted vegetables. It's a bit tangy and a bit sweet, and adds a nice depth of flavor to sweet and savory dishes alike. Pomegranate molasses can be found in specialty food stores or online.
—*Shannon Sarna, South Orange, NJ*

PREP: 25 min. + chilling • **COOK:** 6 hours
MAKES: 8 servings

- 1 tsp. salt
- ½ tsp. ground cinnamon
- ½ tsp. pepper
- ¼ tsp. ground coriander
  Dash crushed red pepper flakes
- 8 bone-in beef short ribs (about 4 lbs.)
- 2 Tbsp. safflower oil
- 1 medium onion, chopped
- 3 garlic cloves, minced
- 1 Tbsp. tomato paste
- 1½ cups dry red wine or pomegranate juice
- 1½ cups chicken or beef stock
- ⅓ cup pomegranate molasses
- 3 Tbsp. soy sauce, optional

Minced fresh parsley and pomegranate seeds

1. Combine the first 5 ingredients; rub over ribs. Refrigerate, covered, at least 2 hours. In a large skillet, heat oil over medium heat. Brown ribs on all sides in batches. Transfer to a 5-qt. slow cooker. Discard drippings, reserving 2 Tbsp. Add onion to drippings; cook and stir over medium-high heat until tender, 8-10 minutes. Add garlic and tomato paste; cook 1 minute longer.
2. Add wine to pan; increase heat to medium-high. Cook 10 minutes until slightly thickened, stirring to loosen browned bits from pan. Transfer to slow cooker. Add the stock, molasses and, if desired, soy sauce, making sure ribs are fully submerged in liquid. Cook, covered, on low 6-8 hours or until ribs are tender. Serve the short ribs with parsley and pomegranate seeds.
1 short rib: 267 cal., 14g fat (5g sat. fat), 55mg chol., 428mg sod., 11g carb. (7g sugars, 0 fiber), 19g pro.

SPICY
TACO MEAT

SPICY TACO MEAT

My husband and I love Tex-Mex food with all the fixings. Cooking the meat in the slow cooker makes prepping the toppings a breeze. We love to make this for parties, keeping the filling warm in the slow cooker and serving the various toppings in bowls so the guests can build their own.

—Rebecca Yankovich, Springfield, VA

PREP: 20 min. • **COOK:** 6 hours
MAKES: 12 servings

- 1 boneless beef chuck roast (4 lbs.)
- 1 tsp. salt
- 1 tsp. pepper
- 1 Tbsp. olive oil
- 1 bottle (12 oz.) beer or
  1 cup beef broth
- 1 can (28 oz.) pickled jalapeno peppers, undrained
- 1 large onion, chopped
- 1 tsp. garlic powder
- 1 tsp. chili powder
  Optional: Corn tortillas (6 in.), crumbled Cotija cheese, lime wedges, fresh cilantro leaves, sliced radishes and sour cream

1. Sprinkle roast with salt and pepper. In a large skillet, heat oil over medium-high heat; brown meat. Transfer the meat to a 5- or 6-qt. slow cooker. Add beer to skillet, stirring to loosen browned bits from pan; pour over meat. In a large bowl, combine jalapenos, onion, garlic powder and chili powder; pour over meat. Cook, covered, on low until tender, 6-8 hours.
2. Remove the roast; shred with 2 forks. Strain cooking juices. Reserve vegetables and 2 cups juices; discard the remaining juices. Skim fat from reserved juices. Return beef and reserved vegetables and cooking juices to the slow cooker; heat through. If desired, serve with optional ingredients.
Freeze option: Freeze cooled meat mixture and juices in freezer containers. To use, partially thaw the mixture in refrigerator overnight. Heat through in a saucepan, stirring occasionally, add water if necessary.
½ cup cooked meat mixture: 307 cal., 21g fat (6g sat. fat), 98mg chol., 829mg sod., 10g carb. (1g sugars, 1g fiber), 31g pro.

SLOW-COOKED
BEEF & VEGGIES

SLOW-COOKED BEEF & VEGGIES

 My husband and I came up with this soothing slow-cooker recipe. It's simple and satisfying with lots of flavor.

—LaDonna Reed, Ponca City, OK

PREP: 15 min. + marinating
COOK: 8 hours • **MAKES:** 2 servings

- 1 boneless beef top round steak (½ lb.), cut into 2 pieces
  Dash seasoned salt, optional
  Dash pepper
  Dash garlic powder
- 1 cup Italian salad dressing
- ½ cup water
- 1 Tbsp. browning sauce, optional
- 2 medium carrots, cut into 2-in. pieces
- 2 medium red potatoes, cubed
- 1 small onion, sliced
- ½ small green pepper, cut into small chunks

1. Sprinkle 1 side of each piece of steak with seasoned salt, if desired, and pepper; sprinkle other side with the garlic powder. Cover and refrigerate steaks for 2-3 hours or overnight.
2. In a 3-qt. slow cooker, combine the salad dressing, water and, if desired, browning sauce. Add the carrots and potatoes; toss to coat. Add steak and coat with sauce. Top with onion and green pepper.
3. Cover and cook on low until meat is tender, 8-9 hours.
1 serving: 505 cal., 22g fat (3g sat. fat), 63mg chol., 1283mg sod., 36g carb. (14g sugars, 5g fiber), 29g pro.

BEEFY AU GRATIN POTATOES

You can vary the taste of this family-favorite casserole by using different soups and potato mixes. I usually dish out hearty helpings with a salad and garlic bread.
—*Eileen Majerus, Pine Island, MN*

PREP: 20 min. • **COOK:** 4 hours
MAKES: 6 servings

- 1 pkg. (5¼ oz.) au gratin potatoes or cheddar and bacon potatoes
- 1 can (15¼ oz.) whole kernel corn, drained
- 1 can (10¾ oz.) condensed cream of potato soup, undiluted
- 1 cup water
- 1 can (4 oz.) chopped green chiles, drained
- 1 can (4 oz.) mushroom stems and pieces, drained
- 1 jar (4 oz.) diced pimientos, drained
- 1 lb. ground beef
- 1 medium onion, chopped

1. Set potato sauce mix aside. Place potatoes in a 3-qt. slow cooker; top with corn. In a bowl, combine soup, water, chiles, mushrooms, pimientos and reserved sauce mix. Mix well and pour a third of the mixture over corn.
2. In a large skillet, cook beef and onion over medium heat until the meat is no longer pink and onion is tender, 5-7 minutes, breaking up the beef into crumbles; drain. Transfer to slow cooker.
3. Top with remaining sauce mixture. Do not stir. Cover and cook on low until potatoes are tender, about 4 hours.
1 serving: 358 cal., 12g fat (4g sat. fat), 54mg chol., 1256mg sod., 38g carb. (6g sugars, 4g fiber), 20g pro.

TEST KITCHEN TIP

Pimientos are roasted sweet red peppers with the skins removed. Store unopened jars in a cool dark place for up to a year. Once opened, refrigerate and use within 2 weeks.

❄

BEEF BARBECUE

We like to keep our freezer stocked with plenty of beef roasts. When we're not in the mood for pot roast, I fix satisfying sandwiches instead. The meat cooks in a tasty sauce while I'm at work. Then I just shred the beef and serve it on rolls with the sauce.
—*Karen Walker, Sterling, VA*

PREP: 5 min. • **COOK:** 6 hours 20 min.
MAKES: 12 servings

- 1 boneless beef chuck roast (3 lbs.)
- 1 cup barbecue sauce
- ½ cup apricot preserves
- ⅓ cup chopped green or sweet red pepper
- 1 small onion, chopped
- 1 Tbsp. Dijon mustard
- 2 tsp. brown sugar
   Sandwich rolls, optional

1. Cut the roast into quarters; place in a greased 5-qt. slow cooker. In a bowl, combine barbecue sauce, preserves, green pepper, onion, mustard and brown sugar; pour over roast. Cover and cook on low until meat is tender, 6-8 hours.
2. Remove roast. When cool enough to handle, shred meat with 2 forks; return to slow cooker and stir gently. Cook, covered, 20-30 minutes longer. Skim fat from the sauce. Serve beef and sauce on sandwich rolls if desired.
Freeze option: Freeze cooled beef mixture in freezer containers. To use, partially thaw in refrigerator overnight. Heat through in a covered saucepan, stirring occasionally; add broth if necessary.
3 oz. cooked beef: 218 cal., 7g fat (0 sat. fat), 78mg chol., 253mg sod., 11g carb. (0 sugars, 1g fiber), 26g pro.

BEEF BARBECUE

GRANDMA'S
OXTAIL STEW

GRANDMA'S OXTAIL STEW

This wonderfully rich soup will warm your soul and your taste buds. Oxtail stew is a favorite family heirloom recipe. Don't let the name of this dish turn you off. Oxtail describes the meaty part of the ox tail (now commonly cow). It is delicious but requires long and slow cooking.
— *Bobbie Keefer, Byers, CO*

- -

PREP: 20 min. • **COOK:** 10 hours
MAKES: 8 servings (3 qt.)

2 lbs. oxtails, trimmed
2 Tbsp. olive oil
4 medium carrots, sliced (about 2 cups)
1 medium onion, chopped
2 garlic cloves, minced
2 cans (14½ oz. each) diced tomatoes, undrained

1 can (15 oz.) beef broth
3 bay leaves
1 tsp. salt
1 tsp. dried oregano
½ tsp. dried thyme
½ tsp. pepper
6 cups chopped cabbage

1. In a large skillet, brown oxtails in oil over medium heat. Remove from pan; place in a 5-qt. slow cooker.
2. Add carrots and onion to the pan drippings; the cook and stir until just softened, 3-5 minutes. Add garlic, cook 1 minute longer. Transfer the vegetable mixture to slow cooker. Add tomatoes, broth, bay leaves, salt, oregano, thyme and pepper; stir to combine.
3. Cook, covered, on low 8 hours. Add the cabbage, cook until cabbage is tender and meat pulls away easily from bones, about 2 hours longer. Remove oxtails; set aside

until cool enough to handle. Remove meat from bones; discard bones and shred meat. Return meat to soup. Discard the bay leaves.

Freeze option: Freeze cooled stew in freezer containers. To use, partially thaw in refrigerator overnight. Heat through in a saucepan, stirring occasionally; add broth if necessary.

1½ cups: 204 cal., 10g fat (3g sat. fat), 34mg chol., 705mg sod., 14g carb. (8g sugars, 5g fiber), 16g pro.

SLOW-SIMMERING BEEF BOURGUIGNON

SLOW-COOKED RUMP ROAST

I enjoy a good pot roast, but was tired of the same old thing. So, I began experimenting. Cooking beef in horseradish sauce gives it a tangy flavor. Even my young children love this roast with its tender veggies and gravy.
—*Mimi Walker, Palmyra, PA*

PREP: 20 min. • **COOK:** 8½ hours
MAKES: 8 servings

- 1   beef rump roast or bottom round roast (3 to 3½ lbs.)
- 2   Tbsp. canola oil
- 4   medium carrots, halved lengthwise and cut into 2-in. pieces
- 3   medium potatoes, peeled and cut into chunks
- 2   small onions, sliced
- ½   cup water
- 6   to 8 Tbsp. horseradish sauce
- ¼   cup red wine vinegar
- ¼   cup Worcestershire sauce
- 2   garlic cloves, minced
- 1½ to 2 tsp. celery salt
- 3   Tbsp. cornstarch
- ⅓   cup cold water

1. In a large skillet, brown roast on all sides in oil over medium-high heat; drain. Place carrots and potatoes in a 5-qt. slow cooker. Top with the meat and onions. Combine the water, horseradish sauce, vinegar, Worcestershire sauce, garlic and celery salt; pour over meat. Cover; cook on low until meat and vegetables are tender, about 8 hours.

2. Combine cornstarch and cold water until smooth; stir into slow cooker. Cover and cook on high until gravy is thickened, about 30 minutes.

Freeze option: Freeze cooled beef and vegetable mixture in freezer containers. To use, partially thaw roast in refrigerator overnight. Microwave, covered, on high in a microwave-safe dish until heated through, stirring gently.

1 serving: 378 cal., 15g fat (3g sat. fat), 113mg chol., 507mg sod., 23g carb. (6g sugars, 2g fiber), 35g pro. **Diabetic exchanges:** 4 lean meat, 1½ starch, 1 fat.

SLOW-SIMMERING BEEF BOURGUIGNON

Warm up cold days with tender chunks of beef simmered in a rich sauce. Serve over steaming noodles.
—*Adele Zuerner, Arden, NC*

PREP: 30 min. • **COOK:** 8 hours
MAKES: 6 servings

- 3   lbs. beef stew meat
- ¾   tsp. salt
- ¾   tsp. pepper
- 3   Tbsp. all-purpose flour
- 1½ cups beef broth
- 1½ cups dry red wine or additional beef broth, divided
- ¾   lb. medium fresh mushrooms, quartered
- 1   large sweet onion, chopped
- 2   medium carrots, sliced
- 1   thick-sliced bacon strip, chopped
- 2   garlic cloves, minced
- 2   Tbsp. Italian tomato paste
     Hot cooked egg noodles

1. Sprinkle beef with salt and pepper. In a large skillet coated with cooking spray, brown beef in batches. Remove with a slotted spoon to a 4- or 5-qt slow cooker. Add flour; toss to coat. Add the broth and 1 cup wine.

2. In the same skillet, add mushrooms, onion, carrots and bacon; cook and stir over medium heat until the carrots are tender. Add garlic; cook 1 minute longer. Add remaining wine, stirring to loosen browned bits from pan; stir in tomato paste. Transfer to slow cooker.

3. Cover and cook on low until beef is tender, 8-10 hours. Serve with noodles.
1½ cups: 428 cal., 20g fat (7g sat. fat), 145mg chol., 843mg sod., 13g carb. (4g sugars, 1g fiber), 47g pro.

SLOW-COOKED
RUMP ROAST

BEEF IN ONION GRAVY

I double this super recipe to feed our family of four so I'm sure to have leftovers to send with my husband to work for lunch. His co-workers tell him he's lucky to have someone who fixes him such special meals. It's our secret that it's an easy slow-cooker dinner!
—*Denise Albers, Freeburg, IL*

- -

PREP: 5 min. + standing • **COOK:** 6 hours
MAKES: 3 servings

- 1 can (10¾ oz.) condensed cream of mushroom soup, undiluted
- 2 Tbsp. onion soup mix
- 2 Tbsp. beef broth
- 1 Tbsp. quick-cooking tapioca
- 1 lb. beef stew meat, cut into 1-in. cubes
       Hot cooked noodles or mashed potatoes

In a 1½-qt. slow cooker, combine the soup, soup mix, broth and tapioca; let stand for 15 minutes. Stir in the beef. Cover and cook on low for 6-8 hours or until meat is tender. Serve the beef over noodles or mashed potatoes.
1 serving: 326 cal., 15g fat (6g sat. fat), 98mg chol., 1220mg sod., 14g carb. (1g sugars, 1g fiber), 31g pro.

MUSHROOM & STEAK STROGANOFF

I rely on this recipe when we have family visiting. I put it in the slow cooker in the morning and when we get home from sightseeing all day, it's ready!
—*Marilyn Shehane, Colorado Springs, CO*

- -

PREP: 15 min. • **COOK:** 6¼ hours
MAKES: 6 servings

- 2 Tbsp. all-purpose flour
- ½ tsp. garlic powder
- ½ tsp. pepper
- ¼ tsp. paprika
- 1¾ lbs. beef top round steak, cut into 1½-in. strips
- 1 can (10¾ oz.) condensed cream of mushroom soup, undiluted
- ½ cup water
- ¼ cup Lipton onion mushroom soup mix
- 2 jars (4½ oz. each) sliced mushrooms, drained
- ½ cup sour cream
- 1 Tbsp. minced fresh parsley
       Hot cooked egg noodles, optional

1. In a large resealable container, combine flour, garlic powder, pepper and paprika. Add beef strips and shake to coat.
2. Transfer to a 3-qt. slow cooker. Combine the soup, water and soup mix; pour over beef. Cover and cook on low until meat is tender, 6-7 hours.
3. Stir in the mushrooms, sour cream and parsley. Cover and cook until sauce is thickened, 15 minutes longer. If desired, serve with noodles.
1 cup: 281 cal., 11g fat (4g sat. fat), 90mg chol., 853mg sod., 11g carb. (2g sugars, 2g fiber), 32g pro.

MUSHROOM & STEAK STROGANOFF

POT ROAST
HASH

HEARTY SHORT RIBS

The whole family will love these ribs! The meat is so tender, it will simply fall off the bone, and the gravy is perfect with either mashed potatoes or rice.
—*Helena Ivy, St. Louis, MO*

PREP: 15 min. • **COOK:** 6 hours
MAKES: 6 servings

- 1 large onion, sliced
- 4 lbs. bone-in beef short ribs
- ½ lb. sliced fresh mushrooms
- 1 can (10¾ oz.) condensed cream of mushroom soup, undiluted
- ½ cup water
- 1 envelope brown gravy mix
- 1 tsp. minced garlic
- ½ tsp. dried thyme
- 1 Tbsp. cornstarch
- 2 Tbsp. cold water
  Hot mashed potatoes

1. Place onion in a 5-qt. slow cooker; top with ribs. Combine the mushrooms, soup, ½ cup water, gravy mix, garlic and thyme; pour over ribs. Cover and cook on low until meat is tender, 6-6½ hours.
2. Remove meat to serving platter; keep warm. Skim the fat from cooking juices; transfer to a small saucepan. Bring juices to a boil.
3. Combine the cornstarch and cold water until smooth. Gradually stir into pan. Bring to a boil. Cook and stir until thickened, about 2 minutes. Serve with mashed potatoes.
1 serving: 317 cal., 18g fat (7g sat. fat), 75mg chol., 769mg sod., 12g carb. (3g sugars, 1g fiber), 27g pro.

❄️
POT ROAST HASH

I love to cook a Sunday-style pot roast on a weeknight. Make it into pot roast hash for any day of the week.
—*Gina Jackson, Ogdensburg, NY*

PREP: 6¼ hours • **COOK:** 15 min.
MAKES: 10 servings

- 1 cup warm water
- 1 Tbsp. beef base
- ½ lb. sliced fresh mushrooms
- 1 large onion, coarsely chopped
- 3 garlic cloves, minced
- 1 boneless beef chuck roast (3 lbs.)
- ½ tsp. pepper
- 1 Tbsp. Worcestershire sauce
- 1 pkg. (28 oz.) frozen potatoes O'Brien

EGGS
- 2 Tbsp. butter
- 10 large eggs
- ½ tsp. salt
- ½ tsp. pepper
  Minced chives

1. In a 5- or 6-qt. slow cooker, whisk water and beef base; add mushrooms, onion and garlic. Sprinkle roast with pepper; transfer to slow cooker. Drizzle mixture with Worcestershire sauce. Cook, covered, on low 6-8 hours or until meat is tender.
2. Remove roast; cool slightly. Shred the meat with 2 forks. In a large skillet, cook the potatoes according to the package directions; stir in shredded beef. Using a slotted spoon, add vegetables from slow cooker to the skillet; heat through. Discard the cooking juices.
3. For the eggs, in another skillet, heat 1 Tbsp. butter over medium-high heat. Break 5 eggs, 1 at a time, into pan. Sprinkle with half of the salt and pepper. Reduce heat to low. Cook until desired doneness, turning after whites are set if desired. Repeat with remaining butter, eggs, salt and pepper. Serve eggs over hash; sprinkle with chives.
Freeze option: Place shredded pot roast and vegetables in a freezer container; top with cooking juices. Cool and freeze. To use, partially thaw in refrigerator overnight. Heat through in a covered saucepan.
⅔ cup hash with 1 egg: 429 cal., 24g fat (8g sat. fat), 281mg chol., 306mg sod., 15g carb. (2g sugars, 2g fiber), 35g pro.

SOUTHERN
POT ROAST

❄ SOUTHERN POT ROAST

Cajun seasoning adds kick to this tender beef roast. I serve it with a corn and tomato mixture. It is an unusual dish, but it's full of flavor.
—*Amber Zurbrugg, Alliance, OH*

- -

PREP: 10 min. • **COOK:** 5 hours
MAKES: 5 servings

- 1   boneless beef chuck roast (2½ lbs.)
- 1   Tbsp. Cajun seasoning
- 1   pkg. (9 oz.) frozen corn, thawed
- ½   cup chopped onion
- ½   cup chopped green pepper
- 1   can (14½ oz.) diced tomatoes, undrained
- ½   tsp. pepper
- ½   tsp. hot pepper sauce

1. Cut roast in half; place in a 5-qt. slow cooker. Sprinkle with Cajun seasoning. Top with corn, onion and green pepper. Combine the tomatoes, pepper and hot pepper sauce; pour over vegetables.
2. Cover and cook on low until meat is tender, 5-6 hours. Serve corn mixture with slotted spoon.
Freeze option: Freeze cooled beef mixture in freezer containers. To use, partially thaw in the refrigerator overnight. Microwave, covered, on high in a microwave-safe dish until heated through, stirring gently.
1 serving: 455 cal., 22g fat (8g sat. fat), 147mg chol., 601mg sod., 17g carb. (5g sugars, 3g fiber), 47g pro.

"I made this for Super Bowl Sunday, and everyone loved it! It was so easy to put together, and it has a wonderful flavor. Would make this again!"
—DEB1856, TASTEOFHOME.COM

BEST EVER ROAST BEEF

❄ BEST EVER ROAST BEEF

This is the best roast beef I've ever had, and it's great for family dinners! Cube the leftover meat and save any extra sauce to make fried rice.
—*Caroline Flynn, Troy, NY*

- -

PREP: 15 min. • **COOK:** 7 hours
MAKES: 12 servings

- 1   boneless beef chuck roast (4 lbs.), trimmed
- 1   large sweet onion, chopped
- 1⅓   cups plus 3 Tbsp. water, divided
- 1   can (10½ oz.) condensed French onion soup
- ½   cup packed brown sugar
- ⅓   cup reduced-sodium soy sauce
- ¼   cup cider vinegar
- 6   garlic cloves, minced
- 1   tsp. ground ginger
- ¼   tsp. pepper
- 3   Tbsp. cornstarch

1. Cut roast in half. Transfer to a 5-qt. slow cooker; add onion and 1⅓ cups water. In a small bowl, combine the soup, brown sugar, soy sauce, vinegar, garlic, ginger and pepper; pour over top. Cover and cook on low until meat is tender, 7-8 hours.
2. Remove meat to a serving platter and keep warm. Skim fat from cooking juices; transfer to a small saucepan. Bring to a boil. Combine cornstarch and remaining water until smooth; gradually stir into the pan. Bring to a boil; cook and stir until thickened, about 2 minutes. Serve with the roast.
Freeze option: Freeze cooled beef mixture in freezer containers. To use, partially thaw in the refrigerator overnight. Microwave, covered, on high in a microwave-safe dish until heated through, stirring gently.
4 oz. cooked beef with ¼ cup gravy: 324 cal., 15g fat (6g sat. fat), 99mg chol., 451mg sod., 15g carb. (11g sugars, 1g fiber), 31g pro.

Poultry

SLOW-COOKER HONEY
TERIYAKI CHICKEN

SLOW-COOKER HONEY TERIYAKI CHICKEN

This recipe is a snap to whip up on a workday and tastes just like Chinese takeout! My kids love it, and they don't even know it's healthy.
—*Rachel Ruiz, Fort Walton Beach, FL*

- -

PREP: 20 min. • **COOK:** 3¾ hours
MAKES: 8 servings

2	lbs. boneless skinless chicken thighs
1	medium onion, thinly sliced
4	garlic cloves, minced
1	Tbsp. minced fresh gingerroot
1	cup chicken broth
¼	cup soy sauce
¼	cup honey
½	to 1 tsp. crushed red pepper flakes
¼	tsp. pepper
3	Tbsp. cornstarch
3	Tbsp. cold water
	Hot cooked rice
	Optional: Minced fresh cilantro and sesame seeds

1. Place chicken in a 3- or 4-qt. slow cooker. Top with onion, garlic and ginger. Combine broth, soy sauce, honey, pepper flakes and pepper; pour over chicken. Cook, covered, on low until chicken is no longer pink, 3½-4 hours. Remove chicken.
2. In a small bowl, mix cornstarch and water until smooth; gradually stir into slow cooker. Cook, covered, on high until sauce is thickened, 15-30 minutes. When chicken is cool enough to handle, shred with 2 forks; return to slow cooker. Serve with rice. If desired, garnish with cilantro and sesame seeds.
⅔ cup: 223 cal., 8g fat (2g sat. fat), 76mg chol., 647mg sod., 14g carb. (9g sugars, 0 fiber), 22g pro. **Diabetic exchanges:** 3 lean meat, 1 starch.

SLOW-COOKER CARIBBEAN MOO SHU CHICKEN

SPICY LEMON CHICKEN

I took a favorite recipe and modified it to work in our slow cooker. We enjoy this tender lemony chicken with rice or buttered noodles.
—*Nancy Rambo, Riverside, CA*

- -

PREP: 20 min. • **COOK:** 4 hours
MAKES: 4 servings

1	medium onion, chopped
⅓	cup water
¼	cup lemon juice
1	Tbsp. canola oil
½ to 1	tsp. salt
½	tsp. each garlic powder, chili powder and paprika
½	tsp. ground ginger
¼	tsp. pepper
4	boneless skinless chicken breast halves (4 oz. each)
4½	tsp. cornstarch
4½	tsp. cold water
	Hot cooked noodles
	Chopped fresh parsley, optional

1. In a greased 3-qt. slow cooker, combine the onion, water, lemon juice, oil and seasonings. Add chicken; turn to coat. Cover and cook on low for 4-5 hours or until a thermometer reads 165°. Remove chicken and keep warm.
2. In a saucepan, combine the cornstarch and cold water until smooth. Gradually add the cooking juices. Bring to a boil; cook and stir for 2 minutes or until thickened. Serve with chicken over noodles. Sprinkle with parsley if desired.
1 serving: 190 cal., 5g fat (1g sat. fat), 66mg chol., 372mg sod., 8g carb. (0 sugars, 1g fiber), 27g pro. **Diabetic exchanges:** 3 lean meat, ½ starch.

SLOW-COOKER CARIBBEAN MOO SHU CHICKEN

A tropical twist on a takeout favorite, this slow-cooker creation is simple, satisfying and destined to become a new favorite for your family!
—*Shannon Kohn, Simpsonville, SC*

- -

PREP: 10 min. • **COOK:** 3 hours
MAKES: 8 servings

6	boneless skinless chicken breast halves (about 6 oz. each)
1½	cups chopped onions (about 2 medium)
1	cup chopped sweet red pepper
⅔	cup chopped dried pineapple
½	cup chopped dried mango
1	can (14½ oz.) fire-roasted diced tomatoes, drained
⅔	cup hoisin sauce
3	Tbsp. hot pepper sauce
16	flour tortillas (6 in.), warmed
4	cups coleslaw mix
½	cup chopped dry roasted peanuts

1. In a 4- or 5-qt. slow cooker, combine first 5 ingredients. In a small bowl, stir together tomatoes, hoisin sauce and hot pepper sauce. Pour tomato mixture over chicken mixture. Cook, covered, on low until chicken is tender, 3-4 hours. Remove the meat. When cool enough to handle, shred with 2 forks; return to slow cooker. Heat through.
2. To serve, divide mixture evenly among tortillas. Top with coleslaw and peanuts.
1 serving: 552 cal., 15g fat (4g sat. fat), 71mg chol., 1122mg sod., 66g carb. (24g sugars, 7g fiber), 35g pro.

TEST KITCHEN TIPS

- Try serving the chicken over steamed jasmine or basmati rice.
- An equal amount of dried apricots may be substituted for either the dried pineapple or mango.

SLOW-COOKER TURKEY BREAST WITH CRANBERRY GRAVY

SLOW-COOKER COUNTRY CAPTAIN CHICKEN

Legend has it that the recipe for country captain chicken was brought to Georgia in the early 1800s by a British sea captain. Although it's traditional to serve this over rice, it's also delicious with noodles or mashed potatoes.

—*Suzanne Banfield, Basking Ridge, NJ*

PREP: 20 min. • **COOK:** 3½ hours
MAKES: 8 servings

- 1 large onion, chopped
- 1 medium sweet red pepper, chopped
- 2 tsp. minced garlic
- 3 lbs. boneless skinless chicken thighs
- 1 Tbsp. curry powder
- 1 tsp. ground cinnamon
- 1 tsp. ground ginger
- 1 tsp. dried thyme
- 1 Tbsp. packed brown sugar
- ½ cup chicken broth
- ½ cup golden raisins or raisins
- 1 can (14½ oz.) diced tomatoes, undrained
  Hot cooked rice
  Chopped fresh parsley, optional

1. Place onion, pepper and garlic in a 6-qt. slow cooker. Arrange chicken pieces over the vegetables.
2. Whisk the next 5 ingredients with the chicken broth. Pour over chicken. Cover and cook on high for 1 hour. Add raisins and tomatoes. Reduce heat to low and cook until a thermometer reads 165°, about 2½ hours. Serve over rice; if desired, sprinkle with parsley.
1 cup: 298 cal., 13g fat (3g sat. fat), 114mg chol., 159mg sod., 13g carb. (9g sugars, 2g fiber), 32g pro. **Diabetic exchanges:** 4 lean meat, 1 vegetable, ½ starch.

SLOW-COOKER TURKEY BREAST WITH CRANBERRY GRAVY

I created this dish when I was craving Thanksgiving dinner, and it was still over a month away. You get all the bells and whistles of Thanksgiving dinner in almost no time. Add a vegetable and some mashed potatoes, and you're done.
—*Cyndy Gerken, Naples, FL*

PREP: 25 min. • **COOK:** 3 hours
MAKES: 12 servings

- 2 boneless skinless turkey breast halves (2 to 3 lbs. each)
- ½ tsp. salt
- ½ tsp. pepper
- 3 fresh thyme sprigs
- 2 Tbsp. butter
- 1 cup whole-berry cranberry sauce
- 1 cup apple cider or juice
- ½ cup chicken stock
- 1 envelope onion soup mix
- 2 Tbsp. maple syrup
- 1 Tbsp. Worcestershire sauce
- ¼ cup all-purpose flour
- ¼ cup water

1. Place turkey in a 5- or 6-qt. slow cooker; sprinkle with salt and pepper. Add thyme and dot with butter. Combine cranberry sauce, cider, stock, soup mix, syrup and Worcestershire; pour over turkey. Cook, covered, on low 3-4 hours or until a thermometer inserted in turkey reads at least 165°. Remove turkey and keep warm.
2. Transfer the remaining cranberry mixture to a large saucepan; discard thyme sprigs. Combine the flour and water until smooth. Bring cranberry mixture to a boil; gradually stir in flour mixture until smooth. Cook and stir until thickened, about 2 minutes. Slice turkey; serve with cranberry gravy. If desired, sprinkle with pepper and garnish with additional thyme sprigs.
5 oz. cooked turkey with ⅓ cup gravy : 259 cal., 4g fat (2g sat. fat), 91mg chol., 537mg sod., 17g carb. (10g sugars, 1g fiber), 36g pro.

SLOW-COOKER COUNTRY
CAPTAIN CHICKEN

BUSY MOM'S CHICKEN FAJITAS

Staying at home with a 9-month-old makes preparing dinner a challenge, but a slow cooker provides an easy way to make a low-fat meal. The tender meat in these fajitas is a hit, and the veggies and beans provide a dose of fiber!
—Sarah Newman, Mahtomedi, MN

PREP: 15 min. • **COOK:** 5 hours
MAKES: 6 servings

- 1 lb. boneless skinless chicken breast halves
- 1 can (16 oz.) kidney beans, rinsed and drained
- 1 can (14½ oz.) diced tomatoes with mild green chiles, drained
- 1 medium green pepper, julienned
- 1 medium sweet red pepper, julienned
- 1 medium sweet yellow pepper, julienned
- 1 medium onion, halved and sliced
- 2 tsp. ground cumin
- 2 tsp. chili powder
- 1 garlic clove, minced
- ¼ tsp. salt
- 6 flour tortillas (8 in.), warmed
   Optional: Shredded lettuce and chopped tomatoes

1. In a 3-qt. slow cooker, combine the first 11 ingredients. Cook, covered, on low until chicken is tender, 5-6 hours. Remove the chicken; cool slightly. Shred and return to slow cooker; heat through.
2. Spoon about ¾ cup chicken mixture down the center of each tortilla. If desired, top with lettuce and tomatoes.
1 serving: 347 cal., 5g fat (1g sat. fat), 42mg chol., 778mg sod., 49g carb. (8g sugars, 7g fiber), 26g pro.

"These were so good after a long day's work when I had little time to cook at night. I added a can of black beans with the kidney beans."
—DA_30303, TASTEOFHOME.COM

NORTH AFRICAN CHICKEN & RICE

NORTH AFRICAN CHICKEN & RICE

I'm always looking to try recipes from different cultures and this one is a huge favorite. We love the spice combinations. This cooks equally well in a slow cooker or pressure cooker.
—Courtney Stultz, Weir, KS

PREP: 10 min. • **COOK:** 4 hours
MAKES: 8 servings

- 1 medium onion, diced
- 1 Tbsp. olive oil
- 8 boneless skinless chicken thighs (about 2 lbs.)
- 1 Tbsp. minced fresh cilantro
- 1 tsp. ground turmeric
- 1 tsp. paprika
- 1 tsp. sea salt
- ½ tsp. pepper
- ½ tsp. ground cinnamon
- ½ tsp. chili powder
- 1 cup golden raisins
- ½ to 1 cup chopped pitted green olives
- 1 medium lemon, sliced
- 2 garlic cloves, minced
- ½ cup chicken broth or water
- 4 cups hot cooked brown rice

In a 3- or 4-qt. slow cooker, combine onion and oil. Place chicken thighs on top of onion; sprinkle with next 7 ingredients. Top with raisins, olives, lemon and garlic. Add broth. Cook, covered, on low until chicken is tender, 4-5 hours. Serve with rice.
1 serving: 386 cal., 13g fat (3g sat. fat), 76mg chol., 556mg sod., 44g carb. (12g sugars, 3g fiber), 25g pro.

SLOW-COOKER CHICKEN CURRY

This festive twist on traditional chicken curry can be tailored to your tastes. Try replacing green beans with fresh sugar snap peas, or use a spicier salsa to turn up the heat.
—*Erin Chilcoat, Central Islip, NY*

- -

PREP: 20 min. • **COOK:** 4½ hours
MAKES: 4 servings

- 4 bone-in chicken breast halves, skin removed (8 oz. each)
- 1 can (15 oz.) cannellini beans, rinsed and drained
- ¾ cup thinly sliced sweet onion
- ½ cup chopped sweet red pepper
- 1 cup peach salsa
- 1 Tbsp. curry powder
- ½ tsp. salt
- ¼ tsp. pepper
- 1 cup fresh green beans, trimmed and cut in half
- 2 Tbsp. cornstarch
- ½ cup cold water
- 1½ cups chicken broth
- 1½ cups uncooked instant rice

1. Place the chicken, cannellini beans, onion and red pepper in 4-qt. slow cooker. In a small bowl, combine the salsa, curry powder, salt and pepper; pour over top.
2. Cover and cook on low until chicken is tender, 4-5 hours. Stir in green beans. Combine cornstarch and water until smooth; gradually stir into slow cooker. Cover and cook on high until sauce is thickened, about 30 minutes.
3. In a large saucepan, bring broth to a boil; stir in rice. Cover and remove from the heat. Let stand until liquid is absorbed and rice is tender, about 5 minutes. Fluff with a fork. Serve with chicken and sauce.
1 chicken breast with ¾ cup rice and ¾ cup sauce: 486 cal., 6g fat (1g sat. fat), 103mg chol., 1132mg sod., 59g carb. (5g sugars, 7g fiber), 46g pro.

LEMON CHICKEN WITH BASIL

No matter when I eat it, this tangy slow-cooked chicken reminds me of summer meals with friends and family.
—*Deborah Posey, Virginia Beach, VA*

- -

PREP: 5 min. • **COOK:** 3 hours
MAKES: 4 servings

- 4 boneless skinless chicken breast halves (6 oz. each)
- 2 medium lemons
- 1 bunch fresh basil leaves (¾ oz.)
- 2 cups chicken stock
  Optional: Additional grated lemon zest and chopped basil

1. Place chicken breasts in a 3-qt. slow cooker. Finely grate enough zest from lemons to measure 4 tsp. Cut lemons in half; squeeze juice. Add zest and juice to slow cooker.
2. Tear basil leaves directly into slow cooker. Add chicken stock. Cook, covered, on low until meat is tender, 3-4 hours. When cool enough to handle, shred meat with 2 forks. If desired, stir in additional lemon zest and chopped basil.
Freeze option: Freeze cooled chicken mixture in freezer containers. To use, partially thaw in refrigerator overnight. Heat through in a saucepan, stirring occasionally; add broth or water if necessary.
1 chicken breast half: 200 cal., 4g fat (1g sat. fat), 94mg chol., 337mg sod., 3g carb. (1g sugars, 0 fiber), 37g pro. **Diabetic exchanges:** 5 lean meat.

SLOW-COOKER
CHICKEN CURRY

SLOW-COOKER CHICKEN
TACO SALAD

SLOW-COOKER CHICKEN TACO SALAD

We use this super-duper chicken across several meals, including it in tacos, sandwiches, omelets and enchiladas. My little guys love helping measure the seasonings.
—*Karie Houghton, Lynnwood, WA*

PREP: 10 min. • **COOK:** 3 hours
MAKES: 6 servings

- 3   tsp. chili powder
- 1   tsp. each ground cumin, seasoned salt and pepper
- ½   tsp. each white pepper, ground chipotle pepper and paprika
- ¼   tsp. dried oregano
- ¼   tsp. crushed red pepper flakes
- 1½ lbs. boneless skinless chicken breasts
- 1   cup chicken broth
- 9   cups torn romaine
      Optional toppings: Sliced avocado, shredded cheddar cheese, chopped tomato or halved cherry tomatoes, sliced green onions and salad dressing of your choice

1. Mix seasonings; rub over chicken. Place in a 3-qt. slow cooker. Add broth. Cook, covered, on low until chicken is tender, 3-4 hours.

2. Remove chicken; cool slightly. Shred with 2 forks. Serve over romaine; top as desired.

Freeze option: Freeze cooled chicken mixture in freezer containers. To use, partially thaw in refrigerator overnight. Heat through in a saucepan, stirring occasionally; add broth or water if necessary.

1½ cups lettuce with 3 oz. cooked chicken: 143 cal., 3g fat (1g sat. fat), 63mg chol., 516mg sod., 4g carb. (1g sugars, 2g fiber), 24g pro. **Diabetic exchanges:** 3 lean meat, 1 vegetable.

CORNISH HENS WITH POTATOES

CORNISH HENS WITH POTATOES

This is a wonderful meal with not much work. This special slow-cooked dinner is delicious. I serve it with green beans and French bread.
—*Deborah Randall, Abbeville, LA*

PREP: 20 min. • **COOK:** 6 hours
MAKES: 4 servings

- 4   Cornish game hens (20 to 24 oz. each)
- 2   Tbsp. canola oil
- 4   large red potatoes, cut into ⅛-in. slices
- 4   bacon strips, cut into 1-in. pieces
      Lemon-pepper seasoning and garlic powder to taste
      Minced fresh parsley

1. In a large skillet, brown hens in oil. Place the potatoes in a 5-qt. slow cooker. Top with the hens and bacon. Sprinkle with lemon pepper and garlic powder.

2. Cover and cook on low until a thermometer inserted in thickest part of thigh reads 170°-175° and potatoes are tender, 6-8 hours. If desired, thicken the cooking juices. Sprinkle the hens with parsley.

1 serving: 995 cal., 67g fat (18g sat. fat), 369mg chol., 367mg sod., 27g carb. (2g sugars, 3g fiber), 66g pro.

❄ BUFFALO PULLED CHICKEN

This simple recipe is a go-to favorite for game day. Buffalo chicken breast is a nice alternative to traditional pulled pork.
—*Kim Ciepluch, Kenosha, WI*

- -

PREP: 5 min. • **COOK:** 3 hours
MAKES: 6 servings

- ½ cup Buffalo wing sauce
- 2 Tbsp. ranch salad dressing mix
- 4 boneless skinless chicken breast halves (6 oz. each)
  Optional: Celery ribs or crusty sandwich buns, crumbled blue cheese, additional wing sauce and ranch salad dressing

1. In a 3-qt. slow cooker, mix wing sauce and dressing mix. Add chicken. Cook, covered, on low until meat is tender, 3-4 hours.
2. Shred chicken with 2 forks. If desired, serve on celery or buns, top with blue cheese and additional wing sauce, and serve with ranch dressing.
Freeze option: Freeze cooled chicken mixture in freezer containers. To use, partially thaw in refrigerator overnight. Heat through in a saucepan, stirring occasionally; add broth or water if necessary.
½ cup chicken mixture: 147 cal., 3g fat (1g sat. fat), 63mg chol., 1288mg sod., 6g carb. (0 sugars, 0 fiber), 23g pro.

🍎 CHICKEN WITH SUGAR PUMPKINS & APRICOTS

When we have family gatherings, we give the slow cooker kitchen duty. This yummy chicken with pumpkin and apricots has the warm flavors of Morocco.
—*Nancy Heishman, Las Vegas, NV*

- -

PREP: 20 min. • **COOK:** 4 hours
MAKES: 8 servings

- 3 pie pumpkins, peeled and cubed (5 to 6 cups each)
- 1 Tbsp. canola oil
- 8 boneless skinless chicken thighs (4 oz. each)
- 1 medium red onion, chopped
- 2 garlic cloves, minced
- ¾ cup dried Turkish apricots, diced
- ½ cup apricot nectar
- ⅓ cup apricot preserves
- 2 Tbsp. lemon juice
- 1 tsp. ground ginger
- 1 tsp. ground cinnamon
- 1 tsp. salt
- ½ tsp. pepper
- 3 Tbsp. minced fresh parsley
  Optional: Hot cooked rice and ½ cup pomegranate seeds

1. Place pumpkin in a 5-qt. slow cooker coated with cooking spray.
2. In a large nonstick skillet, heat oil over medium-high heat; brown chicken thighs on all sides. Transfer chicken to slow cooker. In same skillet, saute onion and garlic 1-2 minutes; transfer to the slow cooker.
3. Add next 8 ingredients to slow cooker. Cook, covered, on low until meat is tender, 4-5 hours. Top with parsley. If desired, serve with hot cooked rice and sprinkle with pomegranate seeds.
Note: If pie pumpkins are unavailable, you may substitute 1 large (5-6 pound) butternut squash, peeled and cut into 1-in. cubes. You should have 15-18 cups of cubed squash.
1 chicken thigh with 1 cup pumpkin: 318 cal., 10g fat (3g sat. fat), 76mg chol., 376mg sod., 36g carb. (20g sugars, 3g fiber), 24g pro. **Diabetic exchanges:** 3 lean meat, 2 starch, ½ fat.

CHICKEN WITH SUGAR
PUMPKINS & APRICOTS

SLOW-COOKED ORANGE
CHIPOTLE CHICKEN

SLOW-COOKED ORANGE CHIPOTLE CHICKEN

Even though this chicken dish cooks for several hours, the hint of citrus keeps things fresh. We're big on spice in our house, so sometimes I use two chipotle peppers.
—*Deborah Biggs, Omaha, NE*

PREP: 10 min. • **COOK:** 4 hours
MAKES: 6 servings

½   cup thawed orange juice concentrate
¼   cup barbecue sauce
1   chipotle pepper in adobo sauce
¼   tsp. salt
¼   tsp. garlic powder
6   boneless skinless chicken breast halves (6 oz. each)
¼   cup chopped red onion
4   tsp. cornstarch
3   Tbsp. cold water
    Grated orange zest

Optional: Hot cooked rice and chopped parsley

1. Place first 5 ingredients in a blender; cover and process until blended.
2. Place chicken and onion in a 3-qt. slow cooker; top with juice mixture. Cook, covered, on low until a thermometer inserted in chicken reads at least 165°, 4-5 hours.
3. Remove chicken from slow cooker; keep warm. Transfer cooking juices to a saucepan; bring to a boil. In a small bowl, mix cornstarch and water until smooth; gradually stir into juices. Return to a boil, stirring constantly; cook and stir until thickened, 1-2 minutes. Spoon over chicken; top with orange zest. If desired, serve with hot cooked rice and sprinkle with parsley.

1 chicken breast with ¼ cup sauce:
246 cal., 4g fat (1g sat. fat), 94mg chol., 315mg sod., 15g carb. (11g sugars, 1g fiber), 35g pro. **Diabetic exchanges:** 5 lean meat, 1 starch.

TEST KITCHEN TIPS

• Some meat can go all day long in the slow cooker and only get more tender and delicious; chicken breast is not one of them. Stick to the 4-5 hour cook time on this or the chicken will become dry.
• Chipotle peppers are spicy, so you don't need much to add smoky heat. Freeze leftovers as individual peppers in ice cube trays, then store in a zip-top bag.

CHICKEN-CRANBERRY HOT DISH

SLOW-COOKER RANCH CHICKEN

This is a fabulous recipe that we have passed around to all our friends, especially those who have young children. It's wonderful for a cold winter night or a hot summer day when you don't want to turn on the oven. Serve it as a weeknight family dinner or for a large group.
—*Sonya Stark, West Jordan, UT*

PREP: 10 min. • **COOK:** 6½ hours
MAKES: 8 servings

- ¾   cup chicken broth
- 1   envelope ranch salad dressing mix
- 2   lbs. boneless skinless chicken breast halves
- 1   can (10½ oz.) condensed cream of chicken soup, undiluted
- 1   pkg. (8 oz.) cream cheese, cubed and softened
  Hot cooked rice or noodles
  Optional: Shredded cheddar cheese, crumbled cooked bacon and chopped green onions

1. In a 4-5-qt. slow cooker, combine broth and dressing mix; add chicken. Cover and cook on low for 6 hours. Remove chicken to cutting board; shred with 2 forks and return to slow cooker.
2. Stir in soup and cream cheese. Cover and cook on low until cream cheese is melted, about 30 minutes. Serve over rice or noodles. Add optional toppings as desired.

⅔ cup: 267 cal., 15g fat (7g sat. fat), 94mg chol., 776mg sod., 7g carb. (1g sugars, 1g fiber), 25g pro.

"I've made this twice now and enjoyed it. Yesterday when I made it, I used chicken breast tenders, so I cooked on low for 5 hours. I also topped it with chopped green peppers."
—TGI, TASTEOFHOME.COM

CHICKEN-CRANBERRY HOT DISH

In my family, we never eat chicken without cranberry sauce! This chicken is fall-off-the-bone tender, and the sauce is divine with mashed potatoes.
—*Lorraine Caland, Shuniah, ON*

PREP: 30 min. • **COOK:** 4 hours
MAKES: 4 servings (2 cups sauce)

- 2   Tbsp. canola oil
- 1   broiler/fryer chicken (4 lbs.), cut up
- ½   tsp. salt
- ¼   tsp. pepper
- 1   medium onion, chopped
- 1   celery rib, chopped
- 1   cup whole-berry cranberry sauce
- ½   cup chili sauce
- 2   Tbsp. brown sugar
- 1   Tbsp. grated lemon zest
- 1   Tbsp. balsamic vinegar
- 1   Tbsp. A.1. steak sauce
- 1   Tbsp. Dijon mustard

1. In a large skillet, heat canola oil over medium-high heat. Brown chicken on both sides in batches; sprinkle with salt and pepper. Transfer to a 4-qt. slow cooker.
2. Add onion and celery to skillet; saute over medium-high heat for 3-4 minutes or until tender. Stir in remaining ingredients. Pour over chicken.
3. Cook, covered, on low until chicken is tender, 4-5 hours. Skim fat from cooking juices; serve juices with chicken.

1 serving with ½ cup sauce: 829 cal., 41g fat (10g sat. fat), 209mg chol., 1140mg sod., 46g carb. (33g sugars, 2g fiber), 66g pro.

SLOW-COOKER
RANCH CHICKEN

Other Entrees

SLOW-COOKER
ARIZONA POBLANO PORK

❄ SLOW-COOKER ARIZONA POBLANO PORK

Living In Arizona and being very fond of the seasonal poblano peppers, I love this easy-to-prepare dish. It can be served in a number of ways—it's great with rice and beans or in a taco with hot sauce.
—*Johnna Johnson, Scottsdale, AZ*

PREP: 20 min. • **COOK:** 3 hours
MAKES: 8 servings

- 1 boneless pork loin roast (3 to 4 lbs.)
- 3 Tbsp. fajita seasoning mix, divided
- 1 Tbsp. olive oil
- 1 can (14½ oz.) fire-roasted diced tomatoes, undrained
- 1 large red onion, chopped
- 1½ cups chopped seeded fresh poblano peppers
- ¼ cup beef broth
- 1 tsp. chili powder
- ¾ tsp. ground cumin
- ½ tsp. garlic powder
- ½ tsp. cayenne pepper
  Optional: Hot cooked rice and a chipotle hot sauce, such as Cholula

1. Sprinkle roast with 2 Tbsp. fajita seasoning. In a large skillet, heat oil over medium heat; brown meat. Transfer meat to a 5- or 6-qt. slow cooker. In a large bowl, combine the next 8 ingredients and the remaining 1 Tbsp. fajita seasoning; pour over meat. Cook, covered, on low until a thermometer inserted in pork reads at least 145°, about 3 hours.
2. Remove roast; cool slightly. Cut pork into bite-sized pieces; return to slow cooker. Heat through. If desired, serve pork with rice and hot sauce.
Freeze option: Place cubed pork in freezer containers; top with cooking juices. Cool and freeze. To use, partially thaw in refrigerator overnight. Heat through in a saucepan, stirring occasionally.
1¼ cups: 274 cal., 10g fat (3g sat. fat), 85mg chol., 588mg sod., 10g carb. (4g sugars, 1g fiber), 34g pro.

COUNTRY FRENCH PORK WITH PRUNES & APPLES

❄️ SMOKY BARBECUE BEANS

Here's a thick and hearty dish that's sure to be popular. Serve it with a crisp salad and your favorite grilled fare for an awesome picnic!
—*Anita Curtis, Camarillo, CA*

PREP: 10 min. • **COOK:** 6 hours
MAKES: 8 servings

- 1 lb. ground beef
- 1 cup chopped onion
- 12 bacon strips, cooked and crumbled
- 2 cans (16 oz. each) pork and beans
- 1 can (16 oz.) kidney beans, rinsed and drained
- 1 can (16 oz.) butter beans, drained
- 1 cup ketchup
- ¼ cup packed brown sugar
- 3 Tbsp. white vinegar
- 1 tsp. liquid smoke, optional
- ½ tsp. salt
- ¼ tsp. pepper

In a skillet, cook the beef and onion until meat is no longer pink; drain. Transfer to a 3-qt. slow cooker. Stir in the remaining ingredients. Cover and cook on low until heated through, 6-7 hours.

Freeze option: Freeze cooled beans in freezer containers. To use, partially thaw in refrigerator overnight. Heat through in a saucepan, stirring occasionally; add water or broth if necessary.

1 serving: 337 cal., 10g fat (4g sat. fat), 36mg chol., 1171mg sod., 44g carb. (16g sugars, 8g fiber), 22g pro.

"What flavor! Thoroughly loved this. Will make again and again. Forget about it being 8 servings, though. We snarfed it down. Seconds all around."
—MARYP2219, TASTEOFHOME.COM

🍎 COUNTRY FRENCH PORK WITH PRUNES & APPLES

The classic flavors of herbes de Provence, apples and dried plums make this easy slow-cooked pork taste like a hearty meal at a French country cafe. For a traditional pairing, serve the pork with braised lentils.
—*Suzanne Banfield, Basking Ridge, NJ*

PREP: 20 min. • **COOK:** 4 hours + standing
MAKES: 10 servings

- 2 Tbsp. all-purpose flour
- 1 Tbsp. herbes de Provence
- 1½ tsp. salt
- ¾ tsp. pepper
- 1 boneless pork loin roast (3 to 4 lbs.)
- 2 Tbsp. olive oil
- 2 medium onions, halved and thinly sliced
- 1 cup apple cider or unsweetened apple juice
- 1 cup beef stock
- 2 bay leaves
- 2 large tart apples, peeled, cored and chopped
- 1 cup pitted dried plums (prunes)

1. Mix flour, herbes de Provence, salt and pepper; rub over pork. In a large skillet, heat oil over medium-high heat. Brown roast on all sides. Place roast in a 5- or 6-qt. slow cooker. Add onions, apple cider, beef stock and bay leaves.

2. Cook, covered, on low 3 hours. Add apples and dried plums. Cook, covered, on low 1-1½ hours longer or until apples and pork are tender. Remove the roast, onions, apples and plums to a serving platter, discarding bay leaves; tent with foil. Let stand 15 minutes before slicing.

4 oz. cooked pork with ¾ cup fruit mixture: 286 cal., 9g fat (3g sat. fat), 68mg chol., 449mg sod., 22g carb. (13g sugars, 2g fiber), 28g pro.

APPLE-CRANBERRY
BREAKFAST RISOTTO

SLOW-COOKER BAKED ZITI

I don't know one family who doesn't have some crazy, hectic weeknights. This recipe was a delicious, easy fix for a busy-weeknight dinner for our family.
—*Christina Addison, Blanchester, OH*

PREP: 10 min. • **COOK:** 2 hours
MAKES: 6 servings

- 1 container (15 oz.) whole-milk ricotta cheese
- 1 large egg, beaten
- 1 tsp. dried basil
- ½ tsp. crushed red pepper flakes, optional
- 1 jar (24 oz.) meatless pasta sauce
- 2 cups uncooked ziti
- ¼ cup water
- 2 cups shredded mozzarella cheese
- ¼ cup minced fresh basil
  Grated Parmesan cheese, optional

1. In a small bowl, stir together ricotta cheese, egg, basil and, if desired, red pepper flakes; set aside. Pour pasta sauce into a 5-qt. slow cooker. Evenly top sauce with pasta; pour water over the top. Drop heaping tablespoons of the ricotta cheese mixture over the pasta. Sprinkle with the mozzarella cheese.
2. Cover; cook on high until heated through and the pasta is tender, 2-2½ hours. Top with fresh basil and, if desired, Parmesan cheese and additional red pepper flakes. Serve immediately.
1½ cups: 379 cal., 17g fat (10g sat. fat), 89mg chol., 886mg sod., 36g carb. (13g sugars, 3g fiber), 23g pro.

APPLE-CRANBERRY BREAKFAST RISOTTO

Cranberries and apples are tart enough to balance the sweetness in this hearty dish that's fun for an after-presents breakfast on Christmas morning.
—*Elizabeth King, Duluth, MN*

PREP: 15 min. • **COOK:** 3 hours
MAKES: 10 servings

- ¼ cup butter, cubed
- 1½ cups uncooked arborio rice
- 2 medium apples, peeled and chopped
- ⅓ cup packed brown sugar
- ¼ tsp. kosher salt
- 1½ tsp. ground cinnamon
- ⅛ tsp. ground nutmeg
- ⅛ tsp. ground cloves
- 3 cups 2% milk
- 2 cups unsweetened apple juice
- 1 cup dried cranberries

1. Heat butter in a 4-qt. slow cooker on high heat until melted. Add rice; stir to coat. Add apples, brown sugar, salt and spices. Stir in milk and apple juice.
2. Cook, covered, on low until rice is tender, 3-4 hours, stirring halfway through cooking. Stir in cranberries during the last 15 minutes of cooking.
¾ cup: 298 cal., 7g fat (4g sat. fat), 18mg chol., 124mg sod., 57g carb. (30g sugars, 2g fiber), 5g pro.

DID YOU KNOW?

Cinnamon comes in two basic types: Ceylon and cassia. Ceylon cinnamon's delicate, complex flavor is ideal for ice creams and dessert sauces. The spicy, bolder cassia cinnamon (often labeled simply as cinnamon) is preferred for baking.

SLOW-COOKER
BAKED ZITI

MEATY SPAGHETTI SAUCE

My homemade spaghetti sauce got rave reviews, but it was so time-consuming to make on the stovetop. My family loves this flavorful slow-cooker version.
—*Arlene Sommers, Redmond, WA*

PREP: 20 min. • **COOK:** 8 hours
MAKES: 12 servings

- 1 lb. lean ground beef (90% lean)
- 1 lb. bulk Italian sausage
- 1 medium green pepper, chopped
- 1 medium onion, chopped
- 8 garlic cloves, minced
- 3 cans (14½ oz. each) Italian diced tomatoes, drained
- 2 cans (15 oz. each) tomato sauce
- 2 cans (6 oz. each) tomato paste
- ⅓ cup sugar
- 2 Tbsp. Italian seasoning
- 1 Tbsp. dried basil
- 2 tsp. dried marjoram
- 1 tsp. salt
- ½ tsp. pepper
  Hot cooked spaghetti
  Shredded Parmesan cheese, optional

1. In a large skillet over medium heat, cook beef and sausage until no longer pink, 10-12 minutes, crumbling meat; drain. Transfer to a 5-qt. slow cooker. Stir in the green pepper, onion, garlic, tomatoes, tomato sauce, paste, sugar and seasonings.
2. Cover and cook on low until bubbly, about 8 hours. Serve with spaghetti. If desired, top with Parmesan.
½ cup: 264 cal., 12g fat (4g sat. fat), 44mg chol., 1119mg sod., 26g carb. (17g sugars, 3g fiber), 15g pro.

CRANBERRY PORK & SWEET POTATOES

With tender pork chops straight from the slow cooker and sweet potatoes flavored with applesauce, cranberry sauce and brown sugar, this is a wonderful meal for the holiday season.
—*Doris Branham, Kingston, TN*

PREP: 10 min. • **COOK:** 6 hours
MAKES: 6 servings

- 1⅔ cups sweetened applesauce (about 15 oz.)
- 3 lbs. sweet potatoes (about 3 large), peeled and cut into 1-in. slices
- ¾ tsp. salt, divided
- ¼ tsp. pepper, divided
- ¼ cup packed brown sugar
- 6 bone-in pork loin chops (6 oz. each)
- 1 can (14 oz.) whole-berry cranberry sauce

1. Place applesauce in a 6-qt. slow cooker. Top with the sweet potatoes; sprinkle with ¼ tsp. salt, ⅛ tsp. pepper and brown sugar.
2. Place pork chops over sweet potatoes; sprinkle with remaining salt and pepper. Spoon cranberry sauce over pork. Cook, covered, on low 6-8 hours or until pork and sweet potatoes are tender.
1 serving: 649 cal., 14g fat (5g sat. fat), 83mg chol., 412mg sod., 101g carb. (58g sugars, 9g fiber), 31g pro.

MEATY SPAGHETTI SAUCE

KASHMIRI LAMB
CURRY STEW

PORK ROAST WITH PLUM SAUCE

The flavors in this roast blend perfectly to create a subtle taste of Asia. If you don't have plum jam, try apricot preserves instead.
—*Jeannie Klugh, Lancaster, PA*

PREP: 20 min. • **COOK:** 5 hours + standing
MAKES: 10 pieces

- 1 boneless pork loin roast (4 lbs.)
- 2 Tbsp. canola oil
- 1 cup sherry
- 2 Tbsp. dried thyme
- 2 Tbsp. soy sauce
- 4 garlic cloves, minced
- 1 Tbsp. ground mustard
- 1½ tsp. ground ginger
- 1 tsp. garlic salt
- ½ tsp. salt
- ½ tsp. pepper
- ½ cup plum jam
- 2 Tbsp. cornstarch
- ¼ cup cold water

1. Cut roast in half. In a large skillet, brown meat in oil on all sides; drain. Transfer to a 4-qt. slow cooker.
2. In a small bowl, combine the sherry, thyme, soy sauce, garlic, mustard, ginger, garlic salt, salt and pepper; pour over pork. Cover and cook on low until meat is tender, 5-6 hours. Remove meat to a serving platter; keep warm. Let stand for 10-15 minutes before slicing.
3. Skim fat from cooking juices; transfer juices to a small saucepan. Add jam. Bring to a boil. Combine cornstarch and water until smooth. Gradually stir into pan. Bring to a boil; cook and stir until thickened, about 2 minutes. Serve with pork.
1 piece: 324 cal., 11g fat (3g sat. fat), 90mg chol., 538mg sod., 14g carb. (10g sugars, 1g fiber), 36g pro. **Diabetic exchanges:** 5 lean meat, 1 starch, ½ fat.

KASHMIRI LAMB CURRY STEW

When I was growing up I was always taught spicy foods are for lovers. So when I was married this was the first meal I made for my husband. Every time we have a spat I make this dish.
—*Amber El, Pittsburgh, PA*

PREP: 25 min. + marinating
COOK: 8 hours
MAKES: 11 servings (2¾ qt.)

- 1 cup plain yogurt
- 2 Tbsp. ghee or butter, melted
- ¼ cup lemon juice
- 4 tsp. curry powder
- 1 Tbsp. cumin seeds
- 1 tsp. each coriander seeds, ground ginger, ground cloves, ground cardamom, sugar and salt
- ½ tsp. each ground cinnamon and pepper
- 3 lbs. lamb stew meat, cut into 1-in. cubes
- 1 large onion, sliced
- 1 medium sweet potato, quartered
- 1 medium Yukon Gold potato, quartered
- 1 large tomato, chopped
- 1 cup frozen peas and carrots
- 3 garlic cloves, minced
- 2 dried hot chiles
- ½ cup chicken broth
- 1½ Tbsp. garam masala
  Optional: Hot cooked basmati rice, sliced green onion, mango chutney and raisins

1. In a large bowl, combine the yogurt, ghee and lemon juice; add curry powder, cumin seeds, coriander, ginger, cloves, cardamom, sugar, salt, cinnamon and pepper. Add lamb, vegetables, garlic and chiles; turn to coat. Cover and refrigerate up to 24 hours.
2. Transfer lamb mixture and marinade to 6-qt. slow cooker; stir in broth and garam masala. Cook, covered, on low until meat is tender, 8-9 hours. If desired, serve with rice, onion, chutney and raisins.
Freeze option: Freeze cooled stew in freezer containers. To use, partially thaw in refrigerator overnight. Heat through in a saucepan, stirring occasionally; add broth if necessary.
1 cup: 261 cal., 10g fat (4g sat. fat), 89mg chol., 384mg sod., 15g carb. (5g sugars, 3g fiber), 28g pro. **Diabetic exchanges:** 4 lean meat, 1 starch.

TEST KITCHEN TIP

Cornstarch needs just a few minutes of boiling to thicken a sauce, gravy or dessert filling. If it cooks too long, the cornstarch will begin to lose its thickening power. Carefully follow the recipe for the best results.

SLOW-COOKER
SPIRAL HAM

SLOW-COOKER SPIRAL HAM

My family loves it when I make this ham. I'm not sure which they love more, though—eating it straightaway or enjoying the leftovers in sandwiches.
—*Angela Lively, Conroe, TX*

PREP: 10 min. • **COOK:** 4 hours
MAKES: 15 servings

- 1 spiral-sliced fully cooked bone-in ham (5 lbs.)
- 1 cup unsweetened pineapple juice
- ½ cup packed brown sugar
- ¼ cup butter, melted
- 2 Tbsp. cider vinegar
- 1 garlic clove, minced
- ½ tsp. crushed red pepper flakes
- 1 medium onion, sliced

1. Place ham in a 5-qt. slow cooker. In a small bowl, combine pineapple juice, brown sugar, butter, cider vinegar, garlic and red pepper flakes; pour over ham. Top with onion slices.
2. Cover and cook ham on low until a thermometer reads 140°, 4-5 hours.

3 oz. ham: 194 cal., 7g fat (3g sat. fat), 75mg chol., 821mg sod., 11g carb. (10g sugars, 0 fiber), 22g pro.

TEST KITCHEN TIP

If you'd rather not use pineapple juice in this recipe, try orange or apple juice. If using apple juice instead, increase the vinegar slightly to help balance the flavors.

PORK & GREEN CHILE STEW

PORK & GREEN CHILE STEW

This easily adaptable stew is ready in 4 hours if cooked on high in a slow cooker, or in less than 8 hours if you cook it low and slow.
—*Paul Sedillo, Plainfield, IL*

PREP: 40 min. • **COOK:** 7 hours
MAKES: 8 servings (2 qt.)

- 2 lbs. boneless pork shoulder butt roast, cut into ¾-in. cubes
- 1 large onion, cut into ½-in. pieces
- 2 Tbsp. canola oil
- 1 tsp. salt
- 1 tsp. coarsely ground pepper
- 4 large potatoes, peeled and cut into ¾-in. cubes
- 3 cups water
- 1 can (16 oz.) hominy, rinsed and drained
- 2 cans (4 oz. each) chopped green chiles
- 2 Tbsp. quick-cooking tapioca
- 2 garlic cloves, minced
- ½ tsp. dried oregano
- ½ tsp. ground cumin
- 1 cup minced fresh cilantro
  Optional: Sour cream and additional cilantro

1. In a large skillet, brown pork and onion in oil in batches. Sprinkle with salt and pepper. Transfer to a 5-qt. slow cooker.
2. Stir in the potatoes, water, hominy, chiles, tapioca, garlic, oregano and cumin. Cover and cook on low until the meat is tender, 7-9 hours, stirring in cilantro during the last 30 minutes of cooking. If desired, serve with sour cream and additional cilantro.

Freeze option: Freeze cooled stew in freezer containers. To use, partially thaw in refrigerator overnight. Heat through in a saucepan, stirring occasionally; add a little broth if necessary.

1 cup: 322 cal., 15g fat (4g sat. fat), 67mg chol., 723mg sod., 25g carb. (3g sugars, 3g fiber), 21g pro. **Diabetic exchanges:** 3 medium-fat meat, 1½ starch, ½ fat.

SLOW-COOKER TROPICAL PORK CHOPS

Pork and fruit go so nicely together. Cook them slowly, then add fresh herbs right before serving to get this light and bright main dish.
—*Roxanne Chan, Albany, CA*

PREP: 15 min. • **COOK:** 3 hours
MAKES: 4 servings

- 2 jars (23½ oz. each) mixed tropical fruit, drained and chopped
- ¾ cup thawed limeade concentrate
- ¼ cup sweet chili sauce
- 1 garlic clove, minced
- 1 tsp. minced fresh gingerroot
- 4 bone-in pork loin chops (¾ in. thick and 5 oz. each)
- 1 green onion, finely chopped
- 2 Tbsp. minced fresh cilantro
- 2 Tbsp. minced fresh mint
- 2 Tbsp. slivered almonds, toasted
- 2 Tbsp. finely chopped crystallized ginger, optional

1. In a 3-qt. slow cooker, combine the first 5 ingredients. Add pork, arranging chops to sit snugly in fruit mixture. Cook, covered, on low until the meat is tender (a thermometer inserted in pork should read at least 145°), 3-4 hours.
2. In a small bowl, mix the onion, herbs, almonds and, if desired, ginger. To serve, remove pork chops from slow cooker. Using a slotted spoon, serve fruit over pork. Sprinkle with herb mixture.
Note: To toast nuts, place in a dry nonstick skillet and heat over low heat until lightly browned, stirring occasionally.
1 serving: 572 cal., 13g fat (4g sat. fat), 69mg chol., 326mg sod., 91g carb. (86g sugars, 3g fiber), 24g pro.

SPICY SAUSAGE FETTUCCINE

I once accidentally bought hot Italian sausage, but still wanted to find a way to use it. I tossed it in the slow cooker with mushrooms, tomatoes and wine, which helped to mellow out the heat. Now I buy the hot stuff on purpose!
—*Judy Batson, Tampa, FL*

PREP: 25 min. • **COOK:** 6 hours
MAKES: 8 servings

- 2 tsp. canola oil
- 8 hot Italian sausage links
- ½ lb. sliced fresh mushrooms
- 1 small sweet onion, chopped
- 2 garlic cloves, minced
- 1 can (14½ oz.) diced tomatoes with mild green chiles, undrained
- ½ cup beef stock
- ½ cup dry white wine or additional stock
- 1 pkg. (12 oz.) fettuccine or tagliatelle Grated Parmesan cheese, optional

1. In a large skillet, heat oil over medium heat; brown the sausages on all sides. Transfer to a 3-qt. slow cooker, reserving drippings in pan.
2. In same skillet, saute mushrooms and onion in drippings over medium heat until tender, 4-5 minutes. Stir in garlic; cook and stir 1 minute. Stir in tomatoes, stock and wine; pour over sausages. Cook, covered, on low 6-8 hours (a thermometer inserted in the sausages should read at least 160°).
3. To serve, cook fettuccine according to package directions; drain. Remove the sausages from slow cooker; cut into thick slices.
4. Skim fat from mushroom mixture. Add fettuccine and sausage; toss to combine. Serve in bowls. If desired, top with cheese.
1⅓ cups: 448 cal., 25g fat (7g sat. fat), 57mg chol., 817mg sod., 37g carb. (5g sugars, 3g fiber), 19g pro.

SPICY SAUSAGE FETTUCCINE

ALL-IN-ONE
SLOW-COOKER
BREAKFAST

SLOW-COOKED RIBS

Nothing says comfort food like a plate of mouthwatering ribs smothered in barbecue sauce. These are delicious and tangy.
—*Sharon Crider, Junction City, KS*

PREP: 15 min. • **COOK:** 6 hours
MAKES: 8 servings

- 4 lbs. boneless country-style pork ribs
- 1 cup barbecue sauce
- 1 cup Catalina salad dressing
- ½ tsp. minced garlic
- 2 Tbsp. all-purpose flour
- ¼ cup cold water

1. Cut ribs into serving-sized pieces. Place in a 5-qt. slow cooker. Combine barbecue sauce and salad dressing; pour over ribs. Sprinkle with garlic. Cover and cook on low until meat is tender, 6-7 hours.
2. Remove the meat to a serving platter; keep warm. Skim fat from cooking juices; transfer juices to a small saucepan; bring to a boil.
3. Combine flour and water until smooth. Gradually stir into the pan. Bring to a boil; cook and stir until thickened, about 2 minutes. Serve with meat.
5 oz. cooked pork: 511 cal., 27g fat (9g sat. fat), 131mg chol., 835mg sod., 24g carb. (19g sugars, 0 fiber), 40g pro.

ALL-IN-ONE
SLOW-COOKER BREAKFAST

Let your slow cooker do the work and don't worry about adding sides because this dish already has everything in it—hash browns, sausage, cheese and eggs. Just sip your coffee, cut up some fresh fruit and breakfast or brunch is served.
—*Debbie Glasscock, Conway, AR*

PREP: 20 min. • **COOK:** 3 hours
MAKES: 6 servings

- 1 lb. bulk pork sausage
- 1 small onion, chopped
- 6 green onions, thinly sliced
- 1 pkg. (30 oz.) frozen shredded hash brown potatoes, thawed
- 2 cups shredded sharp cheddar cheese
- 1 can (10¾ oz.) condensed cream of mushroom soup, undiluted
- 1 cup sour cream
- 6 large eggs
- ¼ tsp. pepper
  Chopped fresh parsley
  Optional: Salsa and additional sour cream

1. In a large skillet, cook sausage, onion and green onions over medium heat until sausage is no longer pink and onions are tender, 6-8 minutes, crumbling sausage, drain. Transfer to a greased 5- or 6-qt. slow cooker. Stir in hash browns, cheese, soup and sour cream until blended.
2. Cook, covered, on high 2½ hours. With the back of a spoon, make 6 wells in the potato mixture. Break an egg in each well. Sprinkle eggs with pepper. Cover and cook until egg whites are completely set and yolks begin to thicken but are not hard, 30-35 minutes longer. Sprinkle with parsley. If desired, serve with salsa and additional sour cream.
1 serving: 654 cal., 44g fat (19g sat. fat), 276mg chol., 1194mg sod., 36g carb. (5g sugars, 3g fiber), 29g pro.

SLOW COOKER | OTHER ENTREES **47**

CHOCOLATE MOLASSES PORK ROAST

HAWAIIAN PULLED PORK LETTUCE WRAPS

We love this easy slow-cooker recipe on Sunday afternoons. It's equally comforting and light for lunch or dinner. We serve ours with sweet potato oven fries and roasted green beans.

—*Arlene Rakoczy, Gilbert, AZ*

- -

PREP: 10 min. • **COOK:** 6 hours
MAKES: 6 servings

- 1 boneless pork shoulder butt roast (3 to 4 lbs.)
- 1 tsp. rubbed sage
- 1 tsp. salt, divided
- ¼ tsp. pepper
- 1 can (20 oz.) unsweetened crushed pineapple, undrained
- 2 Tbsp. minced fresh gingerroot
- 18 Boston or Bibb lettuce leaves
  Thinly sliced green onions, optional

1. Rub roast with sage, ½ tsp. salt and pepper. Place in a 4- or 5-qt. slow cooker. Top with pineapple and ginger. Cook, covered, on low until meat is tender, 6-8 hours.

2. Remove roast; shred with 2 forks. Strain the cooking juices. Reserve pineapple and 1 cup juices; discard the remaining juices. Skim fat from reserved juices. Return pork and cooking juices to slow cooker; stir in remaining ½ tsp. salt. Heat through. Serve in lettuce leaves with reserved pineapple and, if desired, green onions.

Freeze option: Freeze cooled meat mixture and juices in freezer containers. To use, partially thaw in refrigerator overnight. Heat through in a saucepan, stirring occasionally; add water if necessary.

3 wraps: 430 cal., 23g fat (8g sat. fat), 135mg chol., 535mg sod., 16g carb. (14g sugars, 1g fiber), 39g pro.

TEST KITCHEN TIP

Sage and ginger flavor this mildly sweet pork dish. If you'd like yours sweeter, add a drizzle of honey to the pork mixture.

CHOCOLATE MOLASSES PORK ROAST

This new twist on pork roast has a rich molasses flavor with a tantalizing hint of chocolate. It's easy to make, yet elegant enough for entertaining. Serve this with mashed potatoes so as not to waste a drop of the delicious gravy.

—*Avionne Huppert, Adams, NY*

- -

PREP: 20 min. • **COOK:** 6 hours
MAKES: 10 servings

- ½ cup packed brown sugar
- ½ cup maple syrup
- ¼ cup beef broth
- ¼ cup Worcestershire sauce
- ¼ cup ketchup
- ¼ cup molasses
- 2 Tbsp. baking cocoa
- 2 tsp. garlic powder
- 2 tsp. onion powder
- ¾ tsp. salt
- ½ tsp. ground ginger
- ½ tsp. ground mustard
- 1 boneless pork loin roast (4 to 5 lbs.)
- 3 Tbsp. cornstarch
- 3 Tbsp. water

1. In a small bowl, mix the first 12 ingredients. Cut roast in half; place in a 5- or 6-qt. slow cooker. Pour sauce over top. Cover and cook on low until meat is tender, 6-8 hours.

2. Remove pork to a serving platter; keep warm. Skim the fat from cooking juices. Transfer juices to a small saucepan; bring to a boil. In a small bowl, mix cornstarch and water until smooth; gradually stir into pan. Return to a boil; cook and stir until thickened, about 2 minutes. Serve with pork.

5 oz. cooked pork with ⅓ cup sauce: 355 cal., 9g fat (3g sat. fat), 90mg chol., 403mg sod., 33g carb. (27g sugars, 0 fiber), 35g pro.

HAWAIIAN PULLED PORK
LETTUCE WRAPS

in tortillas with toppings of your choice.
Freeze option: Freeze cooled pork mixture in freezer containers. To use, partially thaw in the refrigerator overnight. Microwave, covered, on high in a microwave-safe dish until heated through, stirring occasionally; add water or broth if necessary.

2 tacos: 393 cal., 18g fat (6g sat. fat), 100mg chol., 757mg sod., 25g carb. (2g sugars, 4g fiber), 32g pro.

PORK CHOPS WITH SAUERKRAUT

I pair tender pork chops with tangy sauerkraut in this filling main dish. It's so quick and easy to put together, and it leaves everyone satisfied.
—*Stephanie Miller, Omaha, NE*

- -

PREP: 15 min. • **COOK:** 3 hours
MAKES: 4 servings

- 2 Tbsp. canola oil
- 4 bone-in center-cut pork loin chops (8 oz. each)
- 1 jar (32 oz.) sauerkraut, undrained
- ¾ cup packed brown sugar
- 1 medium green pepper, sliced
- 1 medium onion, sliced

1. Heat oil in a large skillet over medium heat; cook until pork chops are browned on each side, 3-4 minutes. Drain. In a 5-qt. slow cooker, combine the sauerkraut and brown sugar. Top with the pork chops, green pepper and onion.
2. Cover and cook on low until the meat is tender, 3-4 hours. Serve mixture with a slotted spoon.

1 serving: 361 cal., 12g fat (3g sat. fat), 28mg chol., 1536mg sod., 55g carb. (45g sugars, 7g fiber), 12g pro.

PORK CHOPS WITH SAUERKRAUT

❄

SLOW-COOKER CARNITAS

We shared these flavor-packed tacos with friends from church who came over to help us move. The slow cooker makes this recipe extra easy, and I love that whenever I make it, I'm reminded of the wonderful people back in Michigan.
—*Abigail Raines, Hamden, CT*

- -

PREP: 25 min. • **COOK:** 8 hours
MAKES: 12 servings

- ½ cup salsa
- 3 bay leaves
- 1 Tbsp. salt
- 2 tsp. ground cumin
- 2 tsp. dried oregano
- 2 tsp. pepper
- 1½ tsp. garlic powder
- 4 whole cloves
- 1¼ cups water
- 2 medium onions, chopped
- 1 bone-in pork shoulder roast (6 to 7 lbs.)
- 24 corn tortillas (6 in.) or taco shells, warmed
     Optional toppings: Shredded cheese, sour cream and chopped tomato, onion, cilantro and lime wedges

1. In a small bowl, mix first 9 ingredients. Place onions in a 6-qt. slow cooker. Place roast over onions; pour salsa mixture over roast. Cook, covered, on low until pork is tender, 8-10 hours.
2. Remove roast and discard bone. Shred pork with 2 forks. Serve the meat

MY BRAZILIAN
FEIJOADA

Cure your craving for something different
with a savory stew that's tasty with warm
bread. Edamame adds an interesting
protein-packed touch.
—*Erin Chilcoat, Central Islip, NY*

PREP: 20 min. • **COOK:** 8½ hours
MAKES: 6 servings (2 qt.)

  ⅓   cup plus 1 Tbsp. all-purpose flour,
      divided
  1   Tbsp. paprika
  1   tsp. salt
  1   tsp. ground coriander
1½   lbs. boneless pork shoulder butt
      roast, cut into 1-in. cubes
  1   Tbsp. canola oil
2¾   cups cubed peeled butternut squash
  1   can (14½ oz.) diced tomatoes,
      undrained
  1   cup frozen corn, thawed
  1   medium onion, chopped
  2   Tbsp. cider vinegar
  1   bay leaf
2½   cups reduced-sodium chicken broth
1⅔   cups frozen shelled edamame,
      thawed

1. In a large resealable container, combine
⅓ cup flour, paprika, salt and coriander.
Add pork, a few pieces at a time, and
shake to coat.
2. In a large skillet, brown pork in oil in
batches; drain. Transfer to a 5-qt. slow
cooker. Add the squash, tomatoes, corn,
onion, vinegar and bay leaf. In a small
bowl, combine broth and remaining flour
until smooth; stir into slow cooker.
3. Cover and cook on low until pork and
vegetables are tender, 8-10 hours. Stir
in edamame; cover and cook 30 minutes
longer. Discard bay leaf.
Freeze option: Freeze cooled stew in
freezer containers. To use, partially thaw
in refrigerator overnight. Heat through in
a saucepan, stirring occasionally; add broth
if necessary.
1⅓ cups: 371 cal., 16g fat (5g sat. fat),
67mg chol., 635mg sod., 30g carb.
(7g sugars, 5g fiber), 28g pro. **Diabetic
exchanges:** 3 medium-fat meat, 1½ starch,
1 vegetable, ½ fat.

MY BRAZILIAN FEIJOADA

A co-worker's mom used to make this dish
for him and it was his favorite. So I made
him my own version. Instead of sausage
you can use ham hocks, or substitute lean
white meat for the red meat if you prefer.
—*Christiane Counts, Webster, TX*

- -

PREP: 20 min. + soaking • **COOK:** 7 hours
MAKES: 10 servings

  8   oz. dried black beans (about 1 cup)
  2   lbs. boneless pork shoulder butt
      roast, trimmed and cut into 1-in.
      cubes
  3   bone-in beef short ribs (about
      1½ lbs.)
  4   bacon strips, cooked and crumbled
1¼   cups diced onion
  3   garlic cloves, minced
  1   bay leaf
  ¾   tsp. salt
  ¾   tsp. pepper
1½   cups chicken broth
  1   cup water
  ½   cup beef broth
  8   oz. smoked sausage, cut into ½-in.
      slices
      Orange sections
      Hot cooked rice, optional

1. Rinse and sort beans; soak according
to package directions. Meanwhile, place
pork roast, short ribs and bacon in a 6-qt.
slow cooker. Add onion, garlic, bay leaf
and seasonings; pour chicken broth, water
and beef broth over meat. Cook, covered,
on high 2 hours.
2. Stir in beans and sausage. Cook,
covered, on low 5-6 hours, until meat
and beans are tender. Discard bay leaf.
Remove short ribs. When cool enough to
handle, remove meat from bones; discard
bones. Shred meat with 2 forks; return
to slow cooker. Top servings with orange
sections. If desired, serve with rice.
1 serving: 481 cal., 27g fat (11g sat. fat),
123mg chol., 772mg sod., 17g carb. (2g
sugars, 4g fiber), 41g pro.

DID YOU KNOW?

Feijoada is a versatile stew
of beans, various meats and
sausages that's typically served
over rice. Although it originated in
Portugal, feijoada is often called
the national dish of Brazil.

Soups, Sides & Sandwiches

YUMMY PINTO
BEANS

❄ YUMMY PINTO BEANS

I love pinto beans, but I always feel the flavor can easily turn too bland. I added a little this and a little that and came out with this amazing but easy slow-cooker recipe.
—*Erica Vanderpool, Clarksville, TN*

PREP: 15 min. • **COOK:** 8 hours
MAKES: 8 servings

- 1 lb. dried pinto beans
- ¼ cup sliced onions
- 8 cups water
- 1 garlic clove, minced
- 1 Tbsp. chicken bouillon granules
- 1 Tbsp. kosher salt
- 1 tsp. pepper
- 1 tsp. ground cumin
- ½ tsp. dried thyme
- ¼ tsp. dried marjoram
- ¼ tsp. ground coriander
   Fresh thyme sprigs , optional

1. Sort beans and rinse in cold water. Add beans to a greased 3-qt. slow cooker. Add the next 10 ingredients; stir.
2. Cook, covered, on high 2 hours. Reduce heat to low; cook until beans are tender, 6-7 hours. Serve with slotted spoon. If desired, top with fresh thyme sprigs.
Freeze option: Freeze cooled beans in freezer containers. To use, partially thaw in refrigerator overnight. Heat through in a covered saucepan, stirring occasionally; add water if necessary.
¾ cup: 203 cal., 1g fat (0 sat. fat), 0 chol., 1043mg sod., 37g carb. (2g sugars, 9g fiber), 12g pro.

DREAMY POLENTA

—Ann Voccola, Milford, CT

CHICKEN FAJITA CHOWDER

This south-of-the-border chowder is one of my favorite slow-cooker recipes, and it's a winner at family dinners and potlucks alike. We like ours topped with fresh avocado, shredded cheddar cheese and chili-cheese corn chips.

—Nancy Heishman, Las Vegas, NV

PREP: 20 min. • **COOK:** 4 hours
MAKES: 10 servings (about 3½ qt.)

- 3 large tomatoes, chopped
- 1 can (15 oz.) black beans, rinsed and drained
- 6 oz. fully cooked Spanish chorizo links, sliced
- 2 lbs. boneless skinless chicken breasts, cut into 1-in. cubes
- 1 envelope fajita seasoning mix
- 1½ cups frozen corn, thawed
- 1 medium sweet red pepper, chopped
- 1 medium green pepper, chopped
- 6 green onions, chopped
- ¾ cup salsa
- ½ cup chopped fresh cilantro
- 2 cans (14½ oz. each) reduced-sodium chicken broth
- 1 can (10¾ oz.) condensed nacho cheese soup, undiluted
  Optional: Cubed avocado and additional cilantro

1. Place first 12 ingredients in a 6-qt. slow cooker. Cook, covered, on low until chicken is tender, 4-5 hours.
2. Stir in cheese soup; heat through. If desired, top servings with avocado and additional cilantro.

Freeze option: Freeze cooled soup in freezer containers. To use, partially thaw in refrigerator overnight. Heat through in a saucepan, stirring occasionally.

1⅓ cups: 269 cal., 9g fat (3g sat. fat), 64mg chol., 1069mg sod., 20g carb. (5g sugars, 4g fiber), 26g pro.

DREAMY POLENTA

I grew up eating polenta, so it's a must at my holiday gatherings. Traditional recipes require constant stirring, but using my handy slow cooker allows me to turn my attention to the lineup of other foods on my spread.

—Ann Voccola, Milford, CT

PREP: 10 min. • **COOK:** 5 hours
MAKES: 12 servings

- 1 Tbsp. butter
- 5 cups whole milk
- 4 cups half-and-half cream
- 12 Tbsp. butter, cubed, divided
- 2 cups yellow cornmeal
- ¾ tsp. salt
- ½ tsp. minced fresh rosemary
- ¼ tsp. pepper
- 2 cups shredded Asiago cheese

1. Generously grease a 5-qt. slow cooker with 1 Tbsp. butter. Add milk, cream, 6 Tbsp. butter, cornmeal, salt, rosemary and pepper; stir to combine.
2. Cook, covered, on low 5-6 hours or until polenta is thickened, whisking every hour. Just before serving, whisk again; stir in cheese and remaining butter. Garnish with additional rosemary if desired.
¾ cup: 444 cal., 29g fat (18g sat. fat), 100mg chol., 379mg sod., 29g carb. (9g sugars, 1g fiber), 13g pro.

COFFEE-BRAISED PULLED PORK SANDWICHES

RED BEAN VEGETARIAN CHILI

For a vegetarian chili that meat lovers would like, this recipe is healthy and tastes wonderful. I top bowls with shredded cheddar cheese.
—*Connie Barnett, Athens, GA*

PREP: 10 min. • **COOK:** 5 hours
MAKES: 6 servings (2 qt.)

- 1 can (16 oz.) red beans, rinsed and drained
- 2 cans (8 oz. each) no-salt-added tomato sauce
- 2 cups water
- 1 can (14½ oz.) diced tomatoes, undrained
- 1 pkg. (12 oz.) frozen vegetarian meat crumbles
- 1 large onion, chopped
- 1 to 2 Tbsp. chili powder
- 1 Tbsp. ground cumin
- 2 garlic cloves, minced
- 1 tsp. pepper
- ½ tsp. salt
- ½ tsp. cayenne pepper
  Optional: Sour cream and shredded cheddar cheese

In a 4-qt. slow cooker, combine the first 12 ingredients. Cover and cook on low until heated through, 5-6 hours. Serve with sour cream and cheddar cheese if desired.

Note: Vegetarian meat crumbles are a nutritious protein source made from soy. Look for them in the natural foods freezer section.

1⅓ cups: 201 cal., 3g fat (0 sat. fat), 0 chol., 1035mg sod., 27g carb. (5g sugars, 9g fiber), 17g pro.

Lentil & Red Bean Chili: Substitute 1½ cups cooked green lentils for the vegetarian meat crumbles. Decrease cumin to 1½ tsp.; add ¼ tsp. smoked paprika.

COFFEE-BRAISED PULLED PORK SANDWICHES

Adding coffee to meat adds such a deep flavor. And this recipe is so easy—I put it in before work and by the time we all get home, it's ready for us to dig in.
—*Jacquelynn Sanders, Burnsville, MN*

PREP: 30 min. • **COOK:** 8 hours
MAKES: 10 servings

- 1 boneless pork shoulder butt roast (3 to 3½ lbs.)
- ⅓ cup ground coffee beans
- ½ tsp. salt
- ½ tsp. pepper
- 2 Tbsp. canola oil
- 2 celery ribs, chopped
- 1 large carrot, chopped
- 1 medium onion, chopped
- 2 cups chicken stock
- 1½ cups strong brewed coffee
- 2 Tbsp. minced fresh parsley
- 1 tsp. coriander seeds
- 1 tsp. ground cumin
- 1 tsp. whole peppercorns, crushed
- 1 cinnamon stick (3 in.)
- 1 bay leaf
- 10 hoagie or kaiser buns, split
- 10 slices pepper jack cheese

1. Cut roast into thirds. Combine the ground coffee, salt and pepper; rub over roast. In a large skillet, brown meat in oil on all sides; drain.

2. Transfer meat to a 5-qt. slow cooker. Add the celery, carrot, onion, chicken stock, brewed coffee, parsley, coriander seeds, cumin, peppercorns, cinnamon stick and bay leaf; pour over roast.

3. Cover and cook on low until meat is tender, 8-10 hours. When cool enough to handle, shred meat. Skim fat from cooking juices. Strain cooking juices, discarding the vegetables, cinnamon and bay leaf.

4. Spoon about ½ cup pork onto each bun; top with cheese. Serve with cooking juices.

1 sandwich: 458 cal., 23g fat (8g sat. fat), 85mg chol., 689mg sod., 32g carb. (5g sugars, 1g fiber), 31g pro.

"Super good and easy! A crowd pleaser. I bought bone-in shoulder and it was juicier than the boneless."
—SUSANBLACK, TASTEOFHOME.COM

RED BEAN
VEGETARIAN CHILI

CORN & ONION STUFFING

I like something different for a side dish and this is it. This stuffing is perfect with pork, beef or chicken. You can leave it in the slow cooker until it's time to eat—or make it early, refrigerate it until almost serving time, and then reheat it.
—*Patricia Swart, Galloway, NJ*

PREP: 10 min. • **COOK:** 3 hours
MAKES: 8 servings

- 1 can (14¾ oz.) cream-style corn
- 1 pkg. (6 oz.) stuffing mix
- 1 small onion, chopped
- 1 celery rib, chopped
- ¼ cup water
- 2 large eggs
- 1 tsp. poultry seasoning
- ⅛ tsp. pepper
- ¼ cup butter, melted

Combine first 8 ingredients. Transfer to a greased 3-qt. slow cooker. Drizzle with butter. Cook, covered, on low until set, 3-4 hours.
½ cup: 192 cal., 8g fat (4g sat. fat), 63mg chol., 530mg sod., 26g carb. (4g sugars, 1g fiber), 5g pro.

ROSEMARY BEETS

We're a family of beet eaters. For a simple side dish, I use a slow cooker and let the beets mellow with rosemary and thyme.
—*Nancy Heishman, Las Vegas, NV*

PREP: 20 min. • **COOK:** 6 hours
MAKES: 8 servings

- ⅓ cup honey
- ¼ cup white balsamic vinegar
- 1 Tbsp. minced fresh rosemary or 1 tsp. dried rosemary, crushed
- 2 tsp. minced fresh thyme or ¾ tsp. dried thyme
- 1 Tbsp. olive oil
- 2 garlic cloves, minced
- ¾ tsp. salt
- ½ tsp. Chinese five-spice powder
- ½ tsp. coarsely ground pepper
- 5 large fresh beets (about 3½ lbs.), peeled and trimmed
- 1 medium red onion, chopped
- 1 medium orange, peeled and chopped
- 1 cup crumbled feta cheese

1. In a small bowl, whisk first 9 ingredients until blended. Place beets in a greased 4-qt. slow cooker. Add onion and orange. Pour honey mixture over top.
2. Cook, covered, on low 6-8 hours or until beets are tender. Remove beets; cut into wedges. Return to slow cooker. Serve warm, or refrigerate and serve cold. Serve with a slotted spoon; sprinkle with cheese.
¾ cup: 200 cal., 4g fat (2g sat. fat), 8mg chol., 511mg sod., 37g carb. (31g sugars, 5g fiber), 6g pro. **Diabetic exchanges:** 2 vegetable, 1 starch, 1 fat.

ROSEMARY BEETS

SLOW-COOKER SWEET POTATO CHOCOLATE MOLE SOUP

SAUSAGE & CHICKEN GUMBO

This recipe for the classic southern comfort food was the first thing I ever cooked for my girlfriend. It was simple to make, but tasted gourmet. Lucky for me, it was love at first bite.
—*Kael Harvey, Brooklyn, NY*

PREP: 35 min. • **COOK:** 6 hours
MAKES: 6 servings

- ¼ cup all-purpose flour
- ¼ cup canola oil
- 4 cups chicken broth, divided
- 1 pkg. (14 oz.) smoked sausage, cut into ½-in. slices
- 1 cup frozen sliced okra, thawed
- 1 small green pepper, chopped
- 1 medium onion, chopped
- 1 celery rib, chopped
- 3 garlic cloves, minced
- ½ tsp. pepper
- ¼ tsp. salt
- ¼ tsp. cayenne pepper
- 2 cups coarsely shredded cooked chicken
  Hot cooked rice

1. In a heavy saucepan, mix flour and oil until smooth; cook and stir over medium heat until light brown, about 4 minutes. Reduce heat to medium-low; cook and stir until dark reddish brown, about 15 minutes (do not burn). Gradually stir in 3 cups broth; transfer to a 4- or 5-qt. slow cooker.
2. Stir in sausage, vegetables, garlic and seasonings. Cook, covered, on low until flavors are blended, 6-8 hours. Stir in chicken and remaining broth; heat through. Serve with rice.

Freeze option: Freeze cooled gumbo in freezer containers. To use, partially thaw in refrigerator overnight. Heat through in a saucepan, stirring occasionally; add broth if necessary.

1 cup: 427 cal., 31g fat (9g sat. fat), 89mg chol., 1548mg sod., 11g carb. (4g sugars, 1g fiber), 25g pro.

SLOW-COOKER SWEET POTATO CHOCOLATE MOLE SOUP

This recipe is perfect for those days you're craving something just a little bit different. It's spicy, flavorful, and a great excuse to open up a bar of chocolate—if you're the type of person that needs an excuse!
—*Colleen Delawder, Herndon, VA*

PREP: 30 min. • **COOK:** 6 hours
MAKES: 8 servings (2½ qt.)

- 2 Tbsp. olive oil
- 1 large sweet onion, finely chopped
- 2 Tbsp. chili powder
- 1 tsp. dried oregano
- 1 tsp. dried tarragon
- 1 tsp. ground cumin
- ¾ tsp. salt
- ½ tsp. ground cinnamon
- ½ tsp. pepper
- 3 garlic cloves, minced
- 2 Tbsp. tequila, optional
- 1 carton (32 oz.) reduced-sodium vegetable broth
- 1 can (14½ oz.) reduced-sodium chicken broth
- 4 medium sweet potatoes, peeled and cubed
- 2 oz. bittersweet chocolate, finely chopped
  Optional: Cubed avocado, Cotija cheese, chopped onion, corn and cilantro leaves

1. In a large skillet, heat oil over medium-high heat. Add onion and seasonings; cook and stir until onion is tender, 5-7 minutes. Add the garlic; cook 1 minute longer. If desired, add in tequila, stirring constantly.
2. Transfer to a 4- or 5-qt. slow cooker. Add broths and sweet potatoes. Cook, covered, on low until potatoes are tender, 6-8 hours. Stir in chocolate until melted. Cool soup slightly. Process in batches in a blender until smooth. Serve with toppings as desired.

Freeze option: Freeze cooled soup in freezer containers. To use, partially thaw in refrigerator overnight. Heat through in a saucepan, stirring occasionally; add broth if necessary.

1¼ cups: 203 cal., 6g fat (2g sat. fat), 0 chol., 511mg sod., 31g carb. (14g sugars, 5g fiber), 4g pro. **Diabetic exchanges:** 2 starch, 1 fat.

SLOW-COOKER
FRENCH DIP SANDWICHES

SLOW-COOKER FRENCH DIP SANDWICHES

These sandwiches make a standout addition to any buffet line. Make sure to have plenty of small cups of broth for everyone to grab. Dipping perfection!
—Holly Neuharth, Mesa, AZ

PREP: 15 min. • **COOK:** 8 hours
MAKES: 12 servings

- 1 beef rump or bottom round roast (about 3 lbs.)
- 1½ tsp. onion powder
- 1½ tsp. garlic powder
- ½ tsp. Creole seasoning
- 1 carton (26 oz.) beef stock
- 12 whole wheat hoagie buns, split
- 6 oz. Havarti cheese, cut into 12 slices

1. Cut roast in half. Mix onion powder, garlic powder and Creole seasoning; rub onto beef. Place in a 5-qt. slow cooker; add stock. Cook, covered, on low until meat is tender, 8-10 hours.
2. Remove beef; cool slightly. Skim fat from cooking juices. When cool enough to handle, shred beef with 2 forks and return to slow cooker.
3. Place buns on ungreased baking sheets, cut side up. Using tongs, place beef on bun bottoms. Place cheese on bun tops. Broil 3-4 in. from heat until cheese is melted, 1-2 minutes. Close sandwiches; serve with cooking juices.
Note: If you don't have Creole seasoning in your cupboard, you can make your own using ⅛ tsp. each salt, garlic powder and paprika; and a dash each of dried thyme, ground cumin and cayenne pepper.
1 sandwich with ⅓ cup juices: 456 cal., 14g fat (5g sat. fat), 81mg chol., 722mg sod., 50g carb. (9g sugars, 7g fiber), 35g pro.

VEGAN CHILI OLE!

🍎 ❄️
VEGAN CHILI OLE!

I combine ingredients for this hearty chili the night before, start my trusty slow cooker in the morning and come home to a rich, spicy meal at night!
—Marjorie Au, Honolulu, HI

PREP: 35 min. • **COOK:** 6 hours
MAKES: 7 servings

- 1 can (16 oz.) kidney beans, rinsed and drained
- 1 can (15 oz.) black beans, rinsed and drained
- 1 can (14½ oz.) diced tomatoes, undrained
- 1½ cups frozen corn
- 1 large onion, chopped
- 1 medium zucchini, chopped
- 1 medium sweet red pepper, chopped
- 1 can (4 oz.) chopped green chiles
- 1 oz. Mexican chocolate, chopped
- 1 cup water
- 1 can (6 oz.) tomato paste
- 1 Tbsp. cornmeal
- 1 Tbsp. chili powder
- ½ tsp. salt
- ½ tsp. dried oregano
- ½ tsp. ground cumin
- ¼ tsp. hot pepper sauce, optional
  Optional toppings: diced tomatoes and chopped green onions

1. In a 4-qt. slow cooker, combine the first 9 ingredients. Combine water, tomato paste, cornmeal, chili powder, salt, oregano, cumin and, if desired, pepper sauce until smooth; stir into slow cooker. Cover and cook on low until vegetables are tender, 6-8 hours.
2. Serve with toppings of your choice.
Freeze option: Freeze chili in freezer containers. To use, partially thaw in refrigerator overnight. Heat through in a saucepan, stirring occasionally; add water or broth if necessary.
1 cup: 216 cal., 1g fat (0 sat. fat), 0 chol., 559mg sod., 43g carb. (11g sugars, 10g fiber), 11g pro. **Diabetic exchanges:** 2½ starch, 1 lean meat.
Summertime Vegan Chili Ole: Add 1 can garbanzo beans or chickpeas, rinsed and drained. Use fire-roasted diced tomatoes instead of regular and substitute 3 ears fresh corn, removed from the cob, for frozen corn. Substitute 1 cup chopped roasted red and green Hatch chiles for the red pepper and canned green chiles. Top each serving with fresh cilantro leaves.

WILD RICE WITH DRIED BLUEBERRIES

I love the combination of rice and fruit, so this is a go-to Thanksgiving side dish at my house. I toss in mushrooms and toasted almonds; you can also include dried cherries or cranberries if you'd like.
—*Janie Colle, Hutchinson, KS*

- -

PREP: 15 min. • **COOK:** 3¼ hours
MAKES: 16 servings

- 2 Tbsp. butter
- 8 oz. sliced fresh mushrooms
- 3 cups uncooked wild rice
- 8 green onions, sliced
- 1 tsp. salt
- ½ tsp. pepper
- 4 cans (14½ oz. each) vegetable broth
- 1 cup chopped pecans, toasted
- 1 cup dried blueberries

In a large skillet, heat butter over medium heat. Add mushrooms; cook and stir until tender, 4-5 minutes. In a 5-qt. slow cooker, combine rice, mushrooms, onions, salt and pepper. Pour broth over rice mixture. Cook, covered, on low 3-4 hours or until rice is tender. Stir in pecans and blueberries. Cook, covered, 15 minutes longer or until heated through. If desired, top with additional sliced green onions.
¾ cup: 199 cal., 7g fat (1g sat. fat), 4mg chol., 163mg sod., 31g carb. (5g sugars, 4g fiber), 6g pro. **Diabetic exchanges:** 2 starch, 1½ fat.

SLOW-COOKER CLAM & VEGETABLE CHOWDER

New England clam chowder has always been one of my favorite soups—I love mine heavy on the vegetables. This soup is made even better when I put everything in my slow cooker and can forget about it for hours.
—*Erica Schmidt, Kansas City, KS*

- -

PREP: 25 min. • **COOK:** 4½ hours
MAKES: 16 servings (4 qt.)

- 2 lbs. diced red potatoes
- 1 lb. sliced fresh carrots
- 5 thick-sliced bacon strips, cooked and crumbled
- 2 medium onions, chopped
- 2 celery ribs, chopped
- 2 cans (10 oz. each) whole baby clams
- 6 cups water
- 6 garlic cloves, minced
- 1 Tbsp. Worcestershire sauce
- 1 tsp. beef bouillon granules
- ¾ tsp. each dried thyme, salt and pepper
- 2 cups whole milk
- ¼ cup all-purpose flour

1. In a 5- or 6-qt. slow cooker, combine all ingredients except milk and flour. Cook, covered, on high until potatoes and carrots are tender, about 4 hours.
2. In a small bowl, mix milk and flour until smooth, gradually stir into chowder. Cook, covered, on high until thickened, about 30 minutes.
1 cup: 127 cal., 3g fat (1g sat. fat), 23mg chol., 527mg sod., 18g carb. (4g sugars, 2g fiber), 8g pro. **Diabetic exchanges:** 1 starch, 1 lean meat, ½ fat.

WILD RICE WITH DRIED BLUEBERRIES

NAVY BEAN VEGETABLE SOUP

❄ NAVY BEAN VEGETABLE SOUP

My family really likes bean soup, so I came up with this enticing version. The leftovers are, dare I say, even better the next day!
—*Eleanor Mielke, Mitchell, SD*

- -

PREP: 15 min. • **COOK:** 9 hours
MAKES: 12 servings (3 qt.)

  4 **medium carrots, thinly sliced**
  2 **celery ribs, chopped**
  1 **medium onion, chopped**
  2 **cups cubed fully cooked ham**
1½ **cups dried navy beans**
  1 **envelope vegetable recipe mix (Knorr)**
  1 **envelope onion soup mix**
  1 **bay leaf**
  ½ **tsp. pepper**
  8 **cups water**

In a 5-qt. slow cooker, combine the first 9 ingredients. Stir in water. Cover and cook on low until beans are tender, 9-10 hours. Discard bay leaf.

Freeze option: Freeze cooled soup in freezer containers. To use, partially thaw in refrigerator overnight. Heat through in a saucepan, stirring occasionally; add water or broth if necessary.

1 cup: 157 cal., 2g fat (1g sat. fat), 12mg chol., 763mg sod., 24g carb. (4g sugars, 8g fiber), 11g pro.

Country Cassoulet: Instead of cubed ham, add 1½ lbs. smoked ham hocks or pork neck bones or a meaty ham bone to slow cooker. Omit onion soup mix; add ¼ tsp. each dried thyme and rosemary. Remove ham bones at end of cooking; stir 2 cups shredded cooked chicken or turkey and ½ lb. sliced smoked fully cooked sausage into soup. Heat through. Cut meat from ham bones; add to soup.

"I made this soup exactly as is. I did not soak the beans the night before, since the directions did not mention it. I did worry that the beans would be tough, but they weren't. My hubby said that it was one of the best soups that I have ever made. Wow. Thank you, Taste of Home, for making me look good!"
—CINDY_DEMYAN, TASTEOFHOME.COM

SLOW-COOKED
PULLED PORK

CHICKEN & KALE TORTELLINI SOUP

With tender tortellini, chicken, spinach and lots of herbs, this comforting soup is so flavorful. The fact that it's easy to make is just a chilly-night bonus.
—*Emily Hobbs, Springfield, MO*

PREP: 15 min. • **COOK:** 2½ hours
MAKES: 8 servings (3 qt.)

- 1 lb. boneless skinless chicken breasts, cut into 1¼-in. cubes
- 2 garlic cloves, minced
- 1½ tsp. Italian seasoning
- ¼ tsp. pepper
- 6 cups chicken broth
- 1 pkg. (20 oz.) refrigerated cheese tortellini
- 1 can (15 oz.) cannellini beans, rinsed and drained
- 1 jar (7½ oz.) marinated quartered artichoke hearts, drained and coarsely chopped
- 4 cups coarsely chopped fresh kale (about 2 oz.)
     Shaved Parmesan cheese, optional

1. Place first 5 ingredients in a 5- or 6-qt. slow cooker. Cook, covered, on low until chicken is no longer pink, 2-3 hours.
2. Stir in the tortellini, beans, artichoke hearts and kale. Cook, covered, on low until tortellini and the kale are tender, about 30 minutes, stirring halfway through cook time. Serve immediately. If desired, top with cheese.
1½ cups: 386 cal., 12g fat (4g sat. fat), 66mg chol., 1185mg sod., 43g carb. (4g sugars, 4g fiber), 24g pro.

TEST KITCHEN TIP
Chopped fresh spinach can be used instead of kale. Stir it in during the last few minutes of cooking. This soup is loaded with chunky ingredients. If you like yours with more broth, add an extra 1 or 2 cups.

❄ SLOW-COOKED PULLED PORK

Every time I bring this dish to a potluck I get asked, "Where did you get the pork?" People are surprised to hear me say that I made it. When I tell them how simple the recipe is, they are doubly surprised.
—*Betsy Rivas, Chesterfield, MO*

PREP: 20 min. + chilling
COOK: 8 hours • **MAKES:** 10 servings

- 2   Tbsp. brown sugar
- 4½ tsp. paprika
- 2   Tbsp. coarsely ground pepper, divided
- 1   Tbsp. kosher salt
- 1   tsp. chili powder
- ½   tsp. cayenne pepper
- 1   boneless pork shoulder butt roast (3 to 4 lbs.), cut in half
- 1   cup cider vinegar
- ¼   cup beef broth
- ¼   cup barbecue sauce
- 2   Tbsp. Worcestershire sauce
- 1½ tsp. hickory liquid smoke, optional
- 10 kaiser rolls, split

1. In a small bowl, combine the brown sugar, paprika, 1 Tbsp. pepper, salt, chili powder and cayenne. Rub over roast; cover and refrigerate for 8 hours or overnight.
2. Place roast in a 4- or 5-qt. slow cooker. Combine the vinegar, broth, barbecue sauce, Worcestershire sauce, liquid smoke, if desired, and remaining pepper; pour over roast. Cover and cook on low until meat is tender, 8-10 hours.
3. Remove meat from slow cooker; cool slightly. Shred meat with 2 forks and return to the slow cooker; heat through. Using a slotted spoon, place ½ cup on each roll.
Freeze option: Freeze cooled pork mixture in freezer containers. To use, partially thaw in refrigerator overnight. Heat through in a saucepan, stirring occasionally; add broth if necessary.
Note: Kosher salt is a type of coarse salt that is desirable for cooking and canning purposes. The coarser texture makes it ideal for rubbing over meats, seasoning foods during cooking or for decorating the rim of a margarita glass. Kosher salt is not recommended for use in baking or at the table.
1 sandwich: 419 cal., 16g fat (5g sat. fat), 81mg chol., 1076mg sod., 36g carb. (5g sugars, 2g fiber), 29g pro.

CHICKEN & KALE
TORTELLINI SOUP

SLOW-COOKED POTATOES WITH SPRING ONIONS

I love the simplicity of this recipe, as well as its ease of preparation with my slow cooker. Everyone always enjoys roasted potatoes, even my pickiest child! If desired, top with shredded or crumbled cheese.
—Theresa Gomez, Stuart, FL

PREP: 5 min. • COOK: 6 hours
MAKES: 12 servings

- 4 lbs. small red potatoes
- 8 green onions, chopped (about 1 cup)
- 1 cup chopped sweet onion
- ¼ cup olive oil
- ½ tsp. salt
- ½ tsp. pepper

In a 5- or 6-qt. slow cooker, combine all ingredients. Cook, covered, on low until potatoes are tender, 6-8 hours.

1 serving: 157 cal., 5g fat (1g sat. fat), 0 chol., 110mg sod., 26g carb. (2g sugars, 3g fiber), 3g pro. **Diabetic exchanges:** 1½ starch, 1 fat.

CUBED BEEF & BARLEY SOUP

Here's a real stick-to-your-ribs soup. I've also used a chuck roast, rump roast and London broil (cut into bite-sized pieces) with tremendous success.
—Jane Whittaker, Pensacola, FL

PREP: 20 min. • COOK: 8½ hours
MAKES: 8 servings (2 qt.)

- 1½ lbs. beef stew meat, cut into ½-in. cubes
- 1 Tbsp. canola oil
- 1 carton (32 oz.) beef broth
- 1 bottle (12 oz.) beer or nonalcoholic beer
- 1 small onion, chopped
- ½ cup medium pearl barley
- 3 garlic cloves, minced
- 1 tsp. dried oregano
- 1 tsp. dried parsley flakes
- 1 tsp. Worcestershire sauce
- ½ tsp. crushed red pepper flakes
- ½ tsp. pepper
- ¼ tsp. salt
- 1 bay leaf
- 2 cups frozen mixed vegetables, thawed

1. In a large skillet, brown beef in oil; drain. Transfer to a 3-qt. slow cooker.
2. Add the broth, beer, onion, barley, garlic, oregano, parsley, Worcestershire sauce, pepper flakes, pepper, salt and bay leaf. Cover and cook on low, 8-10 hours.
3. Stir in vegetables; cover and cook until meat is tender and vegetables are heated through, 30 minutes longer. Discard bay leaf.

1 cup: 233 cal., 8g fat (2g sat. fat), 53mg chol., 644mg sod., 18g carb. (3g sugars, 4g fiber), 20g pro. **Diabetic exchanges:** 3 lean meat, 1 starch.

Dilly Beef Stew: Omit beer. Add 1 cup chopped carrots to slow cooker and use 1-2 tsp. dill weed instead of oregano and parsley. Substitute thawed peas for the mixed vegetables. Serve stew with mashed potatoes.

CUBED BEEF & BARLEY SOUP

MEXICAN STREET
CORN CHOWDER

CHEESY SPOON BREAD CASSEROLE

I love this spoon bread casserole because it's creamy with a little southwestern kick. This is comfort food at its finest and is a vivid way to add a unique dish to the usual holiday lineup. Sometimes we scoop chili on top.
—*Barbara J. Miller, Oakdale, MN*

- -

PREP: 20 min. • **COOK:** 4 hours
MAKES: 8 servings

- 2 cups shredded cheddar cheese
- 1 can (15¼ oz.) whole kernel corn, drained
- 1 can (14½ oz.) diced tomatoes, drained
- 1 cup sour cream
- ⅔ cup all-purpose flour
- ½ cup yellow cornmeal
- ½ cup butter, melted
- 3 Tbsp. sugar
- 2 Tbsp. taco seasoning
- 2½ tsp. baking powder
- ½ tsp. salt
  Optional toppings: Chopped green onions and minced fresh cilantro

Combine the first 11 ingredients in a greased 3-qt. slow cooker. Cook, covered, on low until a toothpick inserted in the center comes out clean, 4-5 hours. If desired, top with green onions and cilantro.

1 serving: 412 cal., 28g fat (16g sat. fat), 66mg chol., 1028mg sod., 31g carb. (11g sugars, 3g fiber), 11g pro.

MEXICAN STREET CORN CHOWDER

Corn is one of my all-time favorite vegetables, so when it's in season, I always make this super easy soup in the slow cooker.
—*Rashanda Cobbins, Milwaukee, WI*

- -

PREP: 35 min. • **COOK:** 3½ hours
MAKES: 8 servings (2 qt.)

- 10 ears fresh corn (about 5½ cups)
- 1-¼ to 2 cups water
- 6 bacon strips, chopped
- 2 small onions, chopped
- 2 small green peppers, chopped
- 1 jalapeno pepper, seeded and finely chopped
- 1 tsp. ground chipotle pepper
- 2 tsp. salt
- ¾ tsp. ground cumin
- ¼ tsp. pepper
- 1 cup heavy whipping cream
- 1 medium lime, zested and juiced
  Optional toppings: Fresh cilantro, lime wedges, sliced jalapeno, chopped bell pepper and crumbled cotija cheese

1. Cut corn off cobs. Rub the edge of a knife over each cob to milk it; add enough water to cob juice to equal 2 cups. Add corn and liquid to a 5-qt. slow cooker.
2. In a large skillet, cook bacon over medium heat until crisp, 5-7 minutes. Remove with a slotted spoon; drain on paper towels. Discard drippings, reserving 2 Tbsp. in the pan. Add the onions, green peppers and jalapeno to skillet; cook and stir over medium-high heat until soft, 3-4 minutes. Add seasonings and cook 1 minute longer; transfer to slow cooker. Cook on low 3½-4 hours or until corn is tender and mixture has thickened slightly.
3. Stir in cream and lime zest and juice. If desired, puree mixture with an immersion blender to desired consistency. Garnish with reserved bacon. Sprinkle with optional toppings as desired.
Note: Wear disposable gloves when cutting hot peppers; the oils can burn skin. Avoid touching your face.
1 cup: 287 cal., 18g fat (9g sat. fat), 43mg chol., 743mg sod., 29g carb. (10g sugars, 4g fiber), 8g pro.

SWEET POTATO
& SAUSAGE STUFFING

SWEET POTATO & SAUSAGE STUFFING

I love this easy version of a holiday favorite. Slow-cooking the stuffing means that my oven is free for other dishes.
—Kallee Krong-McCreery, Escondido, CA

- -

PREP: 20 min. • **COOK:** 3 hours
MAKES: 8 servings

- 8 oz. bulk pork sausage
- 6 cups dry bread cubes
- 2 cups mashed sweet potatoes
- 1 cup chopped onion
- 1 cup chopped celery
- ¼ cup butter, melted
- 2 tsp. poultry seasoning
- 1 tsp. salt
- 1 tsp. dried tarragon
- ½ tsp. pepper

1. In a large skillet, cook sausage over medium heat until no longer pink, 4-6 minutes, breaking into crumbles; drain and set aside. In a large bowl, combine bread, sweet potatoes, onion and celery. Add sausage to mixture; stir to combine. Stir in melted butter, poultry seasoning, salt, tarragon and pepper.
2. Transfer to a greased 6-qt. slow cooker. Cook, covered, on low 3-4 hours or until heated through, stirring once.

¾ cup: 334 cal., 14g fat (6g sat. fat), 31mg chol., 856mg sod., 47g carb. (8g sugars, 5g fiber), 10g pro.

TEST KITCHEN TIP

This recipe can also be baked in a preheated 350° oven. Transfer the stuffing mixture to a greased 8x8-in. baking dish and bake until golden brown, 30-40 minutes.

HOT PINEAPPLE HAM
SANDWICHES

HOT PINEAPPLE HAM SANDWICHES

Your trusty slow cooker lets you make these warm, gooey sandwiches without heating up the house on a hot day. The mustard and brown sugar give them a richness everybody loves.
—Nancy Foust, Stoneboro, PA

- -

PREP: 25 min. • **COOK:** 3 hours
MAKES: 10 servings

- 2 cans (20 oz. each) unsweetened crushed pineapple, undrained
- 1 medium onion, finely chopped
- ¾ cup packed light brown sugar
- ¼ cup Dijon mustard
- 2½ lbs. thinly sliced deli ham
- 2 Tbsp. cornstarch
- 2 Tbsp. water
- 10 slices Swiss cheese or cheddar cheese, optional
- 10 kaiser rolls, split

1. Mix first 4 ingredients. Place half the mixture in a 5-qt. slow cooker; top with half the ham. Repeat layers. Cook, covered, on low until heated through, 3-4 hours.
2. Using tongs, remove ham from slow cooker, leaving pineapple mixture behind; keep warm. In a large saucepan, mix cornstarch and water until smooth. Stir in pineapple mixture; bring to a boil. Reduce heat; simmer, uncovered, until mixture is slightly thickened, stirring occasionally. Serve ham, pineapple mixture and, if desired, cheese on rolls.

1 sandwich: 468 cal., 8g fat (2g sat. fat), 60mg chol., 1540mg sod., 69g carb. (36g sugars, 2g fiber), 29g pro.

Snacks & Sweets

HOT MULLED WINE

HOT MULLED WINE

For a festive holiday drink or something to keep you warm during those winter months, you'll love this fragrant wine.
—Taste of Home *Test Kitchen*

PREP: 15 min. • **COOK:** 4 hours
MAKES: 5 servings

- 2 cinnamon sticks (3 in.)
- 6 whole cloves
- 1 fresh rosemary sprig
- 1 bottle (750 ml) cabernet sauvignon or other dry red wine
- 1 cup fresh or frozen cranberries
- ⅔ cup sugar
- ⅓ cup bourbon
- ⅓ cup orange juice
- 4 tsp. grated orange zest
  Orange slices, optional

1. Place the cinnamon sticks, cloves and rosemary on a double thickness of cheesecloth; bring up corners of cloth and tie with string to form a bag.
2. In a 1½-qt. slow cooker, combine wine, cranberries, sugar, bourbon, orange juice and zest. Add spice bag. Cover and cook on low until heated through, 4-5 hours. Discard the spice bag. Serve warm and, if desired, garnish with orange slices and additional cinnamon sticks and cranberries.

¾ cup: 129 cal., 0 fat (0 sat. fat), 0 chol., 1mg sod., 31g carb. (29g sugars, 1g fiber), 0 pro.

Hot Mulled Cider: Substitute 4 allspice berries or 2 whole star aniseeds for the rosemary. Substitute 3 cups apple cider for the wine and 1 cup dried mixed fruit (such as apples, apricots and plums) for the cranberries.

TROPICAL
CRANBERRY COBBLER

SPICY APPLE TEA

This recipe has a permanent home in our slow cooker during the cold winter months! Sometimes I'll leave the tea on the "keep warm" setting all day and enjoy the drink with breakfast, brunch or a cozy evening.
—*Karen Lara, Kamloops, BC*

- -

PREP: 15 min. • **COOK:** 2 hours
MAKES: 21 servings (about 4 qt.)

    2 qt. water
    2 qt. unsweetened apple juice
    1 cup packed brown sugar
    4 individual black tea bags
    4 cinnamon sticks (3 in.)
    1 Tbsp. minced fresh gingerroot
    1 Tbsp. whole allspice
    1 Tbsp. whole cloves

1. In a 6-qt. slow cooker, combine the water, apple juice, brown sugar and tea bags. Place the cinnamon sticks, ginger, allspice and cloves on a double thickness of cheesecloth; bring up corners of cloth and tie with string to form a bag. Place in slow cooker.
2. Cover and cook on high until heated through, 2-3 hours. Discard tea bags and spice bag. Serve warm in mugs.
¾ cup: 04 cal., 0 fat (0 sat. fat), 0 chol., 7mg sod., 21g carb. (20g sugars, 0 fiber), 0 pro.

TROPICAL CRANBERRY COBBLER

The sunny island flavors of pineapple and orange go surprisingly well with the tart cranberries in this dessert. A scoop of vanilla ice cream makes it a tasty treat.
—*Jeanne Holt, Saint Paul, MN*

- -

PREP: 20 min. • **COOK:** 4 hours + standing
MAKES: 12 servings

    2 cups fresh or frozen cranberries,
       thawed
    1 can (20 oz.) unsweetened pineapple
       tidbits, drained
    ¾ cup sweetened shredded coconut
    ¾ cup orange marmalade
    ½ cup packed light brown sugar
    6 Tbsp. butter, melted
    TOPPING
    1 pkg. yellow cake mix (regular size)
    1 pkg. (3.4 oz.) instant coconut cream
       pudding mix
    4 large eggs, room temperature
    ¾ cup pineapple-orange juice
    ½ cup butter, melted
    ¼ cup packed light brown sugar
    1 tsp. vanilla extract
       Whipped cream, optional

    ¼ cup sweetened shredded
       coconut, toasted

1. In a greased 6-qt. oval slow cooker, layer cranberries, pineapple and ¾ cup coconut. In a bowl, mix the marmalade, brown sugar and melted butter; spoon evenly over fruit.
2. In a large bowl, combine first 7 topping ingredients; beat on low speed 1 minute. Beat on medium speed 2 minutes. Pour over filling.
3. Cook, covered, on low until top springs back when lightly touched, about 4 hours. Turn off slow cooker. Remove insert; let stand 15 minutes before serving. If desired, serve with whipped cream. Sprinkle cobbler with toasted coconut.
1 serving: 514 cal., 22g fat (13g sat. fat), 98mg chol., 508mg sod., 78g carb. (59g sugars, 2g fiber), 5g pro.

TEST KITCHEN TIP

If you don't have pineapple-orange juice on hand, use apple, grape, plain orange or pineapple juice. Most of the pineapple flavor in this dish comes from the fruit layer.

VERY VANILLA SLOW-COOKER CHEESECAKE

Cinnamon and vanilla give this delectable cheesecake so much flavor.
—*Krista Lanphier, Milwaukee, WI*

PREP: 40 min. • **COOK:** 2 hours + chilling
MAKES: 6 servings

- ¾ cup graham cracker crumbs
- 1 Tbsp. sugar plus ⅔ cup sugar, divided
- ¼ tsp. ground cinnamon
- 2½ Tbsp. butter, melted
- 2 pkg. (8 oz. each) cream cheese, softened
- ½ cup sour cream
- 2 to 3 tsp. vanilla extract
- 2 large eggs, room temperature, lightly beaten

TOPPING

- 2 oz. semisweet chocolate, chopped
- 1 tsp. shortening
  Miniature peanut butter cups or toasted sliced almonds

1. Grease a 6-in. springform pan; place on a double thickness of heavy-duty foil (about 12 in. square). Wrap foil securely around pan.

2. Pour 1 in. water into a 6-qt. slow cooker. Layer two 24-in. pieces of foil. Starting with a long side, roll up the foil to make a 1-in.-wide strip; shape into a circle. Place in bottom of slow cooker to make a rack.

3. In a small bowl, mix cracker crumbs, 1 Tbsp. sugar and cinnamon; stir in the butter. Press onto bottom and about 1 in. up side of prepared pan.

4. In a large bowl, beat the cream cheese and remaining sugar until smooth. Beat in sour cream and vanilla. Add eggs; beat on low speed just until combined. Pour into crust.

5. Place springform pan on foil circle without touching slow cooker sides. Cover slow cooker with a double layer of white paper towels; place lid securely over towels. Cook, covered, on high for 2 hours.

6. Do not remove lid; turn off slow cooker and let cheesecake stand, covered, in slow cooker 1 hour.

7. Remove springform pan from slow cooker; remove foil around pan. Cool cheesecake on a wire rack 1 hour longer. Loosen side from the pan with a knife. Refrigerate overnight, covering when completely cooled.

8. For topping, in a microwave, melt chocolate and shortening; stir until smooth. Cool slightly. Remove rim from springform pan. Pour chocolate mixture over cheesecake; sprinkle with miniature peanut butter cups or almonds.

To make ahead: Cheesecake may be stored in refrigerator 4-6 days before serving. Wrap securely before chilling; top just before serving.

1 piece: 565 cal., 41g fat (24g sat. fat), 180mg chol., 351mg sod., 41g carb. (33g sugars, 1g fiber), 10g pro.

GRANOLA APPLE CRISP

Tender apple slices are tucked beneath a sweet crunchy topping in my comforting dessert. For variety, replace the apples with your favorite fruit.
—*Barbara Schindler, Napoleon, OH*

PREP: 20 min. • **COOK:** 5 hours
MAKES: 8 servings

- 8 medium tart apples, peeled and sliced
- ¼ cup lemon juice
- 1½ tsp. grated lemon zest
- 2½ cups granola with fruit and nuts
- 1 cup sugar
- 1 tsp. ground cinnamon
- ½ cup butter, melted
  Vanilla ice cream, optional

1. In a large bowl, toss the apples, lemon juice and zest. Transfer to a greased 3-qt. slow cooker. Combine the granola, sugar and cinnamon; sprinkle over apples. Drizzle with butter.

2. Cover and cook on low until apples are tender, 5-6 hours. Serve warm; if desired, top with vanilla ice cream and additional ground cinnamon.

1 serving: 382 cal., 17g fat (8g sat. fat), 31mg chol., 153mg sod., 58g carb. (44g sugars, 4g fiber), 3g pro.

Granola Fall Fruit Crisp: Substitute 4 sliced medium Bartlett pears for 4 of the medium tart apples. In the topping, use brown sugar instead of granulated and add 1 Tbsp. minced crystallized ginger.

VERY VANILLA SLOW-COOKER CHEESECAKE

GRANOLA
APPLE CRISP

CHOCOLATE BREAD PUDDING WITH RASPBERRIES

I love chocolate and I love berries, so I was thrilled to find a recipe that combines the two. I like to use egg bread when making this dessert. Since it cooks in the slow cooker, I can tend to other things.
—*Becky Foster, Union, OR*

PREP: 10 min. • **COOK:** 2¼ hours
MAKES: 8 servings

- 6 cups cubed day-old bread (¾-in. cubes)
- 1½ cups semisweet chocolate chips
- 1 cup fresh raspberries
- 4 large eggs
- ½ cup heavy whipping cream
- ½ cup 2% milk
- ¼ cup sugar
- 1 tsp. vanilla extract
  Optional: Whipped cream and additional raspberries

1. In a greased 3-qt. slow cooker, layer half of the bread cubes, chocolate chips and raspberries. Repeat layers. In a bowl, whisk the eggs, cream, milk, sugar and vanilla. Pour over bread mixture.
2. Cover and cook on high 2¼-2½ hours or until a thermometer reads 160°. Let stand 5-10 minutes. If desired, serve with whipped cream and additional raspberries.
1 cup: 352 cal., 19g fat (10g sat. fat), 129mg chol., 189mg sod., 42g carb. (27g sugars, 4g fiber), 8g pro.
White Chocolate Bread Pudding with Blueberries: Use 1½ cups white baking chips, 1 cup fresh blueberries and 1 tsp. lemon extract. Proceed as directed.

SUN-DRIED TOMATO SPINACH-ARTICHOKE DIP

Fresh veggies and crackers will disappear quickly when they're next to this cheesy slow-cooked dip. With smoked Gouda, it has an extra level of flavor that will keep everyone guessing what it is.
—*Katie Stanczak, Hoover, AL*

PREP: 10 min. • **COOK:** 2 hours
MAKES: 3 cups

- 1 pkg. (10 oz.) frozen chopped spinach, thawed and squeezed dry
- 1 pkg. (8 oz.) cream cheese, softened
- 1 cup shredded smoked Gouda cheese
- ½ cup shredded fontina cheese
- ½ cup chopped water-packed artichoke hearts
- ¼ to ½ cup soft sun-dried tomato halves (not packed in oil), chopped
- ⅓ cup finely chopped onion
- 1 garlic clove, minced
  Assorted fresh vegetables and crackers

In a 1½-qt. slow cooker, mix the spinach, cheeses, artichokes, sun-dried tomatoes, onion and garlic. Cook, covered, on low until cheese is melted, 2-3 hours. Stir before serving. Serve with vegetables and crackers.
Note: This recipe was tested with sun-dried tomatoes that can be used without soaking. When using other sun-dried tomatoes that are not oil-packed, cover with boiling water and let stand until soft. Drain before using.
¼ cup: 134 cal., 11g fat (6g sat. fat), 35mg chol., 215mg sod., 4g carb. (2g sugars, 1g fiber), 6g pro.

SUN-DRIED TOMATO
SPINACH-ARTICHOKE DIP

EASY SLOW-COOKER
CINNAMON ROLLS

EASY SLOW-COOKER CINNAMON ROLLS

I love how these cinnamon rolls make use of my slow cooker and are so easy! I can just walk away and come back to perfectly cooked cinnamon rolls ready for the taking!
—*Nina Ward, New Port Richey, FL*

- -

PREP: 30 min. + standing
COOK: 2 hours • **MAKES:** 1 dozen

  1   pkg. (¼ oz.) quick-rise yeast
  ¼   cup warm water (110° to 115°)
  ¼   cup sugar, divided
  ½   cup warm 2% milk (110° to 115°)
  3   Tbsp. butter, softened
  1   large egg, room temperature,
       lightly beaten
  1   tsp. salt
  2½ to 3 cups all-purpose flour
FILLING
  ¼   cup packed brown sugar
  1   Tbsp. ground cinnamon
  3   Tbsp. butter, softened
       Optional: Cream cheese frosting
       and chopped pecans

1. Place a piece of parchment in a 3½-qt. rectangular slow cooker, letting ends extend up sides; spritz the paper with cooking spray. In a small bowl, dissolve yeast in warm water and 1 tsp. sugar. In a large bowl, combine milk, remaining sugar, butter, egg, salt, yeast mixture and 2 cups flour; beat on medium speed until smooth. Stir in enough remaining flour to form a soft dough (dough will be sticky). Turn dough onto a floured surface; knead until smooth and elastic, 6-8 minutes. Let stand 10 minutes.

2. For filling, combine brown sugar and cinnamon. Punch down the dough. Turn onto a lightly floured surface; roll into a 16x10-in. rectangle. Spread butter within ½ in. of edges; sprinkle with brown sugar mixture. Roll up jelly-roll style, starting with a long side; pinch seam to seal. Cut into 12 slices. Place rolls side by side, cut side down, into slow cooker.

3. Cover slow cooker with a double layer of white paper towels; place lid securely over towels. Cook, covered, on high, until rolls are set and edges begin to brown, about 2 hours. To avoid scorching, rotate slow cooker insert a half turn midway through cooking, lifting carefully with oven mitts. Using parchment, lift rolls from slow cooker; cool slightly. If desired, top with cream cheese frosting and chopped pecans.

1 cinnamon roll: 195 cal., 7g fat (4g sat. fat), 32mg chol., 255mg sod., 30g carb. (9g sugars, 1g fiber), 4g pro.

TEST KITCHEN TIP

If you don't have a rectangular slow cooker, not to worry. These rolls can be made in a 5- or 6-qt. round or oval slow cooker as well. To save time, you can use a store-bought cream cheese frosting to top them off.

ALL-DAY
APPLE BUTTER

❄ ALL-DAY APPLE BUTTER

I make several batches of this simple and delicious apple butter to freeze in jars. Depending on the sweetness of the apples used, you can adjust the sugar to taste.
—*Betty Ruenholl, Syracuse, NE*

PREP: 20 min. • **COOK:** 11 hours
MAKES: 4 pints

- 5½ lbs. apples, peeled, cored and finely chopped
- 4 cups sugar
- 2 to 3 tsp. ground cinnamon
- ¼ tsp. ground cloves
- ¼ tsp. salt

1. Place apples in a 3-qt. slow cooker. Combine sugar, cinnamon, cloves and salt; pour over apples and mix well. Cover and cook on high for 1 hour.
2. Reduce the heat to low; cover and cook until thickened and dark brown, 9-11 hours, stirring occasionally (stir mixture more frequently as it thickens to prevent sticking).
3. Uncover slow cooker and cook on low 1 hour longer. If desired, stir with a wire whisk until smooth. Spoon into freezer containers, leaving ½ in. of headspace. Cover and refrigerate or freeze.

Freeze option: Freeze cooled apple butter in freezer containers for up to 3 months. Liquids expand as they freeze, so leave extra room at the top of the container. To use, thaw in refrigerator.

2 Tbsp.: 68 cal., 0 fat (0 sat. fat), 0 chol., 9mg sod., 17g carb. (16g sugars, 1g fiber), 0 pro.

Cranberry-Apple Butter: Soak ½ cup dried cranberries in 1 cup of boiling water 5 minutes; drain. Add cranberries to apples and cook as directed. The apple butter will be pink with a slight tartness from the cranberries.

Easy Apple Butter Dessert: Slice up pound cake and toast in melted butter in a nonstick skillet. Spread slices with mascarpone cheese and top with apple butter or cranberry-apple butter.

SLOW-COOKER BOILED EGGS

🍎 SLOW-COOKER BOILED EGGS

This is my go-to method when I need to make hard-boiled eggs for a crowd. It's a lifesaver and perfect for Easter! I love the walk-away convenience.
—*Rashanda Cobbins, Milwaukee, WI*

PREP: 5 min. • **COOK:** 2 hours + cooling
MAKES: 12 servings

- 12 large eggs
  Cold water

1. Gently place eggs in bottom of 6-qt. slow cooker. Cover with water. Cook, covered, on high 2-3 hours.
2. Remove the eggs from slow cooker; rinse eggs in cold water and place in ice water until completely cooled. Drain and refrigerate. Remove shells; if desired, cut eggs before serving.

1 egg: 72 cal., 5g fat (2g sat. fat), 186mg chol., 71mg sod., 0 carb. (0 sugars, 0 fiber), 6g pro. **Diabetic exchanges:** 1 medium-fat meat.

CIDER CHEESE FONDUE

Cheese lovers are sure to enjoy dipping into this creamy, quick-to-fix fondue that has just a hint of apple. You can also serve this appetizer with pear wedges.
—*Kenny Van Rheenen, Mendota, IL*

PREP: 5 min. • **COOK:** 1½ hours
MAKES: 2⅔ cups

- 2 cups shredded cheddar cheese
- 1 cup shredded Swiss cheese
- 1 Tbsp. cornstarch
- ⅛ tsp. pepper
- ¾ cup apple cider or apple juice
  Cubed French bread and sliced apples and green peppers

In a 1½-qt. slow cooker, combine first 4 ingredients. Place the apple cider in a microwave-safe container; microwave on high until cider is hot, 2-3 minutes. Stir cider into slow cooker. Cook, covered, on low until cheese is melted, 1½ to 2 hours, stirring every 30 minutes. Serve warm with bread, apples and peppers.

¼ cup: 111 cal., 8g fat (6g sat. fat), 28mg chol., 138mg sod., 3g carb. (2g sugars, 0 fiber), 7g pro.

INDULGENT COCONUT RICE PUDDING

This slow-cooked winter dessert is a rich-yet-healthier option for your family that doesn't skimp on flavor. If you can't find turbinado or raw sugar, you can use brown sugar, adjusting to ¾ cup. This can also be made in the oven.
—*Teri Rasey, Cadillac, MI*

- -

PREP: 10 min. • **COOK:** 4 hours + standing
MAKES: 12 servings

- 1 cup uncooked long grain rice
- 5 cups coconut milk, divided
- 2 Tbsp. coconut oil
- 1 cup turbinado (washed raw) sugar
- 1 cup dried cranberries
- 2 tsp. vanilla extract
- 1 tsp. ground cinnamon
  Dash salt
  Optional: Toasted sweetened shredded coconut and additional coconut milk

Place rice in a 3- or 4-qt. slow cooker coated with cooking spray; pour in 4 cups coconut milk. Add coconut oil, distributing it evenly over the top. Add the next 5 ingredients. Cook, covered, on low until rice is tender, 4-5 hours, adding enough remaining coconut milk to reach desired consistency. Let stand, uncovered, 10 minutes. Serve warm. If desired, serve with shredded coconut and additional coconut milk.

½ cup: 340 cal., 18g fat (17g sat. fat), 0 chol., 39mg sod., 43g carb. (28g sugars, 1g fiber), 3g pro.

TEST KITCHEN TIP

Try different flavors inspired by food from other countries. For a taste of India, try a sprinkle of cardamom with golden raisins; for Thailand, cook the pudding first, then stir in fresh mint and fruit, such as mangoes and kiwis.

TROPICAL PULLED PORK SLIDERS

I used what I had in my cupboard to make this Hawaiian-style pork filling, and the results were fantastic. It's a delicious way to fuel up at a party.
—*Shelly Mitchell, Gresham, OR*

- -

PREP: 15 min. • **COOK:** 8 hours
MAKES: 12 servings

- 1 boneless pork shoulder butt roast (3 lbs.)
- 2 garlic cloves, minced
- ½ tsp. lemon-pepper seasoning
- 1 can (20 oz.) unsweetened crushed pineapple, undrained
- ½ cup orange juice
- 1 jar (16 oz.) mango salsa
- 24 whole wheat dinner rolls, split

1. Rub roast with garlic and lemon pepper. Transfer to a 4-qt. slow cooker; top with pineapple and orange juice. Cook, covered, on low until meat is tender, 8-10 hours.
2. Remove roast; cool slightly. Skim fat from cooking juices. Shred pork with 2 forks. Return pork and cooking juices to slow cooker. Stir in salsa; heat through. Serve with rolls.

2 sliders: 422 cal., 15g fat (5g sat. fat), 67mg chol., 674mg sod., 47g carb. (13g sugars, 6g fiber), 26g pro. **Diabetic exchanges:** 3 medium-fat meat, 2 starch, 1 fruit.

INDULGENT COCONUT RICE PUDDING

BUFFALO WING DIP

BUFFALO WING DIP

If you like spice, you'll love this dip.
It's super cheesy, full of rich flavor
and really has that Buffalo wing taste!
—Taste of Home *Test Kitchen*

PREP: 20 min. • **COOK:** 2 hours
MAKES: 6 cups

- 2 pkg. (8 oz. each) cream cheese,
  softened
- ½ cup ranch salad dressing
- ½ cup sour cream
- 5 Tbsp. crumbled blue cheese
- 2 cups shredded cooked chicken
- ½ cup Buffalo wing sauce
- 2 cups shredded cheddar
  cheese, divided
- 1 green onion, sliced
  Tortilla chips and assorted fresh
  vegetables

1. In a small bowl, combine the cream
cheese, dressing, sour cream and blue
cheese. Transfer to a 3-qt. slow cooker.

Layer with the chicken, wing sauce and
1 cup cheddar cheese. Cover and cook
on low until heated through, 2-3 hours.
2. Sprinkle with the remaining cheese
and onion. Serve with tortilla chips
and vegetables.
¼ cup dip: 167 cal., 14g fat (8g sat. fat),
47mg chol., 348mg sod., 2g carb. (0 sugars,
0 fiber), 8g pro.

Buffalo Bean Vegetarian Dip: Instead of
chicken, use 1 can of rinsed and drained
black beans and ¾ cup chopped fresh
mushrooms. Substitute Monterey Jack
cheese for half or all of the cheddar.

ITALIAN OYSTER CRACKERS

My friends and family love these crackers
that are easily made in the slow cooker.
Often I leave them in the slow cooker and
everyone eats them warm.
—Angela Lively, Conroe, TX

PREP: 10 min. • **COOK:** 1 hour
MAKES: 8 servings

- 2 pkg. (9 oz. each) oyster crackers
- ¼ cup canola oil
- 3 garlic cloves, minced
- 1 envelope Italian salad dressing mix
- 1 tsp. dill weed
- ¼ cup butter, melted
- ½ cup grated Parmesan cheese

1. Combine crackers, oil, garlic, Italian
seasoning and dill weed in a 6-qt. slow
cooker. Cook, covered, on low 1 hour.
2. Drizzle melted butter over crackers;
sprinkle with cheese. Stir to coat.
3. Transfer mixture to a baking sheet; let
stand until cool. Store in airtight container.
¾ cup: 407 cal., 20g fat (6g sat. fat), 20mg
chol., 1057mg sod., 49g carb. (2g sugars,
2g fiber), 8g pro.

SLOW-COOKER PEACH COBBLER

CHEESY MEATBALLS

Can meatballs be lucky? My guys think
so. They always want them for game time.
—*Jill Hill, Dixon, IL*

PREP: 1 hour • **COOK:** 4 hours
MAKES: about 9 dozen

  1 **large egg**
  ½ **cup 2% milk**
  2 **Tbsp. dried minced onion**
  4 **Tbsp. chili powder, divided**
  1 **tsp. salt**
  1 **tsp. pepper**
1½ **cups crushed Ritz crackers**
     (about 1 sleeve)
  2 **lbs. ground beef**
  1 **lb. bulk pork sausage**
  2 **cups shredded Velveeta**
  3 **cans (10¾ oz. each) condensed**
     tomato soup, undiluted
2½ **cups water**
  ½ **cup packed brown sugar**

1. Preheat oven to 400°. In a large bowl,
whisk egg, milk, minced onion, 2 Tbsp.
chili powder, salt and pepper; stir in the
crushed crackers. Add beef, sausage and
cheese; mix lightly but thoroughly.
2. Shape mixture into 1-in. balls; place on
greased racks in 15x10x1-in. baking pans.
Bake for 15-18 minutes, or until browned.
3. Meanwhile, in a 5- or 6-qt. slow cooker,
combine soup, water, brown sugar and
remaining chili powder. Gently stir in
meatballs. Cook, covered, on low until
meatballs are cooked through, 4-5 hours.
Freeze option: Freeze cooled meatball
mixture in freezer containers. To use,
partially thaw in refrigerator overnight.
Heat through in a covered saucepan,
stirring; add water if necessary.
Serve as directed.
1 meatball: 52 cal., 3g fat (1g sat. fat),
11mg chol., 134mg sod., 4g carb. (2g
sugars, 0 fiber), 3g pro.

*"The whole family loved these
meatballs. Easy. Might use less tomato
soup next time—lots of sauce. Will
definitely make again."*
—HARDTOUSE, TASTEOFHOME.COM

**SLOW-COOKER
PEACH COBBLER**

SLOW-COOKER PEACH COBBLER

Unlike conventional cobblers, the topping
of this dessert is on the bottom. Placing
the batter underneath the peaches helps
it cook through evenly in the slow cooker.
It's a simple but tasty treat that everyone
will enjoy.
—Taste of Home *Test Kitchen*

PREP: 15 min. • **COOK:** 1¾ hours
MAKES: 8 servings

1¼ **cups all-purpose flour, divided**
  2 **Tbsp. sugar**
  1 **tsp. baking powder**
  ¼ **tsp. ground cinnamon**
  ⅛ **tsp. salt**
  1 **large egg, room temperature**
  ¼ **cup 2% milk, warmed**
  2 **Tbsp. butter, melted**
  6 **cups sliced peeled fresh peaches**
     (about 6 large)
  2 **Tbsp. brown sugar**
  1 **Tbsp. lemon juice**
  1 **Tbsp. vanilla extract**
     Vanilla ice cream, optional

1. Whisk together 1 cup flour, sugar,
baking powder, cinnamon and salt.
In another bowl, whisk together egg,
milk and melted butter. Add to the dry
ingredients, stirring just until moistened
(batter will be thick). Spread onto bottom
of a greased 5-qt. slow cooker.
2. Combine peaches, the remaining
¼ cup flour, brown sugar, lemon juice
and vanilla; spoon over batter. Cook,
covered, on high until peach mixture
is bubbly, 1¾-2 hours. If desired,
serve with vanilla ice cream.
1 serving: 198 cal., 6g fat (3g sat. fat), 35mg
chol., 145mg sod., 33g carb. (17g sugars, 2g
fiber), 4g pro.

CHEESY MEATBALLS

UPSY-DAISY PLUM PUDDING

Baking is not my favorite thing to do, but a sweet plum pudding is always in order.
—*Judy Batson, Tampa, FL*

PREP: 25 min. • **COOK:** 4 hours.
MAKES: 8 servings

- 7 oz. medium red plums, halved, pitted and sliced
- 1 cup frozen unsweetened blackberries, thawed
- 2 Tbsp. mixed berry jelly
- ½ cup butter, softened
- ½ cup sugar
- 2 large eggs, room temperature
- 1 cup self-rising flour
- ⅓ cup ground almonds
- ⅛ tsp. almond extract
  Sweetened whipped cream, optional

1. Pour 1 in. water into a 6-qt. slow cooker. Layer two 24-in. pieces of foil; roll foil up lengthwise to make a 1-in.-thick tube. Shape into a ring; place in slow cooker to make a rack.

2. Toss the plums and blackberries with jelly; arrange in bottom of greased 2-qt. baking dish. For batter, in a large bowl, cream butter and sugar until light and fluffy, 5-7 minutes. Add eggs, 1 at a time, beating well after each addition. Add the flour to the creamed mixture just until moistened. Stir in almonds and extract. Spread batter over fruit mixture; cover with foil.

3. Fold an 18x12-in. piece of aluminum foil lengthwise into thirds, making a sling. Use sling to lower the baking dish onto foil rack, not allowing the sides to touch slow cooker. Cook, covered, on high until a toothpick inserted in the center comes out clean, about 4 hours.

4. Remove baking dish from slow cooker using sling. Run a knife around edge of baking dish; invert cake onto serving plate. Serve warm. Top with sweetened whipped cream if desired.

1 piece: 283 cal., 15g fat (8g sat. fat), 77mg chol., 296mg sod., 34g carb. (20g sugars, 2g fiber), 4g pro.

BUTTER PECAN SYRUP

My family loves butter pecan anything, and this recipe is perfect over vanilla ice cream, cake or waffles. It's a special treat my family enjoys.
—*Angela Lively, Conroe, TX*

PREP: 10 min. • **COOK:** 3 hours
MAKES: 2 cups

- 1 cup packed brown sugar
- 5 tsp. cornstarch
  Dash salt
- 1 cup water
- ⅓ cup butter, cubed
- ¾ cup chopped pecans, toasted
- 1 tsp. vanilla extract
  Vanilla ice cream

In a 1½-qt. slow cooker, mix the brown sugar, cornstarch and salt. Whisk in water. Cover and cook on high until thickened and bubbly, 3-3½ hours, stirring every 30 minutes. Whisk in butter until melted. Stir in chopped pecans and vanilla. Serve with ice cream.

¼ cup: 251 cal., 15g fat (5g sat. fat), 20mg chol., 87mg sod., 30g carb. (27g sugars, 1g fiber), 1g pro.

UPSY-DAISY
PLUM PUDDING

SLOW-COOKER
CARAMELIZED ONIONS

PUMPKIN PIE HOT CHOCOLATE

Spiked hot chocolate is the ultimate holiday cocktail! Made in a slow cooker and perfect for feeding a crowd, this creamy twist on a classic is a must-make for the holidays.
—*Becky Hardin, Saint Peters, MO*

PREP: 10 min. **COOKING:** 2 hours.
MAKES: 10 servings

  4 cups whole milk
  2 cups heavy whipping cream
  1 can (14 oz.) sweetened condensed milk
  1 pkg. (12 oz.) semisweet chocolate chips
  1 cup vodka
  1 cup canned pumpkin
  1 Tbsp. pumpkin pie spice
    Optional: Miniature marshmallows or whipped cream

1. In a 4-qt. slow cooker, combine all the ingredients. Cook, covered, on low, 2 hours, stirring occasionally, until the mixture is hot and chocolate is melted.
2. If desired, garnish with marshmallows or whipped cream.
1 cup: 575 cal., 34g fat (21g sat. fat), 77mg chol., 111mg sod., 52g carb. (47g sugars, 3g fiber), 9g pro.

❄️
SLOW-COOKER CARAMELIZED ONIONS

Caramelized onions make any meal taste better. Toss them on a burger or sandwich, or in scrambled eggs or omelets.
—*Heather Ingersoll, Seattle, WA*

- -

PREP: 10 min. • **COOK:** 6 hours
MAKES: 8 servings

  4 large sweet onion, thinly sliced
  2 Tbsp. butter
  ¼ tsp. salt
  ¼ tsp. pepper

1. Add all ingredients to 5-qt. slow cooker. Cover and cook on high, stirring mixture occasionally, until the onions are browned and tender, about 5 hours. Uncover slow cooker and cook 1 additional hour, or until most of the liquid has evaporated. Serve as desired. Refrigerate onions in airtight container.

Freeze option: Freeze cooled onions in freezer containers up to 3 months. To use, thaw in refrigerator.
¼ cup: 79 cal., 3g fat (2g sat. fat), 8mg chol., 110mg sod., 13g carb. (8g sugars, 2g fiber), 1g pro.

TEST KITCHEN TIP

The beauty of making these onions in the slow cooker (as opposed to on the stovetop) is that you don't have to stir them constantly. You should stir this onion recipe occasionally throughout the 5 hours that they're in the slow cooker, just to make sure they don't burn on the bottom. You'll know they're done when they're browned and tender.

CORNMEAL-CRUSTED
CATFISH
PAGE 143

90

116

119

132

Stovetop Suppers

Simple, everyday, delicious—those are the recipes we reach for time and again. When you want a satisfying meal that comes together fast and fabulous, just look here. You will find more than 100 express-lane dinners and dishes that highlight the season's best. Smart cooking starts with these timesaving suppers!

Beef & Ground Beef

CHEESEBURGER QUESADILLAS

I created these super fun cheeseburger quesadilla mashups in honor of my family's two favorite foods. They are so yummy and easy to make!
—*Jennifer Stowell, Deep River, IA*

TAKES: 25 min. • **MAKES:** 4 quesadillas

- 1 lb. ground beef
- 1 cup ketchup
- ⅓ cup prepared mustard
- 4 bacon strips, cooked and crumbled
- 2 Tbsp. Worcestershire sauce
- ⅔ cup mayonnaise
- 2 Tbsp. 2% milk
- 2 Tbsp. dill pickle relish
- ¼ tsp. pepper
- 8 flour tortillas (8 in.)
- 1 cup shredded cheddar cheese
  Optional: Shredded lettuce and chopped tomatoes

1. In a large skillet, cook beef over medium heat until no longer pink, 6-8 minutes, crumbling beef; drain. Stir in ketchup, mustard, bacon and Worcestershire sauce; bring to a boil. Reduce the heat; simmer, uncovered, 5-7 minutes or until slightly thickened, stirring occasionally.

2. Meanwhile, in a small bowl, combine mayonnaise, milk, relish and pepper.

3. Preheat the griddle over medium heat. Sprinkle 4 tortillas with cheese; top with beef mixture and remaining tortillas. Place on griddle; cook until tortillas are golden brown and cheese is melted, 1-2 minutes on each side. Serve with the sauce and, if desired, lettuce and tomatoes.

1 quesadilla with about ¼ cup sauce: 1002 cal., 60g fat (17g sat. fat), 110mg chol., 2115mg sod., 75g carb. (18g sugars, 4g fiber), 39g pro.

"Delicious! The whole family loved them. My 14-year-old son said that it's the best thing I've ever made!"
—ANITARX, TASTEOFHOME.COM

CHEESEBURGER QUESADILLAS

BEEF WITH RAMEN NOODLES

SESAME BEEF & MUSHROOM NOODLES

This beef, mushroom and noodle dish is a tasty way to fix a quick dinner.
—*Sherry Johnston, Green Cove Springs, FL*

TAKES: 30 min. • **MAKES:** 4 servings

- 3 pkg. (3 oz. each) beef ramen noodles
- 1 lb. ground beef
- 1 lb. fresh mushrooms, thinly sliced
- 2¾ cups water
- ⅓ cup coarsely chopped fresh cilantro leaves
- 2 Tbsp. sesame oil

1. Break noodles into small pieces; reserve ¼ cup.
2. In a large skillet, cook beef over medium heat until no longer pink, 6-8 minutes, breaking into crumbles; drain. Add mushrooms and contents of ramen seasoning packets; cook and stir until the mushrooms are tender, 3-4 minutes longer. Add remaining noodles and water. Bring to a boil; cook until the noodles are tender, 3-4 minutes, stirring occasionally.
3. Remove from heat; stir in cilantro and sesame oil. Top with reserved ramen noodles.
1½ cups: 565 cal., 30g fat (12g sat. fat), 70mg chol., 1264mg sod., 46g carb. (5g sugars, 3g fiber), 28g pro.

TEST KITCHEN TIP
Beef top sirloin steak works well in this dish because it cooks quickly, while staying tender. If you have some other cuts of beef you'd like to use, however, consider round steak or flank steak.

BEEF WITH RAMEN NOODLES

I made up this recipe when I was hungry for Chinese food. Everyone who tries it likes it, but each time I make it, I change something slightly. Heat any leftovers in the microwave or in a skillet the next day for a tasty lunch.
—*Annette Hemsath, Sutherlin, OR*

TAKES: 25 min. • **MAKES:** 2 servings

- 1 pkg. (3 oz.) beef ramen noodles
- 1 Tbsp. cornstarch
- 1 cup beef broth, divided
- 1 Tbsp. vegetable oil
- ½ lb. beef top sirloin steak, cut into thin strips
- 1 Tbsp. soy sauce
- 1 can (14 oz.) whole baby corn, rinsed and drained
- 1 cup fresh broccoli florets
- ½ cup chopped sweet red pepper
- ½ cup shredded carrot
- 2 green onions, cut into 1-in. pieces
- ¼ cup peanuts

1. Set aside seasoning packet from noodles. Cook noodles according to package directions. Drain; keep warm.
2. In a small bowl, combine cornstarch and ¼ cup broth until smooth; set aside.
3. In a large skillet, heat oil over medium heat; add beef. Cook and stir until beef is no longer pink, 3-5 minutes. Add soy sauce; cook until most of the liquid has evaporated, about 1 minute. Remove beef and keep warm.
4. In the same skillet over medium heat, add the corn, broccoli, red pepper, carrot, onions and remaining ¾ cup broth. Stir in contents of reserved seasoning packets. Cook and stir until vegetables are crisp-tender, 4-6 minutes.
5. Stir reserved cornstarch mixture and add to skillet. Bring to a boil; cook and stir until thickened, 1-2 minutes. Add reserved beef and noodles to skillet; heat through. Top with peanuts.
1½ cups: 601 cal., 28g fat (8g sat. fat), 46mg chol., 2086mg sod., 47g carb. (7g sugars, 8g fiber), 40g pro.

SUPER SWISS STEAK

This is one of my very favorite recipes. I've made it countless times in more than 45 years of marriage. Our children always asked for it on their birthdays, and it has a wonderful flavor!

—*Vicky Reinhold, Sturgis, SD*

- -

PREP: 10 min. • **COOK:** 1½ hours
MAKES: 10 servings

- ¼ cup all-purpose flour
- 1 tsp. salt, divided
- ½ tsp. pepper
- 2½ lbs. beef top round steak (about 1 in. thick), cut into serving-size pieces
- 2 Tbsp. canola oil
- 1 can (14½ oz.) stewed tomatoes
- 1 can (10¾ oz.) condensed tomato soup, undiluted
- 1 large onion, sliced
- 1 bay leaf
- ¼ tsp. dried marjoram
- ¼ tsp. dried thyme
- ¼ tsp. paprika
- ⅛ tsp. ground cloves, optional

1. In a large resealable container, combine flour, ½ tsp. salt and pepper. Add beef, a few pieces at a time, and shake to coat. Remove steak from container; flatten to ¾-in. thickness.
2. In a large skillet, brown steak on both sides in oil over medium-high heat. In a large bowl, combine the tomatoes, tomato soup, onion, bay leaf, marjoram, thyme, paprika, cloves if desired, and remaining salt; pour over beef.
3. Bring to a boil. Reduce heat; cover and simmer until the meat is tender, 1¼-1¾ hours. Discard bay leaf.

4 oz cooked steak: 214 cal., 6g fat (2g sat. fat), 64mg chol., 522mg sod., 11g carb. (5g sugars, 1g fiber), 27g pro.

STOVETOP CHEESEBURGER PASTA

Cheeseburgers are delicious in any form, but I'm partial to this creamy pasta dish that seriously tastes just like the real thing. It's weeknight comfort in a bowl.

—*Tracy Avis, Peterborough, ON*

- -

TAKES: 30 min. • **MAKES:** 8 servings

- 1 pkg. (16 oz.) penne pasta
- 1 lb. ground beef
- ¼ cup butter, cubed
- ½ cup all-purpose flour
- 2 cups 2% milk
- 1¼ cups beef broth
- 1 Tbsp. Worcestershire sauce
- 3 tsp. ground mustard
- 2 cans (14½ oz. each) diced tomatoes, drained
- 4 green onions, chopped
- 3 cups shredded Colby-Monterey Jack cheese, divided
- ⅔ cup grated Parmesan cheese, divided

1. Cook pasta according to package directions; drain.
2. Meanwhile, in a Dutch oven, cook beef over medium heat until no longer pink, 5-7 minutes, breaking it into crumbles.

Remove from pan with a slotted spoon; pour off drippings.
3. In same pan, melt butter over low heat; stir in flour until smooth. Cook and stir until lightly browned, 2-3 minutes (do not burn). Gradually whisk in milk, broth, Worcestershire sauce and mustard. Bring to a boil, stirring constantly; cook and stir until thickened, 1-2 minutes. Stir in the tomatoes; return to a boil. Reduce heat; simmer, covered, 5 minutes.
4. Stir in green onions, pasta and beef; heat through. Stir in half the cheeses until melted. Sprinkle with remaining cheeses; remove from heat. Let stand, covered, until cheeses are melted.

1½ cups: 616 cal., 29g fat (17g sat. fat), 98mg chol., 727mg sod., 56g carb. (7g sugars, 3g fiber), 33g pro.

TEST KITCHEN TIP

For some fun crunch and color, top with shredded iceberg lettuce just before serving. Try topping with sliced pickles, too!

STOVETOP CHEESEBURGER PASTA

CURRIED
BEEF STEW

GINGERED PEPPER STEAK

This wonderfully tender steak is a treat even for the folks not watching their diets. When my mother-in-law shared the recipe, she said it cooks up in no time—and she was right!
—*Susan Adair, Somerset, KY*

TAKES: 20 min. • **MAKES:** 4 servings

  2 tsp. cornstarch
  2 tsp. sugar
  ¼ tsp. ground ginger
  ¼ cup reduced-sodium soy sauce
  1 Tbsp. cider or white wine vinegar
  1 lb. beef flank steak, cut into
     ¼-in.-thick strips
  2 tsp. canola oil, divided
  2 medium green peppers, julienned
     Hot cooked rice, optional

1. Mix first 5 ingredients until smooth. Add beef; toss to coat.
2. In a large skillet, heat 1 tsp. oil over medium-high heat; stir-fry peppers until crisp-tender, 2-3 minutes. Remove from the pan.
3. In same pan, heat remaining oil over medium-high heat; stir-fry beef until browned, 2-3 minutes. Stir in peppers. If desired, serve over rice.
1 cup stir-fry: 224 cal., 11g fat (4g sat. fat), 54mg chol., 644mg sod., 7g carb. (4g sugars, 1g fiber), 23g pro. **Diabetic exchanges:** 3 lean meat, 1 vegetable, ½ fat.

CURRIED BEEF STEW

My mother, who was Japanese, made a dish very similar to this. After a lot of experimenting, I came up with a version that is very close to the one she used to make. This beef curry stew recipe is special to me because it brings back memories of my mother.
—*Gloria J. Gowins, Massillon, OH*

PREP: 15 min. • **COOK:** 2 hours
MAKES: 4 servings

  ¾   lb. beef stew meat (1- to 1½-in.
      pieces)
  ¼   tsp. salt
  ⅛   tsp. pepper
  2   Tbsp. all-purpose flour
  1   Tbsp. canola oil
  1   large onion, cut into ¾-in. pieces
  2   Tbsp. curry powder
  2   tsp. reduced-sodium soy sauce
  2   bay leaves
  3   cups beef stock
  1½ lbs. potatoes (about 3 medium), cut
      into 1-in. cubes
  2   large carrots, thinly sliced
  1   Tbsp. white vinegar
      Hot cooked brown rice, optional

1. Sprinkle beef with salt and pepper; toss with flour. In a Dutch oven, heat oil over medium heat; cook beef and onion until lightly browned, stirring occasionally. Stir in curry powder, soy sauce, bay leaves and stock; bring to a boil. Reduce heat; simmer, covered, 45 minutes.
2. Stir in potatoes and carrots; return to a boil. Reduce heat; simmer, covered, until meat and vegetables are tender, 1-1¼ hours, stirring occasionally. Remove the bay leaves; stir in vinegar. If desired, serve with rice.
Freeze option: Freeze the cooled stew in freezer containers. To use, partially thaw in refrigerator overnight. Heat through in a saucepan, stirring occasionally; add water if necessary.
1½ cups: 362 cal., 10g fat (3g sat. fat), 53mg chol., 691mg sod., 44g carb. (7g sugars, 7g fiber), 24g pro. **Diabetic exchanges:** 3 starch, 3 lean meat, ½ fat.

VEAL SCALLOPINI

My husband and I like to enjoy this fabulous veal dish on birthdays and other special occasions.
—*Karen Bridges, Downers Grove, IL*

TAKES: 25 min. • **MAKES:** 2 servings

- 2 Tbsp. all-purpose flour
- ⅛ tsp. salt
- ⅛ tsp. pepper
- 1 large egg
- ½ to ¾ lb. veal cutlets or boneless skinless chicken breasts, flattened to ¼-in. thickness
- 2 Tbsp. olive oil
- 4 oz. fresh mushrooms, halved
- 1 cup chicken broth
- 2 Tbsp. Marsala wine
  Hot cooked spaghetti

1. In a shallow bowl, combine the flour, salt and pepper. In another shallow bowl, lightly beat the egg. Dip veal in egg, then coat with flour mixture.

2. In a large skillet, brown veal in oil on both sides. Stir in the mushrooms, broth and wine. Bring to a boil. Reduce heat; simmer, uncovered, 5-10 minutes or until the mushrooms are tender and a thermometer inserted in center of veal reaches 160°. Serve with spaghetti.

1 serving: 395 cal., 27g fat (7g sat. fat), 180mg chol., 697mg sod., 10g carb. (3g sugars, 1g fiber), 25g pro.

Chicken Scallopini: Substitute boneless skinless chicken breasts, flattened to ¼-in. thickness, for the veal. Prepare as directed, adding a few more minutes cooking time as needed for chicken juices to run clear.

STUFFED WHOLE CABBAGE

STUFFED WHOLE CABBAGE

My husband's great about trying new recipes. I had to experiment with this one before getting just right.
—*Wyn Jespersen, Suffield, CT*

PREP: 30 min. • **COOK:** 1½ hours
MAKES: 8 servings

SAUCE
- 1 can (28 oz.) diced tomatoes, undrained
- 1 can (6 oz.) tomato paste
- 1 garlic clove, minced
- 1½ tsp. dried oregano
- 1 tsp. dried thyme
- 1 tsp. brown sugar
- ½ tsp. salt

FILLING
- 1 large head cabbage (4 lbs.), such as savoy
- 2 tsp. vegetable oil
- 1 medium onion, chopped
- 1 lb. ground beef
- ¾ cup cooked rice
- 1 large egg, beaten
- 1 tsp. salt
- ½ tsp. pepper
- 1¼ cups water, divided
- 3 Tbsp. cornstarch
- 2 Tbsp. shredded Parmesan cheese
  Optional: Fresh thyme and oregano leaves

1. Combine sauce ingredients; set aside. Line a medium bowl with cheesecloth, allowing 6 in. to overhang edge of bowl. Place cabbage in bowl with core facing up. Remove core and center of cabbage, leaving a 1-in. shell. Discard core; chop center cabbage leaves.

2. Heat large skillet over medium heat; add oil. Cook onion and 1 cup chopped cabbage in oil until tender, 4-5 minutes. Remove from the heat and cool slightly. In a small bowl, combine the beef, onion mixture, 1 cup sauce, rice, egg, salt and pepper. Spoon mixture into cabbage shell. Gather cheesecloth around cabbage and twist tightly to securely enclose cabbage leaves and filling.

3. Place 1 cup water, remaining chopped cabbage and remaining sauce in a Dutch oven; mix well. Carefully add the stuffed cabbage, with the twisted cheesecloth facing down. Bring to a boil. Reduce heat; simmer, covered, until whole cabbage is tender and a thermometer inserted in the middle of the cabbage reads 165°, 1-1¼ hours. Remove cabbage and discard cheesecloth. Place cabbage on a serving platter; keep warm.

4. Combine cornstarch and remaining ¼ cup water; add to Dutch oven. Bring to a boil, stirring constantly. Boil until thickened, about 2 minutes. Cut cabbage into wedges; serve with sauce and Parmesan cheese. If desired, sprinkle with fresh thyme and oregano leaves.

1 serving: 306 cal., 14g fat (5g sat. fat), 64mg chol., 724mg sod., 31g carb. (14g sugars, 8g fiber), 17g pro.

PASTA NAPOLITANA

This is the ultimate meat lovers pasta and is my copycat version of the Olive Garden's pasta. Rich and hearty with tremendous flavors, this delish dish will disappear quickly. I always make extra sauce as it freezes very well.
—*John Pittman, Northampton, PA*

PREP: 30 min. • **COOK:** 2 hours
MAKES: 8 servings

- 8   bacon strips
- 1   lb. ground beef
- 1   lb. bulk Italian sausage
- 1   Tbsp. olive oil
- 1   large onion, chopped
- 1   can (6 oz.) tomato paste
- 1   jar (24 oz.) marinara sauce
- 1   can (14½ oz.) chicken broth
- ½   cup dry red wine
- 1   can (8 oz.) mushroom stems and pieces
- ⅓   cup pepperoni, chopped
- 1   Tbsp. sugar
- 1   Tbsp. garlic powder
- 1   Tbsp. dried oregano
- 1   Tbsp. dried basil
- 2   tsp. dried parsley flakes
- 1   tsp. dried rosemary, crushed
- 1   tsp. dried marjoram
- 1   tsp. rubbed sage
- 1   tsp. seasoned salt
- 1   tsp. pepper
- ½   to 1 tsp. crushed red pepper flakes
- 1   tsp. Worcestershire sauce
      Hot cooked spaghetti
      Grated Parmesan cheese

1. In a Dutch oven, cook bacon strips over medium heat; drain and set aside. Discard drippings. In same pan, cook ground beef and sausage in olive oil until the beef is no longer pink, breaking meat into crumbles. Add the onion; cook until tender, about 5 minutes. Drain. Add tomato paste; cook and stir until fragrant, about 5 minutes.
2. Stir in the bacon, marinara sauce, broth, wine, mushrooms, pepperoni, sugar, garlic powder, oregano, basil, parsley, rosemary, marjoram, sage, seasoned salt, pepper, pepper flakes and Worcestershire sauce. Bring to a boil; reduce the heat. Simmer, covered, stirring occasionally, until thickened and flavors have combined, about 2 hours. Serve with spaghetti and Parmesan cheese.
1 serving: 427 cal., 28g fat (9g sat. fat), 82mg chol., 1591mg sod., 19g carb. (10g sugars, 4g fiber), 24g pro.

WASABI BEEF FAJITAS

Beef fajitas get an eastern spin with gingerroot, sesame oil and wasabi, a type of Japanese horseradish. You can find it in the Asian section at your local supermarket.
—*Taste of Home Test Kitchen*

TAKES: 20 min. • **MAKES:** 8 servings

- 2   tsp. cornstarch
- 3   Tbsp. reduced-sodium soy sauce
- 2   tsp. prepared wasabi
- 2   tsp. minced fresh gingerroot
- 1   garlic clove, minced
- 2   Tbsp. sesame oil, divided
- 1   lb. uncooked beef stir-fry strips
- 12 green onions with tops, cut in half lengthwise
- 1   large sweet red pepper, julienned
- 8   flour tortillas (8 in.), warmed
- 1   cup coleslaw mix

1. In a small bowl, mix cornstarch, soy sauce, wasabi, ginger and garlic until blended. In a large skillet, heat 1 Tbsp. oil over medium-high heat. Add beef; stir-fry 4-6 minutes or until no longer pink. Remove from pan.
2. Stir-fry green onions and red pepper in the remaining oil 2-3 minutes or until vegetables are crisp-tender.
3. Stir cornstarch mixture and add to pan. Bring to a boil; cook and stir 1-2 minutes or until sauce is thickened. Return beef to pan; heat through. Serve with tortillas and coleslaw mix.
1 fajita: 287 cal., 9g fat (2g sat. fat), 23mg chol., 507mg sod., 32g carb. (2g sugars, 3g fiber), 17g pro. **Diabetic exchanges:** 2 starch, 2 lean meat, ½ fat.

PASTA NAPOLITANA

**BBQ BEEF &
VEGETABLE STIR-FRY**

MEATBALLS & GRAVY

Christmas was the time when our family forgot about the food budget and splurged on one special meal. I can still envision Grandmother making dozens of these little meatballs! The spices gives them a taste that makes them authentically Norwegian.
—*Karen Hoylo, Duluth, MN*

PREP: 15 min. • **COOK:** 25 min.
MAKES: 6 servings

- 1   large egg
- ½   cup 2% milk
- 1   Tbsp. cornstarch
- 1   medium onion, finely chopped
- 1   tsp. salt
    Dash pepper
- ¼   tsp. ground nutmeg
- ¼   tsp. ground allspice
- ¼   tsp. ground ginger
- 1½   lbs. lean ground beef (90% lean)
- 3   to 4 Tbsp. butter

GRAVY
- 1   Tbsp. butter
- 2   Tbsp. all-purpose flour
- 1   cup beef broth
- ½   cup whole milk or
    half-and-half cream
    Salt and pepper to taste
    Minced fresh parsley, optional

1. In a large bowl, beat the egg, milk, cornstarch, onion, salt, pepper, nutmeg, allspice and ginger. Add the beef; mix lightly but thoroughly. Shape into 1½-in. meatballs. (Mixture will be very soft. For easier shaping, rinse your hands in cold water frequently.)
2. In a large skillet over medium heat, brown the meatballs in butter, half at a time, for about 10 minutes or until no longer pink. Remove meatballs to paper towels to drain, reserving 1 Tbsp. drippings in skillet.
3. For gravy, add butter to drippings. Stir in flour. Add broth and milk. Bring to a boil; cook and stir for 2 minutes or until thickened. Season with salt and pepper. Return meatballs to skillet; heat through on low. Garnish with parsley if desired.
3 meatballs: 302 cal., 18g fat (9g sat. fat), 117mg chol., 712mg sod., 8g carb. (4g sugars, 1g fiber), 25g pro.

🍎
BBQ BEEF & VEGETABLE STIR-FRY

This was a spur-of-the-moment experiment when we wanted something nice and filling, but also easy. I had steak, peppers and onions on hand, and this is what my mind created. We make it often. For something different, try it in tortillas for fajitas.
—*Rochelle Dickson, Potwin, KS*

TAKES: 25 min. • **MAKES:** 4 servings

- 1   beef top sirloin steak (1 lb.), cut into thin strips
- 3   Tbsp. reduced-sodium soy sauce
- 1   garlic clove, minced
- ¼   tsp. pepper
- 2   Tbsp. vegetable oil, divided
- 1   large sweet onion, halved and sliced
- 1   medium green pepper, cut into thin strips
- 1   medium sweet red pepper, cut into thin strips
- ¼   cup barbecue sauce
- 3   cups hot cooked brown rice

1. Toss the beef with soy sauce, garlic and pepper. Heat 1 Tbsp. oil in a large nonstick skillet over medium-high heat. Add beef mixture; stir-fry 2-3 minutes or until beef is browned. Remove from pan.
2. Add remaining 1 Tbsp. oil to pan. Add vegetables; stir-fry 3-4 minutes or until crisp-tender. Stir in barbecue sauce and beef; heat through. Serve with rice.
1 cup beef mixture with ¾ cup rice: 387 cal., 6g fat (2g sat. fat), 46mg chol., 673mg sod., 51g carb. (12g sugars, 5g fiber), 30g pro. **Diabetic exchanges:** 3 starch, 3 lean meat, 1 vegetable.

MEATBALLS
& GRAVY

EASY SALISBURY STEAK

This dish can be made in 25 minutes or made ahead and reheated with the gravy in the microwave. I often double the recipe and freeze one batch of the cooked steaks and gravy for an even faster meal on an especially busy night.
—Carol Callahan, Rome, GA

TAKES: 25 min. • **MAKES:** 4 servings

- ⅓ cup chopped onion
- ¼ cup crushed saltines
- 1 large egg white, lightly beaten
- 2 Tbsp. 2% milk
- 1 Tbsp. prepared horseradish
- ¼ tsp. salt, optional
- ⅛ tsp. pepper
- 1 lb. lean ground beef (90% lean)
- 1 jar (12 oz.) beef gravy
- 1½ cups sliced fresh mushrooms
- 2 Tbsp. water
  Hot cooked noodles, optional

1. In a large bowl, combine the onion, saltines, egg white, milk, horseradish, salt if desired, and pepper. Crumble beef over mixture. Shape into 4 oval patties.
2. In a large skillet over medium heat, cook patties until no pink remains and a thermometer reads 160°, 5-6 minutes per side.
3. Remove patties and keep warm. Add gravy, mushrooms and water to skillet; cook until heated through, 3-5 minutes. Serve with patties and, if desired, noodles.
1 serving: 253 cal., 11g fat (4g sat. fat), 78mg chol., 582mg sod., 11g carb. (2g sugars, 1g fiber), 26g pro. **Diabetic exchanges:** 3 lean meat, ½ starch.

TAKEOUT BEEF FRIED RICE

Transform leftover cooked beef into a quick dinner for six. You can use chuck roast or flank steak.
—Taste of Home *Test Kitchen*

TAKES: 30 min. • **MAKES:** 6 servings

- 1 Tbsp. plus 1 tsp. canola oil, divided
- 3 large eggs
- 1 can (11 oz.) mandarin oranges
- 2 medium sweet red peppers, chopped
- 1 cup fresh sugar snap peas, trimmed
- 1 small onion, thinly sliced
- 3 garlic cloves, minced
- ½ tsp. crushed red pepper flakes
- 4 cups cold cooked rice
- 2 cups cooked beef, sliced across grain into bite-sized pieces
- 1 cup beef broth
- ¼ cup reduced-sodium soy sauce
- ½ tsp. salt
- ¼ tsp. ground ginger

1. In a large skillet, heat 1 Tbsp. oil over medium-high heat. Whisk the eggs until blended; pour into skillet. Mixture should set immediately at its edge. As eggs set, push cooked portions toward center, letting uncooked egg flow underneath. When eggs are thickened and no liquid egg remains, remove to a cutting board and chop. Meanwhile, drain oranges, reserving 2 Tbsp. juice.
2. In same skillet, heat remaining 1 tsp. oil over medium-high heat. Add peppers, sugar snap peas and onion; cook and stir until crisp-tender, 1-2 minutes. Add garlic and pepper flakes; cook 1 minute longer. Add remaining ingredients and reserved juice; heat through. Gently stir in eggs and drained oranges.
1⅓ cups: 367 cal., 9g fat (2g sat. fat), 136mg chol., 793mg sod., 45g carb. (11g sugars, 3g fiber), 26g pro. **Diabetic exchanges:** 3 starch, 3 lean meat, 1 fat.

TAKEOUT BEEF FRIED RICE

GROUND BEEF SPAGHETTI SKILLET

WEEKDAY BEEF STEW

Beef stew capped with puff pastry adds comfort and joy to the weeknight menu. Make a salad and call your crowd to the table.

—Daniel Anderson, Kenosha, WI

- -

TAKES: 30 min. • **MAKES:** 4 servings

1   sheet frozen puff pastry, thawed
1   pkg. (15 oz.) refrigerated beef roast au jus
2   cans (14½ oz. each) diced tomatoes, undrained
1   pkg. (16 oz.) frozen vegetables for stew
¾   tsp. pepper
2   Tbsp. cornstarch
1¼   cups water

1. Preheat oven to 400°. Unfold the puff pastry. Using a 4-in. round cookie cutter, cut out 4 circles. Place 2 in. apart on a greased baking sheet. Bake until golden brown, 14-16 minutes.
2. Meanwhile, shred beef roast with 2 forks; transfer to a large saucepan. Add tomatoes, vegetables and pepper; bring to a boil. In a small bowl, mix the cornstarch and water until smooth; stir into beef mixture. Return to a boil, stirring constantly; cook and stir until thickened, 1-2 minutes.
3. Ladle stew into 4 bowls; top each serving with a pastry round.
1½ cups with 1 pastry round: 604 cal., 25g fat (8g sat. fat), 73mg chol., 960mg sod., 65g carb. (10g sugars, 9g fiber), 32g pro.

GROUND BEEF SPAGHETTI SKILLET

I remember my grandma making this stovetop supper many times—we always loved Granny's spaghetti! My husband and I now enjoy making this for our dinner. You can easily use ground turkey instead of ground beef if that's what you happen to have on hand.

—Jill Thomas, Washington, IN

- -

TAKES: 30 min. • **MAKES:** 4 servings

1   lb. ground beef
1   medium green pepper, chopped
1   small onion, chopped
2   garlic cloves, minced
1½   cups water
1   can (14½ oz.) diced tomatoes, undrained
1   can (8 oz.) tomato sauce
1   Tbsp. chili powder
1   Tbsp. grape jelly
½   tsp. salt
6   oz. uncooked thin spaghetti, halved

1. In a Dutch oven, cook beef, green pepper, onion and garlic over medium heat, breaking beef into crumbles, until meat is no longer pink and vegetables are tender, 8-10 minutes; drain.
2. Add water, tomatoes, tomato sauce, chili powder, jelly and salt. Bring to a boil. Stir in spaghetti. Reduce heat; simmer, covered, until the spaghetti is tender, 6-8 minutes.
1½ cups: 431 cal., 15g fat (5g sat. fat), 70mg chol., 843mg sod., 47g carb. (10g sugars, 5g fiber), 28g pro.

TEST KITCHEN TIP
Serve with a side of crusty French bread or a leafy salad to make a hearty, delicious meal.

STEAK WITH
CREAMY
PEPPERCORN SAUCE

STEAK WITH CREAMY PEPPERCORN SAUCE

My wife and I both love spicy foods. This is one of her favorite dishes. I have been cooking it as a treat on her birthday for years.
—*David Collin, Martinez, CA*

- -

PREP: 5 min. + chilling • **COOK:** 15 min.
MAKES: 4 servings

- 2 to 3 Tbsp. whole black peppercorns, crushed
- 1½ tsp. white pepper
- 4 boneless beef top loin steaks (12 oz. each)
- 1 tsp. salt
- ¼ cup butter, melted
- ¼ cup Worcestershire sauce
- 1 tsp. hot pepper sauce
- ¼ cup half-and-half cream

1. Combine peppercorns and pepper; rub over both sides of steaks. Chill for 1 hour.
2. Sprinkle salt in a large skillet; heat on high until salt begins to brown. Add steaks and brown on both sides. Add the butter; reduce heat to medium-high; cook steaks 1-2 minutes on each side.
3. Add Worcestershire and hot pepper sauce; cook until the meat reaches desired doneness (for medium-rare, a thermometer should read 135°; medium, 140°; medium-well, 145°), 2-3 minutes longer. Remove steaks and keep warm. Add cream to the skillet; cook and stir until smooth. Serve with steaks.
Note: Top loin steak may be labeled as strip steak, Kansas City steak, New York strip steak, ambassador steak or boneless club steak in your region.
1 serving: 487 cal., 17g fat (7g sat. fat), 157mg chol., 919mg sod., 5g carb. (2g sugars, 0 fiber), 73g pro.

TEST KITCHEN TIP

You can use 1 Tbsp. of whole green peppercorns instead of 1 Tbsp. of the black peppercorns. White pepper can also be replaced with 1 Tbsp. of crushed whole white peppercorns.

CAJUN BEEF & RICE

CAJUN BEEF & RICE

Dirty rice from a restaurant or box can end up having a surprisingly high amount of sodium and fat. This fast recipe is a hearty, healthy way to trim it down.
—*Raquel Haggard, Edmond, OK*

- -

TAKES: 30 min. • **MAKES:** 4 servings

- 1 lb. lean ground beef (90% lean)
- 3 celery ribs, chopped
- 1 small green pepper, chopped
- 1 small sweet red pepper, chopped
- ¼ cup chopped onion
- 2 cups water
- 1 cup instant brown rice
- 1 Tbsp. minced fresh parsley
- 1 Tbsp. Worcestershire sauce
- 2 tsp. reduced-sodium beef bouillon granules
- 1 tsp. Cajun seasoning
- ¼ tsp. crushed red pepper flakes
- ¼ tsp. pepper
- ⅛ tsp. garlic powder

1. In a large skillet, cook beef, celery, green and red peppers, and onion over medium heat until the beef is no longer pink, 8-10 minutes; crumble beef; drain.
2. Stir in remaining ingredients. Bring to a boil. Reduce heat; simmer, covered, until rice is tender, 12-15 minutes.
Note: Worcestershire sauce is a commercially produced thin, dark brown sauce used as a condiment or to season meats, gravies, sauces and salad dressings. It's generally made of soy sauce, vinegar, garlic, onions, tamarind, molasses and various seasonings and is widely available in supermarkets. White wine Worcestershire sauce, which is pale in color, is also available.
1½ cups: 291 cal., 10g fat (4g sat. fat), 71mg chol., 422mg sod., 23g carb. (3g sugars, 2g fiber), 25g pro. **Diabetic exchanges:** 3 lean meat, 1 starch, 1 vegetable.

SOUTHWESTERN BEEF BURRITOS

We became better acquainted with Mexican food after moving to Arizona from the Midwest. I got this tasty recipe from my brother-in-law, who ran a Mexican restaurant.

—*Jacqueline Hergert, Payson, AZ*

PREP: 15 min. • **COOK:** 2¼ hours
MAKES: 8 servings

- 2 to 2½ lbs. beef top round steak, cut into 1-in. cubes
- 2 Tbsp. canola oil
- 2 large onions, chopped
- 2 garlic cloves, minced
- 1 can (15 oz.) enchilada sauce
- 1 can (14½ oz.) diced tomatoes, undrained
- 1 to 2 cans (4 oz. each) chopped green chiles
- 1 tsp. salt
- ¼ tsp. pepper
- 2 Tbsp. all-purpose flour
- ¼ cup cold water
- 8 flour tortillas (10 in.)
  Optional: Diced tomatoes, sliced ripe olives, shredded cheddar cheese, sour cream, chopped green onions, shredded lettuce and guacamole

1. In a large skillet over medium heat, brown meat in oil; drain. Add onions and garlic; cook and stir 2 minutes. Add the enchilada sauce, tomatoes, chiles, salt and pepper; bring to a boil. Reduce heat; cover and simmer until meat is tender, about 2 hours.
2. Combine flour and water; add to beef mixture, stirring constantly. Bring to a boil; cook and stir until thickened, about 1 minute.
3. Warm tortillas; spoon ½ cup filling, off center, on each one. Fold sides and bottom of tortilla over filling, then roll up. Spoon a little more filling over the top of burritos. Serve immediately. If desired, garnish with the tomatoes, olives, cheese, sour cream, onions, lettuce and guacamole.
1 serving: 446 cal., 12g fat (3g sat. fat), 64mg chol., 973mg sod., 43g carb. (6g sugars, 9g fiber), 34g pro.

ONE-PAN ROTINI WITH
TOMATO CREAM SAUCE

ONE-PAN ROTINI WITH TOMATO CREAM SAUCE

I like to make one-pan recipes and this one was proclaimed a clear winner by my family. Bonus: It's also easy to clean up. Serve with crusty bread to dip into the sauce.

—*Angela Lively, Conroe, TX*

PREP: 15 min. • **COOK:** 30 min.
MAKES: 6 servings

- 1 lb. lean ground beef (90% lean)
- 1 medium onion, chopped
- 2 garlic cloves, minced
- 1 tsp. Italian seasoning
- ½ tsp. pepper
- ¼ tsp. salt
- 2 cups beef stock
- 1 can (14½ oz.) fire-roasted diced tomatoes, undrained
- 2 cups uncooked spiral pasta
- 1 cup frozen peas
- 1 cup heavy whipping cream
- ½ cup grated Parmesan cheese

1. In a large skillet, cook beef and onion over medium heat until beef is no longer pink and onion is tender, 5-10 minutes, breaking beef into crumbles; drain. Add the garlic and seasonings; cook 1 minute longer. Add the stock and tomatoes; bring to a boil. Add pasta and peas; reduce heat. Simmer, covered, until the pasta is tender, 10-12 minutes.
2. Gradually stir in cream and cheese; heat through (do not allow to boil).
1 cup: 443 cal., 23g fat (13g sat. fat), 98mg chol., 646mg sod., 33g carb. (6g sugars, 3g fiber), 25g pro.

TEST KITCHEN TIP

For an extra boost of flavor, stir in cooked sausage and serve with additional cheese.

MOROCCAN APPLE BEEF STEW

I love the mix of sweet and savory flavors in this hearty stew. It's the perfect blend of adventurous and comforting, and makes a fun dish to share with guests.
—Trisha Kruse, Eagle, ID

PREP: 20 min. • **COOK:** 2 hours
MAKES: 8 servings (2 qt.)

- 1¼ tsp. salt
- ½ tsp. ground cinnamon
- ½ tsp. pepper
- ¼ tsp. ground allspice
- 2½ lbs. beef stew meat, cut into 1-in. pieces
- 2 to 3 Tbsp. olive oil
- 1 large onion, chopped (about 2 cups)
- 3 garlic cloves, minced
- 1 can (15 oz.) tomato sauce
- 1 can (14½ oz.) beef broth
- 1 cup pitted dried plums (prunes), coarsely chopped
- 1 Tbsp. honey
- 2 medium Fuji or Gala apples, peeled and cut into 1½-in. pieces
  Hot cooked rice or couscous, optional

1. Mix the salt, cinnamon, pepper and allspice; sprinkle over beef and toss to coat. In a Dutch oven, heat 2 Tbsp. oil over medium heat.

2. Brown beef in batches, adding more oil as necessary. Remove beef with a slotted spoon.

3. Add onion to same pan; cook and stir until tender, 6-8 minutes. Add garlic; cook 1 minute longer. Stir in tomato sauce, broth, dried plums and honey. Return beef to pan; bring to a boil. Reduce heat; simmer, covered, 1½ hours.

4. Add apples; cook, covered, until beef and apples are tender, 30-45 minutes longer. Skim fat. If desired, serve stew with rice or couscous.

Freeze option: Freeze cooled stew in freezer containers. To use, partially thaw in refrigerator overnight. Heat through in a saucepan, stirring occasionally; add broth if necessary.

1 cup: 339 cal., 13g fat (4g sat. fat), 88mg chol., 905mg sod., 24g carb. (14g sugars, 2g fiber), 29g pro.

GERMAN MEATBALLS & GRAVY

These meatballs are a celebration of my heritage. I love making them for my family, especially because they are a quick meal.
—Marshelle Greenmyer-Bittner, Lisbon, ND

PREP: 30 min. • **COOK:** 35 min.
MAKES: 8 servings

- 1 large egg
- 3½ cups 2% milk, divided
- ½ tsp. Worcestershire sauce
- 1 cup finely shredded uncooked peeled potatoes
- 2 Tbsp. finely chopped onion
- 2 tsp. salt
- ½ tsp. ground nutmeg
- ¼ tsp. ground ginger
- ¼ tsp. ground allspice
- ⅛ tsp. pepper
- 2 lbs. ground beef
- ¼ cup butter, cubed
- ¼ cup all-purpose flour
  Hot mashed potatoes, optional

1. In a large bowl, combine the egg, ½ cup milk, Worcestershire sauce, shredded potatoes, onion, salt, nutmeg, ginger, allspice and pepper. Crumble beef over mixture and mix lightly but thoroughly. Shape into 48 balls.

2. In a large skillet over medium heat, cook meatballs in butter in batches until no longer pink; remove and keep warm.

3. Stir flour into drippings until blended; gradually add the remaining milk. Bring to a boil; cook and stir until thickened, about 2 minutes. Return meatballs to the pan; heat through. If desired, serve meatballs with mashed potatoes.

6 meatballs: 383 cal., 24g fat (11g sat. fat), 127mg chol., 745mg sod., 13g carb. (5g sugars, 1g fiber), 28g pro.

MOROCCAN
APPLE BEEF STEW

BEEFY
CHILI DOGS

❄ BEEFY CHILI DOGS

For years people have told me I make the best hot dog chili out there. It's timeless and family-friendly, and I usually carry the recipe with me because people ask for it.
—*Vicki Boyd, Mechanicsvlle, VA*

TAKES: 30 min.
MAKES: 8 servings (2 cups chili)

- 1   lb. ground beef
- 1   tsp. chili powder
- ½   tsp. garlic powder
- ½   tsp. paprika
- ¼   tsp. cayenne pepper
- 1   cup ketchup
- 8   hot dogs
- 8   hot dog buns, split
     Optional: Shredded cheddar cheese and chopped onion

1. For chili, in a large skillet, cook the beef over medium heat 5-7 minutes or until no longer pink, breaking into crumbles; drain. Transfer beef to a food processor; pulse until finely chopped.
2. Return beef to skillet; stir in seasonings and ketchup. Bring to a boil. Reduce heat; simmer, covered, 15-20 minutes to allow flavors to blend, stirring occasionally.
3. Meanwhile, cook hot dogs according to package directions. Serve in buns with chili. If desired, top with cheese and onion.
Freeze option: Freeze cooled chili in a freezer container. To use, partially thaw in refrigerator overnight. Heat through in a saucepan, stirring occasionally; add water if necessary.
1 hot dog with ¼ cup chili: 400 cal., 22g fat (9g sat. fat), 60mg chol., 1092mg sod., 31g carb. (11g sugars, 1g fiber), 19g pro.

TEST KITCHEN TIP
Toast the hot dog buns with a bit of butter in the skillet for a minute to add some crunch to every bite.

ZUCCHINI BEEF SKILLET

ZUCCHINI BEEF SKILLET

This is a speedy summer recipe that uses up those abundant garden goodies: zucchini, tomatoes and green peppers.
—*Becky Calder, Kingston, MO*

TAKES: 30 min. • **MAKES:** 4 servings

- 1   lb. ground beef
- 1   medium onion, chopped
- 1   small green pepper, chopped
- 2   tsp. chili powder
- ¾   tsp. salt
- ¼   tsp. pepper
- 3   medium zucchini, cut into ¾-in. cubes
- 2   large tomatoes, chopped
- ¼   cup water
- 1   cup uncooked instant rice
- 1   cup shredded cheddar cheese

1. In a large skillet, cook beef with onion and pepper over medium-high heat until no longer pink, 5-7 minutes; crumble the beef; drain.
2. Stir in seasonings, vegetables, water and rice; bring to a boil. Reduce heat; simmer, covered, until rice is tender, 10-15 minutes. Sprinkle with cheese. Remove from heat; let stand until cheese is melted.
2 cups: 470 cal., 24g fat (11g sat. fat), 98mg chol., 749mg sod., 33g carb. (8g sugars, 4g fiber), 32g pro.

Poultry

LEFTOVER TURKEY
CROQUETTES

LEFTOVER TURKEY CROQUETTES

I grew up with a family that looked forward to leftovers from big meals, especially on the day after Thanksgiving. But we didn't just reheat turkey and mashed potatoes in the microwave—we took our culinary creativity to a new level with recipes likes these mini croquettes. They're delicious dipped in sour cream or leftover gravy.
—*Meredith Coe, Charlottesville, VA*

PREP: 20 min. • **COOK:** 20 min.
MAKES: 6 servings

- 2 cups mashed potatoes (with added milk and butter)
- ½ cup grated Parmesan cheese
- ½ cup shredded Swiss cheese
- 1 shallot, finely chopped
- 2 tsp. minced fresh rosemary or ½ tsp. dried rosemary, crushed
- 1 tsp. minced fresh sage or ¼ tsp. dried sage leaves
- ½ tsp. salt
- ¼ tsp. pepper
- 3 cups finely chopped cooked turkey
- 1 large egg
- 2 Tbsp. water
- 1¼ cups panko bread crumbs
- ¼ cup butter, divided
  Sour cream, optional

1. In a large bowl, combine the mashed potatoes, cheeses, shallot, rosemary, sage, salt and pepper; stir in turkey. Shape into twelve 1-in.-thick patties.
2. In a shallow bowl, whisk egg and water. Place bread crumbs in another shallow bowl. Dip croquettes in the egg mixture, then in bread crumbs, patting to help the coating adhere.
3. In a large skillet, heat 2 Tbsp. butter over medium heat. Add half of croquettes; cook until browned, 4-5 minutes on each side. Remove and keep warm. Repeat. If desired, serve with sour cream.
2 croquettes: 383 cal., 19g fat (10g sat. fat), 144mg chol., 734mg sod., 22g carb. (2g sugars, 2g fiber), 29g pro.

GRANDPA FREY'S CHICKEN MULLIGAN

Grandpa's mulligan never tasted exactly the same from batch to batch. Still, I could always pick out his creation at a church supper. The basic flavors were always present. Try it with bread and butter.
—*Valerie Frey, Athens, GA*

PREP: 25 min. • **COOK:** 1½ hours
MAKES: 10 servings (3¾ qt.)

- 1 broiler/fryer chicken (about 4 lbs.), cut into pieces
- 1 lb. potatoes, peeled and cut into ½-in. cubes
- 1 large onion, diced
- 6 oz. unsmoked bacon strips, halved, or pork belly, cut into 1-in. pieces
- 1½ tsp. kosher salt, or to taste
- 1 to 4 cups chicken stock (only as needed)
- 1 can (14½ oz.) diced tomatoes, or about 1 lb. fresh tomatoes, blanched, peeled and diced
- 8 oz. uncooked thin spaghetti, broken into 1-in. pieces, or elbow macaroni
- ¼ tsp. pepper, or to taste
- 1 can (14¾ oz.) cream-style corn, or fresh creamed corn

1. Put chicken, potatoes, onion, bacon and salt into an 8-qt. stockpot. Add enough cold water to just cover the ingredients and place on the stove over medium heat.
2. When the water comes just to a boil, reduce heat and simmer, covered, until the chicken is tender and falling off the bone (45-90 minutes, depending on the chicken and stove setting).
3. Skim off the froth across the top and discard. Lift chicken from the pot, cool slightly, and pull meat from the bones in small pieces. Discard skin and bones and place meat back in stew. Remove bacon and discard.
4. If at this point much of the liquid has steamed off, add chicken stock so there is enough liquid to fully cook the pasta. Add tomatoes, noodles and pepper.
5. Increase heat until mulligan is bubbling gently. Cook until noodles are soft. Add corn and stir periodically for 10 minutes. If bottom begins to scorch, reduce heat slightly and stir more often. Noodles should be soft and beginning to break down so they add to creaminess.
6. Serve hot, preferably in a large bowl with a piece of fresh cornbread.
Freeze option: Freeze cooled stew in freezer containers. To use, partially thaw in refrigerator overnight. Heat through in a saucepan, stirring occasionally; add broth if necessary.
1½ cups: 460 cal., 21g fat (6g sat. fat), 95mg chol., 650mg sod., 34g carb. (5g sugars, 3g fiber), 33g pro.

GRANDPA FREY'S CHICKEN MULLIGAN

TURKEY MOLE WITH RICE

Here's a wonderful Tex-Mex treat. The chipotle pepper and cocoa in the mole sauce make this dish out of this world.
—*Trisha Kruse, Eagle, ID*

PREP: 20 min. • **COOK:** 15 min.
MAKES: 4 servings

- 1½ cups chunky salsa
- ¼ cup plus 2 Tbsp. unsalted peanuts, divided
- 1 chipotle pepper in adobo sauce
- 1 Tbsp. lime juice
- ¼ tsp. baking cocoa
- 1 pkg. (20 oz.) turkey breast tenderloins, cut into 1-in. pieces
- 2 tsp. olive oil
- ⅓ cup reduced-sodium chicken broth
- 2 cups cooked brown rice
- 2 Tbsp. minced fresh cilantro

1. In a food processor, combine the salsa, ¼ cup peanuts, chipotle pepper, lime juice and cocoa; cover and process mixture until blended.
2. In a large skillet, cook turkey in oil over medium heat until no longer pink, 6-8 minutes. Add broth and salsa mixture. Bring to a boil. Reduce the heat; simmer, uncovered, for 10 minutes. Serve with rice; sprinkle with cilantro and remaining nuts.
1 serving: 393 cal., 12g fat (2g sat. fat), 69mg chol., 514mg sod., 32g carb. (4g sugars, 3g fiber), 39g pro.

**VIETNAMESE CHICKEN
BANH MI SANDWICHES**

SOUTHWEST CHICKEN DINNER

My family loves to order those gigantic takeout Tex-Mex burritos, but they can be expensive and we always have leftovers. So I created a lighter, no-guilt alternative with the bold flavors we love, but missing the calorie-laden tortilla.

—*Marquisha Turner, Denver, CO*

TAKES: 30 min. • **MAKES:** 4 servings

- 2 cups water
- 2 Tbsp. olive oil, divided
- ½ tsp. salt
- ¼ tsp. pepper
- 1 cup uncooked long grain rice
- 1 Tbsp. taco seasoning
- 4 boneless skinless chicken breast halves (4 oz. each)
- 1 cup canned black beans or pinto beans, rinsed and drained
- ¼ cup chopped fresh cilantro
- 1 tsp. grated lime zest
- 2 Tbsp. lime juice
  Optional: Pico de gallo, shredded Mexican cheese blend, sour cream, avocado, shredded lettuce and lime wedges

1. In a large saucepan, combine water, 1 Tbsp. oil, and the salt and pepper; bring to a boil. Stir in rice. Reduce heat; simmer, covered, 15-17 minutes or until liquid is absorbed and rice is tender.

2. Meanwhile, sprinkle taco seasoning over both sides of chicken. In a large skillet, heat remaining 1 Tbsp. oil over medium heat. Add the chicken; cook 4-5 minutes on each side or until a thermometer reads 165°.

3. In a microwave, heat the beans until warmed. To serve, gently stir cilantro, lime zest and lime juice into rice; divide among 4 bowls. Cut chicken into slices. Place the chicken and beans over rice; top individual bowls as desired.

1 serving: 398 cal., 7g fat (1g sat. fat), 63mg chol., 678mg sod., 52g carb. (1g sugars, 3g fiber), 30g pro.

VIETNAMESE CHICKEN BANH MI SANDWICHES

My version of the classic Vietnamese sandwich combines the satisfying flavor of chicken sausage with tangy vegetables pickled in rice vinegar. Stuff the ingredients in a hoagie bun and lunch is ready to go!

—*Angela Spengler, Niceville, FL*

TAKES: 25 min. • **MAKES:** 4 servings

- 1 pkg. (12 oz.) fully cooked spicy chicken sausage links
- 2 tsp. olive oil, divided
- ⅓ cup hoisin sauce
- 1 Tbsp. honey
- 2 tsp. reduced-sodium soy sauce
- 1 garlic clove, minced
- ¼ tsp. Chinese five-spice powder
- 1 medium onion, thinly sliced
- ½ cup shredded cabbage
- ½ cup shredded carrots
- 2 tsp. rice vinegar
- 4 hoagie buns, split
- 4 lettuce leaves

1. Cut each sausage in half lengthwise. In a large skillet, brown sausage in 1 tsp. oil. Remove and keep warm.

2. Add the hoisin, honey, soy sauce, garlic and five-spice powder to the skillet. Bring to a boil. Cook and stir until garlic is tender and sauce is thickened. Return sausages to pan; toss to coat.

3. In a skillet, saute the onion, cabbage and carrots in remaining oil until crisp-tender. Stir in vinegar. Serve the sausage in buns with lettuce and onion mixture.

Note: Hoisin sauce is a common soy-based ingredient in Chinese cuisine that's used to flavor sauces for stir-fry dishes or as a condiment for moo shu pork or Peking duck. Its flavor profile is sweet, salty and spicy. Hoisin sauce can be found in the Asian section of the grocery store.

1 sandwich: 452 cal., 15g fat (3g sat. fat), 66mg chol., 1,331mg sod., 57g carb., 3g fiber, 25g pro.

SOUTHWEST
CHICKEN DINNER

HOISIN TURKEY LETTUCE WRAPS

I'm married to a marathon runner, which means dinners need to be healthy but flavor-packed. These low-carb wraps are quick and easy. He loves the health aspect, I love the taste!
—*Melissa Pelkey Hass, Waleska, GA*

- -

TAKES: 30 min. • **MAKES:** 4 servings

- 1 lb. lean ground turkey
- ½ lb. sliced fresh mushrooms
- 1 medium sweet red pepper, diced
- 1 medium onion, finely chopped
- 1 medium carrot, shredded
- 1 Tbsp. sesame oil
- ¼ cup hoisin sauce
- 2 Tbsp. balsamic vinegar
- 2 Tbsp. reduced-sodium soy sauce
- 1 Tbsp. minced fresh gingerroot
- 2 garlic cloves, minced
- 8 Bibb or Boston lettuce leaves

In a large skillet, cook the turkey with vegetables in sesame oil over medium-high heat until the turkey is no longer pink, 8-10 minutes, breaking up the meat into crumbles. Stir in hoisin sauce, vinegar, soy sauce, ginger and garlic; cook and stir over medium heat until sauce is slightly thickened, about 5 minutes. Serve in lettuce leaves.

2 wraps: 292 cal., 13g fat (3g sat. fat), 79mg chol., 629mg sod., 19g carb. (11g sugars, 3g fiber), 26g pro. **Diabetic exchanges:** 3 lean meat, 1 starch, 1 vegetable, 1 fat.

MANGO CHICKEN THIGHS WITH BASIL-COCONUT SAUCE

MANGO CHICKEN THIGHS WITH BASIL-COCONUT SAUCE

This recipe brings the restaurant to my home kitchen. And it's easy, too! The meal comes together quickly and fills my kitchen with wonderful aromas. Plus, if there are any leftovers, with a quick reheat the next day, they're just as good!
—*Kathi Jones-DelMonte, Rochester, NY*

- -

PREP: 20 min. • **COOK:** 30 min.
MAKES: 4 servings

- 4 boneless skinless chicken thighs (about 1 lb.)
- ½ tsp. salt
- ¼ tsp. pepper
- 1 Tbsp. olive oil
- 3 garlic cloves, minced
- 1 Tbsp. minced fresh gingerroot
- 1 can (13.66 oz.) coconut milk
- 1 medium mango, peeled and chopped
- 4 green onions, sliced
- ½ cup thinly sliced fresh basil, divided
- ¼ cup miso paste
- 2 tsp. Sriracha chili sauce
- 2 cups cooked jasmine rice
- 2 medium limes, quartered

1. Sprinkle chicken with salt and pepper. In a large skillet, heat oil over medium heat. Brown chicken on both sides. Add garlic and ginger; cook 1 minute longer.
2. Stir in coconut milk, mango, green onions, ¼ cup basil, miso paste and chili sauce. Cook and stir until sauce is slightly reduced and a thermometer inserted in chicken reads 170°, about 20 minutes. Sprinkle with remaining basil. Serve with rice and limes.

1 serving: 552 cal., 28g fat (18g sat. fat), 76mg chol., 1209mg sod., 46g carb. (17g sugars, 4g fiber), 28g pro.

TEST KITCHEN TIP

This recipe also works well with seafood. It's particularly good with shrimp or scallops, but it's also great with clams or mussels. If you want to go meatless, try tofu and vegetables. Like it spicy? Turn up the heat with an additional splash of Sriracha.

BUFFALO CHICKEN TENDERS

These chicken tenders get a spicy kick from homemade Buffalo sauce. They taste like they're from a restaurant, but are so easy to make at home. Blue cheese salad dressing for dipping takes them over the top.
—*Dahlia Abrams, Detroit, MI*

TAKES: 20 min. • **MAKES:** 4 servings

- 1 lb. chicken tenderloins
- 2 Tbsp. all-purpose flour
- ¼ tsp. pepper
- 2 Tbsp. butter, divided
- ⅓ cup Louisiana-style hot sauce
- 1¼ tsp. Worcestershire sauce
- 1 tsp. minced fresh oregano
- ½ tsp. garlic powder
  Blue cheese salad dressing, optional

1. Toss chicken with flour and pepper. In a large skillet, heat 1 Tbsp. butter over medium heat. Add chicken; cook until no longer pink, 4-6 minutes per side. Remove from pan.
2. Mix hot sauce, Worcestershire sauce, oregano and garlic powder. In the same skillet, melt remaining butter; stir in sauce mixture. Add the chicken; heat through, turning to coat. If desired, serve with blue cheese dressing.

1 serving: 184 cal., 7g fat (4g sat. fat), 71mg chol., 801mg sod., 5g carb. (1g sugars, 0 fiber), 27g pro. **Diabetic exchanges:** 3 lean meat, 1½ fat.

BUFFALO CHICKEN TENDERS

CHICKEN BROCCOLI STIR-FRY

This easy recipe offers a scrumptious but mild Asian flavor in a nicely balanced protein dish the whole family will love.
—*Clara Coulson Minney, Washington Court House, OH*

PREP: 20 min. + marinating
COOK: 15 min. • **MAKES:** 4 servings

- ½ cup reduced-sodium chicken broth
- 6 Tbsp. reduced-sodium soy sauce
- ¼ cup water
- ¼ cup rice vinegar
- 2 garlic cloves, minced
  Dash cayenne pepper
- 1 lb. boneless skinless chicken breasts, cut into ¾ in. cubes
- 2 tsp. cornstarch
- 4 tsp. canola oil, divided
- 2 cups fresh broccoli florets
- 1 cup sliced fresh mushrooms
- ½ cup canned sliced water chestnuts
- ½ cup canned bamboo shoots
- 2 green onions, thinly sliced
- 2 cups hot cooked rice

1. In a large bowl, combine the first 6 ingredients. Remove ¾ cup of marinade; cover and refrigerate. Add the chicken to remaining marinade in bowl; toss to coat. Refrigerate for 1-2 hours.
2. Drain chicken, discarding marinade. In a small bowl, combine the cornstarch and reserved marinade until smooth; set aside.
3. In a large skillet or wok, heat 2 tsp. oil over medium-high heat. Add chicken; stir-fry until no longer pink. Remove and keep warm. Stir-fry broccoli in remaining oil for 2 minutes. Add the mushrooms; stir-fry 2 minutes longer. Add the water chestnuts, bamboo shoots and onions; cook until vegetables are crisp-tender, 1-2 minutes longer.
4. Stir cornstarch mixture and add to the pan. Bring to a boil; cook and stir until thickened, about 2 minutes. Add chicken; heat through. Serve with rice.

1 serving: 316 cal., 8g fat (1g sat. fat), 63mg chol., 719mg sod., 32g carb. (2g sugars, 2g fiber), 28g pro. **Diabetic exchanges:** 3 lean meat, 1½ starch, 1 vegetable, 1 fat.

NUTTY CHICKEN STRIPS

NUTTY CHICKEN STRIPS

I enjoy cooking things that feature unique flavors. These chicken strips, seasoned with curry, are great way to enjoy a classic with a twist.
—*Betsy Baertlein, Mazeppa, MN*

PREP: 20 min. • **COOK:** 20 min.
MAKES: 6 servings

- 1 cup plain yogurt
- 2 Tbsp. minced fresh cilantro
- 1 Tbsp. honey

CHICKEN
- 1 large egg
- ½ cup 2% milk
- 1 cup soft bread crumbs
- ½ cup chopped almonds
- 2 Tbsp. minced fresh cilantro
- 1½ tsp. curry powder
- 1½ lbs. boneless skinless chicken breasts, cut into 1-in.-wide strips
- ¼ cup all-purpose flour
- ¼ cup canola oil

1. Mix yogurt, cilantro and honey. Refrigerate, covered, until serving.
2. In a shallow bowl, whisk together the egg and milk. In another bowl, toss bread crumbs with almonds, cilantro and curry powder. Toss chicken strips with flour to coat lightly; shake off excess. Dip both sides in egg mixture, then in the crumb mixture.
3. In a large skillet, heat oil over medium heat. In batches, cook chicken until golden brown, 5-6 minutes per side. Drain strips on paper towels. Serve with sauce.
Note: To make soft bread crumbs, tear bread into pieces and place in a food processor or blender. Cover and pulse until soft crumbs form. A slice of bread yields ½–¾ cup crumbs.

4 oz. cooked chicken with 1½ Tbsp. sauce: 365 cal., 20g fat (3g sat. fat), 101mg chol., 132mg sod., 16g carb. (7g sugars, 2g fiber), 30g pro.

Pecan Parmesan Chicken Strips: Omit almond, cilantro, curry powder, flour and yogurt dipping sauce. Reduce the bread crumbs to ½ cup. Combine with ⅓ cup each grated Parmesan cheese and ground pecans, 1 tsp. dried oregano, ½ tsp. each seasoned salt and dried basil and ¼ tsp. pepper. Proceed as directed. Serve with warmed spaghetti sauce if desired.

CHICKEN CREOLE

CHICKEN CREOLE

I like food that has a little zip to it, and this Creole chicken recipe hits the spot every time. It's especially good served over rice.
—*Dolly Hall, Wheelwright, KY*

PREP: 15 min. • **COOK:** 20 min.
MAKES: 4 servings

- 4 boneless skinless chicken breast halves (1½ lbs.), cut into 1-in. cubes
- ½ tsp. salt, divided
- ¼ tsp. pepper
- 1 Tbsp. vegetable oil
- 1 cup finely chopped onion
- ½ cup finely sliced celery
- ½ cup diced green pepper
- 2 garlic cloves, minced
- 1 can (14½ oz.) diced tomatoes, undrained
- ½ cup water
- 1½ tsp. paprika
   Dash cayenne pepper
- 1 bay leaf
- 2 tsp. cornstarch
- 1 Tbsp. cold water
   Hot cooked rice, optional

1. Sprinkle chicken with ¼ tsp. salt and pepper. Heat large cast-iron or other heavy skillet over medium heat, brown chicken in oil; remove and set aside. In the same skillet, saute onion, celery, green pepper and garlic until tender. Stir in the tomatoes, water, paprika, remaining ¼ tsp. salt, cayenne pepper and bay leaf; bring to a boil. Reduce the heat; cover and simmer 10 minutes.
2. Return chicken to skillet. Whisk the cornstarch and cold water until smooth; stir into the chicken mixture and bring to a boil. Simmer, uncovered, until chicken is tender, 10-15 minutes. Remove bay leaf before serving. If desired, serve with rice.

1¼ cups: 265 cal., 8g fat (2g sat. fat), 94mg chol., 553mg sod., 12g carb. (6g sugars, 3g fiber), 36g pro. **Diabetic exchanges:** 5 lean meat, 2 vegetable.

"Found this recipe years ago and have made it ever since. Paprika is the key to making this dish taste good! My family absolutely loves it!"
—CHARIHIBNER, TASTEOFHOME.COM

SAGE & PROSCIUTTO CHICKEN SALTIMBOCCA

The Italian word saltimbocca means to jump into one's mouth. This wonderful dish, flavored with prosciutto and fresh sage leaves, fulfills that promise.
—*Trisha Kruse, Eagle, ID*

TAKES: 25 min. • **MAKES:** 4 servings

- ½ cup plus 2 tsp. all-purpose flour, divided
- 4 boneless skinless chicken breast halves (6 oz. each)
- ½ tsp. salt
- ¼ tsp. pepper
- 8 fresh sage leaves
- 8 thin slices prosciutto or deli ham
- 2 Tbsp. olive oil
- 1 Tbsp. butter
- ½ cup chicken broth
- 2 Tbsp. lemon juice
- 2 Tbsp. white wine or additional chicken broth
  Optional: Lemon slices and fresh sage

1. Place ½ cup flour in a shallow bowl; set aside. Flatten the chicken breasts to ¼-in. thickness. Sprinkle both sides with the salt and pepper; top each breast half with 2 sage leaves and 2 slices prosciutto, pressing to adhere. Dip the chicken sides only in flour to coat.

2. In a large skillet, heat oil and butter over medium heat; cook chicken for 3-4 minutes on each side or until lightly browned and chicken is no longer pink. Remove and keep warm.

3. In a small bowl, whisk the chicken broth, lemon juice, wine and remaining flour; add to the skillet, stirring to loosen browned bits from pan. Bring to a boil; cook and stir for 1 minute or until sauce is thickened. Spoon over chicken. Top chicken with lemon and sage if desired.

1 chicken breast half with 2 Tbsp. sauce: 355 cal., 17g fat (5g sat. fat), 128mg chol., 1070mg sod., 5g carb. (0 sugars, 0 fiber), 43g pro.

CREAMY CHICKEN & PASTA

Rich, creamy and laced with wine, this homemade sauce is one my family loves. Use it over pasta and chicken for a dinner you'll be proud to serve. I also add capers to lend a salty, lemony flavor to pasta.
—*Elaine Moser, Spokane, WA*

TAKES: 30 min. • **MAKES:** 5 servings

- 2 cups uncooked penne pasta
- 2 cups sliced fresh mushrooms
- 1 cup sliced green onions
- 2 Tbsp. butter
- ½ cup white wine or chicken broth
- 1 tsp. minced garlic
- 1 Tbsp. all-purpose flour
- ⅓ cup water
- 1 cup heavy whipping cream
- 2 cups cubed cooked chicken
- 2 Tbsp. capers, drained
- ¼ tsp. salt
- ⅛ tsp. pepper
  Shredded Parmesan cheese

1. Cook pasta according to the package directions. Meanwhile, in a large skillet, saute mushrooms and onions in butter for 4-5 minutes or until tender. Add wine and garlic. Bring to a boil; cook until the liquid is reduced by half, about 5 minutes.

2. Combine flour and water until smooth; gradually add to mushroom mixture. Bring to a boil. Reduce the heat; cook and stir for 2 minutes or until thickened. Stir in cream. Bring to a boil. Reduce the heat; simmer, uncovered, for 4-5 minutes or until the mixture is heated through.

3. Add the pasta, chicken, capers, salt and pepper to cream sauce. Cook for 3-4 minutes or until heated through. Sprinkle with Parmesan cheese.

1 cup: 431 cal., 25g fat (14g sat. fat), 121mg chol., 420mg sod., 27g carb. (3g sugars, 2g fiber), 23g pro.

TEST KITCHEN TIP

Capers are the small, green flower buds of a bush that grows in the Mediterranean. Pickled in wine, vinegar or brine, capers lend a salty, lemony flavor to sauces, salads, veggies and main dishes. They can be found near the olives and pickles in grocery stores.

CREAMY CHICKEN & PASTA

EASY MEDITERRANEAN CHICKEN

COUNTRY FRIED CHICKEN

This is one of our favorite recipes to take along on a picnic. We like to eat the chicken cold, along with a salad and watermelon.
—*Rebekah Miller, Rocky Mount, VA*

PREP: 20 min. • **COOK:** 40 min.
MAKES: 4 servings

- 1 cup all-purpose flour
- 2 tsp. garlic salt
- 2 tsp. pepper
- 1 tsp. paprika
- ½ tsp. poultry seasoning
- 1 large egg
- ½ cup 2% milk
- 1 broiler/fryer chicken (3 to 3½ lbs.), cut up
  Oil for frying

1. In a resealable container, combine the flour and seasonings. In a shallow bowl, beat egg and milk. Dip chicken pieces into egg mixture, then add to container, a few pieces at a time, and shake to coat.
2. In a large skillet or Dutch oven, heat ¼ in. of oil to 375°. Fry the chicken, a few pieces at a time, 7-10 minutes on each side or until the chicken is golden brown and the juices run clear. Drain chicken on paper towels.

1 serving: 526 cal., 24g fat (7g sat. fat), 189mg chol., 1051mg sod., 27g carb. (2g sugars, 1g fiber), 48g pro.

"Well worth the effort. Reminds me of summer days at my grandma's house for dinner."
—BEARGUY64, TASTEOFHOME.COM

EASY MEDITERRANEAN CHICKEN

Friends and family love this special chicken recipe. I changed a few things to make it healthier, but it tastes just as good.
—*Kara Zilis, Oak Forest, IL*

TAKES: 30 min. • **MAKES:** 4 servings

- 4 boneless skinless chicken breast halves (4 oz. each)
- 1 Tbsp. olive oil
- 1 can (14½ oz.) no-salt-added stewed tomatoes
- 1 cup water
- 1 tsp. dried oregano
- ¼ tsp. garlic powder
- 1½ cups instant brown rice
- 1 pkg. (12 oz.) frozen cut green beans
- 12 pitted Greek olives, halved
- ½ cup crumbled feta cheese

1. In a large nonstick skillet, brown chicken in oil on each side. Stir in the tomatoes, water, oregano and garlic powder. Bring to a boil; reduce heat. Cover and simmer 10 minutes.
2. Stir in the rice and green beans. Return to a boil. Cover and simmer until a thermometer reads 165° and rice is tender, 8-10 minutes longer. Stir in the olives; sprinkle with cheese.

1 serving: 417 cal., 12g fat (3g sat. fat), 70mg chol., 386mg sod., 44g carb. (6g sugars, 6g fiber), 31g pro. **Diabetic exchanges:** 3 lean meat, 2 starch, 2 vegetable, 1 fat.

CHICKEN & GOAT CHEESE
SKILLET

CHICKEN & GOAT CHEESE SKILLET

My husband was completely bowled over by this on-a-whim skillet meal. I can't wait to make it again soon!
—*Ericka Barber, Eureka, CA*

- -

TAKES: 20 min. • **MAKES:** 2 servings

- ½   lb. boneless skinless chicken breasts, cut into 1-in. pieces
- ¼   tsp. salt
- ⅛   tsp. pepper
- 2   tsp. olive oil
- 1   cup cut fresh asparagus (1-in. pieces)
- 1   garlic clove, minced
- 3   plum tomatoes, chopped
- 3   Tbsp. 2% milk
- 2   Tbsp. herbed fresh goat cheese, crumbled
      Hot cooked rice or pasta
      Additional goat cheese, optional

1. Toss chicken with salt and pepper. In a large skillet, heat oil over medium-high heat; saute the chicken until no longer pink, 4-6 minutes. Remove from the pan; keep warm.

2. Add asparagus to skillet; cook and stir over medium-high heat 1 minute. Add garlic; cook and stir 30 seconds. Stir in tomatoes, milk and 2 Tbsp. cheese; cook, covered, over medium heat until cheese begins to melt, 2-3 minutes. Stir in the chicken. Serve with rice. If desired, top with additional cheese.

1½ cups chicken mixture: 251 cal., 11g fat (3g sat. fat), 74mg chol., 447mg sod., 8g carb. (5g sugars, 3g fiber), 29g pro. **Diabetic exchanges:** 4 lean meat, 2 fat, 1 vegetable.

TEST KITCHEN TIP

An unopened package of goat cheese can last a couple of months in the refrigerator. But an opened package of goat cheese, if stored correctly, will last up to 2 weeks. To keep it as fresh as possible, wrap cheese twice—once in the original packaging, waxed paper or parchment and a second time in heavy-duty foil. If the cheese starts to get moldy, throw it away.

TURKEY CABBAGE STEW

Chock-full of ground turkey, cabbage, carrots and tomatoes, this stew delivers down-home comfort food fast!
—*Susan Lasken, Woodland Hills, CA*

- -

TAKES: 30 min. • **MAKES:** 6 servings

- 1   lb. lean ground turkey
- 1   medium onion, chopped
- 3   garlic cloves, minced
- 4   cups chopped cabbage
- 2   medium carrots, sliced
- 1   can (28 oz.) diced tomatoes, undrained
- ¾   cup water
- 1   Tbsp. brown sugar
- 1   Tbsp. white vinegar
- 1   tsp. salt
- 1   tsp. dried oregano
- ¼   tsp. dried thyme
- ¼   tsp. pepper

1. Cook the turkey, onion and garlic in a large saucepan over medium heat until meat is no longer pink, 5-7 minutes, breaking up turkey into crumbles; drain.

2. Add the remaining ingredients. Bring to a boil; cover and simmer until the vegetables are tender, 12-15 minutes.

Freeze option: Freeze cooled stew in freezer containers. To use, partially thaw in refrigerator overnight. Heat through in a saucepan, stirring occasionally; add broth if necessary.

1 cup: 180 cal., 6g fat (2g sat. fat), 52mg chol., 674mg sod., 16g carb. (10g sugars, 5g fiber), 17g pro. **Diabetic exchanges:** 2 vegetable, 2 lean meat.

TURKEY CABBAGE STEW

TURKEY BREAST TENDERLOINS WITH RASPBERRY SAUCE

Sweet and tangy raspberry sauce is a perfect complement to versatile turkey tenderloins. In fact, the sauce is so good, you'll be tempted to eat it with a spoon.
—*Deirdre Cox, Kansas City, MO*

TAKES: 30 min. • **MAKES:** 2 servings

2   turkey breast tenderloins (5 oz. each)
⅛   tsp. salt
⅛   tsp. pepper
2   tsp. olive oil
1   tsp. cornstarch
¼   cup cranberry-raspberry juice
2   Tbsp. Heinz 57 steak sauce
2   Tbsp. red raspberry preserves
½   tsp. lemon juice

1. Sprinkle turkey with salt and pepper. In a large nonstick skillet over medium heat, brown turkey in oil on all sides. Cover and cook until a thermometer reads 165°, 10-12 minutes. Remove and keep warm.
2. Combine cornstarch and juice until smooth; add to the pan. Stir in the steak sauce, preserves and lemon juice. Bring to a boil; cook and stir until thickened, about 1 minute. Slice turkey; serve with sauce.
1 tenderloin with ¼ cup sauce: 275 cal., 6g fat (1g sat. fat), 69mg chol., 425mg sod., 22g carb. (19g sugars, 0 fiber), 33g pro.

ITALIAN SAUSAGE VEGGIE SKILLET

🍎 ITALIAN SAUSAGE VEGGIE SKILLET

We love Italian sausage sandwiches, but because the bread isn't diet friendly for me, I created this flavorful skillet recipe to satisfy my craving. If you like some heat, use hot peppers in place of the sweet ones.
—*Tina Howells, Salem, OH*

TAKES: 30 min. • **MAKES:** 6 servings

4   cups uncooked whole wheat spiral pasta
1   lb. Italian turkey sausage, casings removed
1   medium onion, chopped
1   garlic clove, minced
2   medium zucchini, chopped
1   large sweet red pepper, chopped
1   large sweet yellow pepper, chopped
1   can (28 oz.) diced tomatoes, drained
¼   tsp. salt
¼   tsp. pepper

1. Cook pasta according to package directions; drain.
2. Meanwhile, in large skillet, cook the sausage and onion over medium-high heat until the sausage is no longer pink, 5-7 minutes. Add garlic and cook 1 minute longer. Add zucchini and peppers; cook until crisp-tender, 3-5 minutes. Add the tomatoes, salt and pepper. Cook and stir until vegetables are tender and begin to release their juices, 5-7 minutes. Serve with pasta.
1⅓ cups: 251 cal., 6g fat (1g sat. fat), 28mg chol., 417mg sod., 35g carb. (4g sugars, 6g fiber), 16g pro. **Diabetic exchanges:** 2 vegetable, 2 lean meat, 1½ starch.

GARLIC CHICKEN WITH HERBS

Pan-roasting garlic cloves turns them into rich, creamy deliciousness. This chicken is also fantastic with a loaf of crusty bread or mashed potatoes on the side.
—*Kathy Fleming, Lisle, IL*

TAKES: 30 min. • **MAKES:** 4 servings

- 4 boneless skinless chicken thighs (about 1 lb.)
- ½ tsp. salt
- ¼ tsp. pepper
- 1 Tbsp. butter
- 10 garlic cloves, peeled and halved
- ¼ cup white wine or chicken broth
- 1½ tsp. minced fresh rosemary
- ½ tsp. minced fresh sage
- 1 cup chicken broth
  Hot cooked rice of your choice

1. Sprinkle chicken thighs with salt and pepper. In a large skillet, heat the butter over medium-high heat; brown chicken on both sides. Remove from the pan, reserving drippings.

2. In same skillet, saute garlic in drippings over medium-high heat until light golden brown. Add wine and herbs; bring to a boil, stirring to loosen browned bits from pan. Cook until mixture is almost evaporated. Add broth and chicken; bring to a boil. Reduce heat; simmer, covered, until a thermometer inserted in chicken reads at least 170°, 10-12 minutes.

3. To serve, spoon pan juices over chicken. Serve with rice.

1 serving: 214 cal., 12g fat (3g sat. fat), 76mg chol., 487mg sod., 3g carb. (0 sugars, 0 fiber), 22g pro. **Diabetic exchanges:** 3 lean meat, ½ fat.

SWEET CHILI & ORANGE CHICKEN

My husband loves this simple chicken dish so much that he often requests it when he comes home from deployment. The sweet chili sauce adds just the right amount of heat to the bright citrusy sauce.
—*Jessica Eastman, Bremerton, WA*

TAKES: 20 min. • **MAKES:** 4 servings

- 1 lb. boneless skinless chicken breasts, cut into 1-in. pieces
- ¼ tsp. salt
- ¼ tsp. pepper
- 2 Tbsp. butter
- ¾ cup sweet chili sauce
- ⅓ cup thawed orange juice concentrate
  Hot cooked jasmine or other rice
  Minced fresh basil

1. Toss chicken with salt and pepper. In a large skillet, heat the butter over medium-high heat; stir-fry chicken until no longer pink, 5-7 minutes. Remove from pan; keep warm.

2. Add chili sauce and juice concentrate to skillet; cook and stir until heated through. Stir in chicken. Serve with rice; sprinkle with basil.

½ cup chicken mixture: 309 cal., 9g fat (4g sat. fat), 78mg chol., 1014mg sod., 33g carb. (31g sugars, 1g fiber), 24g pro.

GARLIC CHICKEN WITH HERBS

CHICKEN WITH
GARLIC-TOMATO SAUCE

CHICKEN WITH GARLIC-TOMATO SAUCE

My husband and I came up with this new favorite. It reminds us of an entree served at an Italian eatery.
—*Angela Schellenberg, Steinbach, MB*

- -

TAKES: 30 min. • **MAKES:** 4 servings

- 4   boneless skinless chicken breast halves (4 oz. each)
- ¼   tsp. pepper
- 2   tsp. olive oil, divided
- 2   plum tomatoes, seeded and chopped
- 2   garlic cloves, minced
- 2   medium carrots, halved and thinly sliced
- 1   cup Italian tomato sauce
- ¾   cup reduced-sodium chicken broth
- ¼   cup tomato paste
- 1   tsp. dried rosemary, crushed
     Hot cooked pasta
     Minced fresh rosemary, optional

1. Sprinkle both sides of chicken with pepper. In a large nonstick skillet over medium-high heat, brown the chicken on each side in 1 tsp. oil. Remove and keep warm.

2. In the same skillet, saute the tomatoes and garlic in remaining oil for 1 minute. Add carrots; saute 2-3 minutes longer. Combine the tomato sauce, broth, tomato paste and rosemary; stir into skillet. Bring to a boil.

3. Return chicken to the pan. Reduce heat; cover and simmer until a thermometer reaches 165° and carrots are crisp-tender, 10-12 minutes. Serve with the pasta. If desired, sprinkle with additional rosemary.
1 serving: 197 cal., 5g fat (1g sat. fat), 63mg chol., 510mg sod., 10g carb. (5g sugars, 3g fiber), 26g pro. **Diabetic exchanges:** 3 lean meat, 2 vegetable.

DID YOU KNOW?

This chicken pasta dish relies on the aromatic boost of garlic for its delicious flavor. When shopping for garlic, look for firm, fresh heads with tight, papery skin and free of sprouts. Remember to remove the paperlike layer before mincing.

GARLIC-MUSHROOM TURKEY SLICES

GARLIC-MUSHROOM TURKEY SLICES

My daughter is a picky eater, and even she likes this enticing dish! There's minimal fat, and it's delicious, easy and affordable for weeknight dining.
—*Rick Fleishman, Beverly Hills, CA*

- -

TAKES: 30 min. • **MAKES:** 4 servings

- ½   cup all-purpose flour
- ½   tsp. dried oregano
- ½   tsp. paprika
- ¾   tsp. salt, divided
- ¼   tsp. pepper, divided
- 1   pkg. (17.6 oz.) turkey breast cutlets
- 1   Tbsp. olive oil
- ½   lb. sliced fresh mushrooms
- ¾   cup reduced-sodium chicken broth
- ¼   cup dry white wine or additional broth
- 2   garlic cloves, minced

1. In a large shallow dish, mix the flour, oregano, paprika, ½ tsp. salt and ⅛ tsp. pepper. Dip cutlets in flour mixture to coat both sides; shake off excess.

2. In a large nonstick skillet, heat oil over medium heat. In batches, add turkey and cook until no longer pink, 1-2 minutes on each side; remove from pan.

3. Add remaining ingredients to skillet; stir in the remaining salt and pepper. Cook, uncovered, until mushrooms are tender, 4-6 minutes, stirring occasionally. Return turkey to the pan; heat through, turning to coat.
1 serving: 218 cal., 4g fat (1g sat. fat), 77mg chol., 440mg sod., 8g carb. (1g sugars, 1g fiber), 34g pro. **Diabetic exchanges:** 4 lean meat, ½ starch, ½ fat.

COCONUT-LIME CHICKEN

Tangy lime combines with sweet coconut in this tropical dish. Fragrant jasmine rice is a wonderful accompaniment.
—*Trisha Kruse, Eagle, ID*

- -

PREP: 20 min. • **COOK:** 15 min.
MAKES: 4 servings

- 1   cup uncooked jasmine rice
- 1   cup water
- ¾   cup light coconut milk
- ½   tsp. sugar
- ½   tsp. salt
- ¼   cup lime juice
- 2   Tbsp. reduced-sodium soy sauce
- 1   Tbsp. grated lime zest
- 1   Tbsp. minced fresh gingerroot
- 1   Tbsp. rice vinegar
- 1   Tbsp. honey
- 1   lb. boneless skinless chicken breasts, cut into 1-in. cubes
- 2   tsp. canola oil
- 1   tsp. sesame oil
- ¼   cup sweetened shredded coconut
- 1   Tbsp. minced fresh cilantro

1. In a large saucepan, bring the rice, water, coconut milk, sugar and salt to a boil. Reduce the heat; cover and simmer until liquid is absorbed and rice is tender, 15-20 minutes.

2. Meanwhile, in a small bowl, combine the lime juice, soy sauce, lime zest, ginger, vinegar and honey; set aside. In a large skillet, saute the chicken in canola and sesame oils until no longer pink. Add lime mixture to the pan. Bring to a boil; cook and stir 2 minutes. Sprinkle with coconut and cilantro. Fluff rice with a fork and serve with chicken mixture.

⅔ cup chicken mixture with ¾ cup rice: 415 cal., 11g fat (5g sat. fat), 63mg chol., 671mg sod., 48g carb. (8g sugars, 1g fiber), 27g pro.

"We like lots of sauce, so I doubled it. We loved this meal and will definitely be making it again."
—CINDYMARZA, TASTEOFHOME.COM

TURKEY TENDERLOIN SUPREME

We're a busy hockey and figure skating family, so we're always on the go. This fast skillet supper makes a good home-cooked meal when there's little time.
—*Nancy Levin, Chesterfield, MO*

- -

TAKES: 25 min. • **MAKES:** 4 servings

- 4   turkey breast tenderloin slices (¾ in. thick and 4 oz. each)
- ½   cup all-purpose flour
- 1   Tbsp. butter
- 3   green onions, thinly sliced
- 1   can (10¾ oz.) condensed cream of chicken soup, undiluted
- ½   cup water

Lightly dredge turkey with flour, shaking off excess. In a large skillet, heat butter over medium heat. Add turkey; cook until browned. Add the onions; cook and stir, 1-2 minutes. Combine soup and water; pour over the turkey. Bring to a boil. Reduce heat; cover and simmer until a thermometer reads 165°, 8-10 minutes.

1 serving: 174 cal., 3g fat (1g sat. fat), 59mg chol., 323mg sod., 8g carb. (5g sugars, 1g fiber), 28g pro. **Diabetic exchanges:** 3 lean meat, 1 fruit, 1 vegetable.

TURKEY TENDERLOIN SUPREME

WEEKNIGHT PASTA SQUIGGLES

PUMPKIN-CHORIZO BOW TIES

Chicken sausage is a convenient way to add flavor to healthy dishes. If your family doesn't like spicy food, skip the red pepper flakes and use a milder sausage.
—*Sharon Ricci, Mendon, NY*

TAKES: 25 min. • **MAKES:** 4 servings

- 3 cups uncooked multigrain bow tie pasta
- 1 tsp. canola oil
- 1 pkg. (12 oz.) fully cooked chorizo chicken sausage links or other spicy chicken sausage, cut into ¼-in. slices
- 1 cup fat-free half-and-half
- 1 cup canned pumpkin
- ½ cup shredded Mexican cheese blend
- ⅛ tsp. garlic powder
- ⅛ tsp. crushed red pepper flakes
- 1 Tbsp. minced fresh cilantro

1. Cook pasta according to the package directions. Meanwhile, in a large skillet, heat oil over medium-high heat. Add sausage; cook and stir for 4-6 minutes or until browned. Stir in half-and-half, pumpkin, cheese blend, garlic powder and pepper flakes; heat through.
2. Drain pasta. Add to sausage mixture; toss to coat. Sprinkle with cilantro.
1¼ cups: 506 cal., 15g fat (5g sat. fat), 78mg chol., 732mg sod., 60g carb. (11g sugars, 6g fiber), 32g pro.

WEEKNIGHT PASTA SQUIGGLES

This zesty pasta dish is ideal for busy weeknights. It's low on ingredients and easy to prep, and it tastes so comforting when the weather turns cool. A salad on the side makes it a meal.
—*Stacey Brown, Spring, TX*

TAKES: 30 min. • **MAKES:** 8 servings

- 1 pkg. (19½ oz.) Italian turkey sausage links, casings removed
- 1 can (28 oz.) whole plum tomatoes with basil
- 1 can (14½ oz.) no-salt-added whole tomatoes
- 4 cups uncooked spiral pasta (about 12 oz.)
- 1 can (14½ oz.) reduced-sodium chicken broth
- ¼ cup water
- ½ cup crumbled goat or feta cheese

1. In a Dutch oven, cook and crumble sausage over medium-high heat until no longer pink, 5-7 minutes. Meanwhile, coarsely chop tomatoes, reserving juices.
2. Add tomatoes and reserved juices to sausage; stir in pasta, broth and water. Bring to a boil. Reduce heat to medium; cook, uncovered, until pasta is al dente, 15-18 minutes, stirring occasionally. Top with cheese.
1½ cups: 278 cal., 7g fat (2g sat. fat), 34mg chol., 622mg sod., 38g carb. (5g sugars, 4g fiber), 16g pro. **Diabetic exchanges:** 2½ starch, 2 medium-fat meat.

Pork

SAUCY MUSHROOM PORK CHOPS

SAUCY MUSHROOM PORK CHOPS

I came up with this easy way to dress up ordinary pork chops. My husband loved them, and the sauce was great over mashed potatoes.
—*Karlene Lantz, Felton, CA*

TAKES: 30 min. • **MAKES:** 6 servings

- 6 boneless pork loin chops (4 oz. each)
- ¼ tsp. salt
- ¼ tsp. pepper
- 2 tsp. olive oil, divided
- 1 cup sliced fresh mushrooms
- ⅓ cup chopped onion
- 1 garlic clove, minced
- ½ cup white wine or reduced-sodium chicken broth
- 1 can (10¾ oz.) reduced-fat reduced-sodium condensed cream of mushroom soup, undiluted
- ½ cup reduced-sodium chicken broth

1. Sprinkle pork chops with salt and pepper. Heat a large nonstick skillet over medium-high heat; add 1 tsp. oil. Brown chops on both sides, 2-3 minutes; remove and keep warm. In the same skillet, saute the mushrooms and onion in remaining oil until tender. Add garlic; cook 1 minute longer.
2. Add wine, stirring up any browned bits; cook until the liquid is reduced by half, 4-6 minutes. Stir in soup and broth; bring to a boil. Return pork chops to the pan. Reduce heat; simmer, uncovered, until a thermometer reads 145°, 8-10 minutes.
1 serving: 217 cal., 9g fat (3g sat. fat), 59mg chol., 380mg sod., 6g carb. (2g sugars, 0 fiber), 23g pro. **Diabetic exchanges:** 3 lean meat, ½ starch.

TEST KITCHEN TIP

No garlic press? Slice the peeled clove the way you'd slice an onion, making several vertical cuts into the clove, almost to the base. Then make horizontal cuts into the clove to get similarly sized pieces.

PORK PARMESAN

I came up with this entree by substituting pork for veal. You could even use chicken.
—*Kenna Robinson, Sault Ste. Marie, ON*

- -

TAKES: 25 min. • **MAKES:** 6 servings

½	cup dry bread crumbs
¼	cup grated Parmesan cheese
¼	tsp. salt
⅛	tsp. pepper
⅛	tsp. paprika
1	large egg
6	boneless pork loin chops (4 oz. each)
2	Tbsp. vegetable oil
½	cup tomato sauce
6	slices part-skim mozzarella cheese

1. In a shallow bowl, combine the bread crumbs, Parmesan cheese, salt, pepper and paprika. In another bowl, beat egg. Dip each pork chop in the egg, then coat with crumb mixture.

2. In a large skillet, cook the pork chops in oil over medium heat until juices run clear, 6-8 minutes on each side. Top each chop with the tomato sauce and cheese; cover and simmer until cheese is melted, about 1 minute.

Note: To prepare recipe in a microwave, place breaded pork chops on a microwave-sate plate. (Omit oil.) Microwave on high for 4 minutes. Rotate plate and microwave 4 minutes longer or until juices run clear. Top each chop with the tomato sauce and cheese; microwave 1-2 minutes or until cheese is melted.

1 serving: 213 cal., 13g fat (5g sat. fat), 62mg chol., 497mg sod., 9g carb. (1g sugars, 0 fiber), 15g pro.

"Easy and good! After browning the chops on the stovetop, I cooked them in my slow cooker on low for 4½ hours with the sauce mixture on top. I placed the cheese on top during last 30 minutes."
—OJC0806, TASTEOFHOME.COM

**CHINESE PORK
FRIED RICE**

🍎 CHINESE PORK FRIED RICE

Here's an all-time classic scaled down for two. The vegetables add color and crunch to this savory dinner.
—*Peggy Vaught, Glasgow, WV*

- -

TAKES: 25 min. • **MAKES:** 2 servings

1	boneless pork loin chop (6 oz.), cut into ½-in. pieces
¼	cup finely chopped carrot
¼	cup chopped fresh broccoli
¼	cup frozen peas
1	green onion, chopped
1	Tbsp. butter
1	large egg, lightly beaten
1	cup cold cooked long grain rice
4½	tsp. reduced-sodium soy sauce
⅛	tsp. garlic powder
⅛	tsp. ground ginger

1. In a large skillet, saute the pork, carrot, broccoli, peas and onion in butter until the pork is no longer pink, 3-5 minutes. Remove from skillet and set aside.

2. In same skillet, cook and stir egg over medium heat until completely set. Stir in the rice, soy sauce, garlic powder, ginger and pork mixture; heat through. If desired, garnish with additional green onions.

1 cup: 338 cal., 13g fat (6g sat. fat), 163mg chol., 597mg sod., 29g carb. (3g sugars, 2g fiber), 24g pro. **Diabetic exchanges:** 3 lean meat, 2 starch.

BLT SKILLET

SAUSAGE RATATOUILLE

You'll feel like a great chef when you serve this veggie-packed dish that party guests will rave about. Don't let the ingredient list fool you—pantry staples and an easy-cook method make this one a cinch.
—*Janine Freeman, Blaine, WA*

PREP: 20 min. • **COOK:** 25 min.
MAKES: 10 servings

- 2   lbs. sweet Italian sausage links
- ½   lb. fresh green beans, trimmed and cut into 2-in. pieces
- 2   medium green peppers, julienned
- 1   large onion, chopped
- 5   shallots, chopped
- 2   garlic cloves, minced
- 2   Tbsp. butter
- 2   Tbsp. olive oil
- 4   medium zucchini, quartered and sliced
- 5   plum tomatoes, chopped
- ½   tsp. sugar
- ½   tsp. salt
- ¼   tsp. pepper
- ¼   tsp. crushed red pepper flakes
- ⅛   tsp. ground allspice
- ¼   cup minced fresh parsley
- ⅓   cup grated Parmesan cheese
      Hot cooked rice

1. In a large skillet, cook sausage over medium heat until no longer pink; drain. Remove and cut into ½-in. slices.
2. In the same skillet, in batches cook beans, green peppers, onion, shallots and garlic in butter and oil over medium heat until tender. Stir in the zucchini, tomatoes, sugar, salt, pepper, red pepper flakes and allspice. Cook and stir for 6-8 minutes or until the vegetables are tender.
3. Stir in sausage and parsley; heat through. Sprinkle with the Parmesan cheese. Serve with rice.
1¼ cups: 337 cal., 26g fat (8g sat. fat), 57mg chol., 752mg sod., 15g carb. (6g sugars, 3g fiber), 14g pro.

🍎
BLT SKILLET

This weeknight meal is fast and is reminiscent of a BLT, with its chunks of bacon and tomato. The whole wheat linguine gives the skillet dish extra flavor and texture.
—*Edrie O'Brien, Denver, CO*

TAKES: 25 min. • **MAKES:** 2 servings

- 4   oz. uncooked whole wheat linguine
- 4   bacon strips, cut into 1½-in. pieces
- 1   plum tomato, cut into 1-in. pieces
- 1   garlic clove, minced
- 1½ tsp. lemon juice
- ¼   tsp. salt
- ¼   tsp. pepper
- 2   Tbsp. grated Parmesan cheese
- 1   Tbsp. minced fresh parsley

1. Cook linguine according to package directions. Meanwhile, in a large skillet, cook bacon over medium heat until crisp. Remove to paper towels; drain, reserving 1 tsp. drippings.
2. In the drippings, saute the tomato and garlic 1-2 minutes or until heated through. Stir in bacon, lemon juice, salt and pepper.
3. Drain linguine; add to skillet. Sprinkle with cheese and parsley; toss to coat.
1½ cups: 314 cal., 11g fat (4g sat. fat), 23mg chol., 682mg sod., 46g carb. (2g sugars, 7g fiber), 14g pro.

SAUSAGE
RATATOUILLE

DIJON-HONEY PORK CHOPS

Lemon pepper is our seasoning of choice for these pork chops. With the flavorful honey-orange Dijon sauce, there's no need to pass the salt.
—*Shirley Goehring, Lodi, CA*

TAKES: 20 min. • **MAKES:** 4 servings

4	boneless pork loin chops (5 oz. each)
1	tsp. salt-free lemon-pepper seasoning
2	tsp. canola oil
½	cup orange juice
1	Tbsp. Dijon mustard
1	Tbsp. honey

1. Sprinkle pork chops with lemon pepper. In a large nonstick skillet, heat oil over medium heat. Brown chops on both sides.
2. In a small bowl, whisk orange juice, mustard and honey until blended; pour over chops. Bring to a boil. Reduce heat; simmer, covered, 5-8 minutes or until a thermometer inserted in pork reads 145°.
3. Remove chops from pan; keep warm. Bring sauce to a boil; cook until mixture is reduced to ¼ cup, stirring occasionally. Serve with chops.
1 pork chop with 1 Tbsp. sauce: 244 cal., 11g fat (3g sat. fat), 68mg chol., 134mg sod., 9g carb. (7g sugars, 0 fiber), 28g pro.
Diabetic exchanges: 4 lean meat, ½ starch.

CURRIED PORK & GREEN TOMATOES

When the tomatoes are green in the garden, my husband and sons are thrilled to know this dish will appear on several weekly menus. I've passed the recipe on more times than I can count.
—*Coleen Frederick, Redwater, AB*

TAKES: 30 min. • **MAKES:** 4 servings

1	large onion, finely chopped
2	Tbsp. butter
4	large fresh green tomatoes, cubed
¼	cup all-purpose flour
1	to 2 tsp. curry powder
½	tsp. salt
¼	tsp. pepper
¼	tsp. sugar
	Pinch ground cardamom, optional
2	cups chicken broth
2	cups cubed cooked pork
	Hot cooked rice

In a medium skillet, saute onion in butter. Add tomatoes; cover and simmer for 10-12 minutes or until tender. Combine flour, curry, salt, pepper, sugar and, if desired, cardamom; slowly stir into the tomatoes. Add broth and pork; simmer, uncovered, 3-5 minutes or until sauce thickens. Serve over rice.
1½ cups: 275 cal., 13g fat (6g sat. fat), 79mg chol., 879mg sod., 17g carb. (6g sugars, 2g fiber), 24g pro.

CURRIED PORK & GREEN TOMATOES

LOADED HUEVOS RANCHEROS
WITH ROASTED
POBLANO PEPPERS

LOADED HUEVOS RANCHEROS WITH ROASTED POBLANO PEPPERS

This is a unique but very tasty version of huevos rancheros. It's similar to a cowboy hash, as the potatoes take the place of the corn tortillas.

—*Joan Hallford, North Richland Hills, TX*

PREP: 15 min. + standing • **COOK:** 20 min.
MAKES: 4 servings

- 1 poblano pepper
- ½ lb. fresh chorizo or bulk spicy pork sausage
- 4 cups frozen O'Brien potatoes, thawed
- ½ cup shredded pepper jack cheese
- 1 tsp. smoked paprika
- ½ tsp. kosher salt
- ½ tsp. garlic powder
- ½ tsp. pepper
- 4 large eggs
  Optional: Salsa, sour cream and minced fresh cilantro

1. Place the poblano pepper in a 12-in. cast-iron or other ovenproof skillet. Broil 4 in. from heat until skin blisters, rotating with tongs until all sides are blistered and blackened, about 5 minutes. Immediately place pepper in a small bowl; let stand, covered, 20 minutes.
2. Peel off and discard the charred skin. Remove stems and seeds. Finely chop pepper; set aside.
3. In the same skillet, cook chorizo over medium heat 6-8 minutes or until cooked through, breaking into crumbles; drain. Add potatoes; cook and stir until tender, 8-10 minutes. Stir in cheese, paprika, kosher salt, garlic powder and pepper.

4. With the back of a spoon, make 4 wells in the potato mixture. Break an egg in each well. Cook, covered, on medium-low until the egg whites are completely set and yolks begin to thicken but are not hard, 5-7 minutes. Serve with roasted pepper and, if desired, salsa, sour cream and cilantro.
1 serving: 426 cal., 26g fat (10g sat. fat), 251mg chol., 1114mg sod., 20g carb. (2g sugars, 3g fiber), 24g pro.

DID YOU KNOW?
Poblanos are a mild pepper and are sold fresh, young and dark green. Once ripened and dried, they're called ancho or ancho chile peppers and hold much more heat.

PORK MEATBALLS

❄ PORK MEATBALLS

This recipe is one of my favorites. My mom used to make the moist, flavorful meatballs often. They were part of our traditional dinner on Shrove Tuesday and served with homemade gnocchi.

—*Joan Newberry, Indiana, PA*

PREP: 15 min. • **COOK:** 30 min.
MAKES: 2 servings

- 1 large egg, lightly beaten
- 1 slice bread, crumbled
- 1 garlic clove, minced
- ¼ cup grated Romano or Parmesan cheese
- ½ tsp. salt
- ½ tsp. dried parsley flakes
- ¼ tsp. pepper
- ¾ lb. ground pork
- 1 can (14½ oz.) beef broth

1. In a bowl, combine first 7 ingredients. Crumble ground pork over mixture and mix lightly but thoroughly. Shape into ten 2-in. balls.

2. In a saucepan, bring the broth to a boil. Place meatballs in the broth. Reduce heat; cover and simmer for 15 minutes. Turn the meatballs; cook for 15 minutes or until the meatballs are cooked through, turning occasionally. Remove with a slotted spoon. If desired, sprinkle with additional cheese and parsley.

Freeze option: Freeze cooled meatball mixture in freezer containers. To use, partially thaw in refrigerator overnight. Heat through in a covered saucepan, stirring occasionally; add water or broth if necessary.

5 meatballs: 511 cal., 33g fat (14g sat. fat), 235mg chol., 1731mg sod., 8g carb. (2g sugars, 0 fiber), 43g pro.

QUICK TACOS AL PASTOR

🍎 QUICK TACOS AL PASTOR

My husband and I tried pork and pineapple tacos at a truck stand in Hawaii. Something about them was so tasty, I decided to make my own version at home.

—*Lori McLain, Denton, TX*

TAKES: 25 min. • **MAKES:** 4 servings

- 1 pkg. (15 oz.) refrigerated pork roast au jus
- 1 cup well-drained unsweetened pineapple chunks, divided
- 1 Tbsp. canola oil
- ½ cup enchilada sauce
- 8 corn tortillas (6 in.), warmed
- ½ cup finely chopped onion
- ¼ cup chopped fresh cilantro
  Optional: Crumbled queso fresco, salsa verde and lime wedges

1. Coarsely shred pork, reserving juices. In a small bowl, crush half the pineapple with a fork.

2. In a large nonstick skillet, heat oil over medium-high heat. Add whole pineapple chunks; cook 2-3 minutes or until lightly browned, turning occasionally. Remove from pan.

3. Add the enchilada sauce and crushed pineapple to same skillet; stir in pork and reserved juices. Cook over medium-high heat for 4-6 minutes or until the liquid is evaporated, stirring occasionally.

4. Serve in tortillas with pineapple chunks, onion and cilantro. If desired, top with queso fresco and salsa, and serve with lime wedges.

2 tacos: 317 cal., 11g fat (3g sat. fat), 57mg chol., 573mg sod., 36g carb. (12g sugars, 5g fiber), 24g pro. **Diabetic exchanges:** 3 lean meat, 2 starch, 1 fat.

PORK SLAW SKILLET

Tender, moist slices of pork tenderloin and crispy slaw combine in this recipe. I've been serving it to family and friends for nearly 30 years, and it's still a hit.
—*Jerry Harrison, St. Mary's, GA*

TAKES: 20 min. • **MAKES:** 4 servings

> 2 pork tenderloins (about ¾ lb. each) cut into ¼-in. slices
>   Salt and pepper to taste
> 2 Tbsp. canola oil
> **SLAW**
> 1 Tbsp. all-purpose flour
> ½ cup water
> 2 Tbsp. cider vinegar
> 1 Tbsp. sugar
> 1 Tbsp. prepared mustard
> 2 tsp. Worcestershire sauce
> 1 tsp. salt
> ½ to 1 tsp. celery seed
>   Dash pepper
> 7 cups shredded cabbage
> 1½ cups shredded carrots
> 1 medium onion, chopped
> 1 cup chopped green pepper, optional

1. Season the pork with salt and pepper. In a large skillet, heat oil over medium heat. Add pork, cook until lightly browned, 2-3 minutes on each side. Remove and keep warm.

2. In a large bowl, combine the flour and water until smooth. Stir in vinegar, sugar, mustard, Worcestershire sauce, salt, celery seed and pepper; pour into skillet; add cabbage, carrots, onion and, if desired, green pepper. Cook and stir over medium heat until mixture comes to a boil. Cook and stir for 2 minutes or until thickened and vegetables are crisp-tender. Top with pork; cover and cook until a thermometer reads 145°. Let stand 5 minutes before serving.

1¼ cups: 248 cal., 10g fat (2g sat. fat), 47mg chol., 732mg sod., 20g carb. (12g sugars, 5g fiber), 20g pro.

🍎 CURRIED SQUASH & SAUSAGE

This stovetop supper is simple to make, and it charms my whole family of curry lovers. My kids even like it cold and ask to have it packed that way in their school lunches. It's on our regular rotation.
—*Colette Lower, York, PA*

PREP: 15 min. • **COOK:** 20 min.
MAKES: 8 servings

> 1 lb. mild bulk Italian sausage
> 1 Tbsp. olive oil
> 1 medium onion, chopped
> 1 medium green pepper, chopped
> 1 large acorn squash or 6 cups butternut squash, seeded, peeled and cubed (½ in.)
> 1 large unpeeled apple, cubed (½ in.)
> 2 to 3 tsp. curry powder
> 1 tsp. salt
> 3 cups cooked small pasta shells
> ¼ cup water

1. In a stockpot, cook and crumble the sausage over medium heat until no longer pink, 5-6 minutes; remove from the pan.

2. In the same pan, heat oil. Add onion and pepper; cook and stir for 3 minutes. Add squash; cook for 5 minutes. Stir in the apple, curry powder and salt; cook until vegetables are crisp-tender, 3-4 minutes.

3. Return sausage to pan; add pasta and water. Heat through.

1⅓ cups: 385 cal., 18g fat (5g sat. fat), 38mg chol., 735mg sod., 44g carb. (7g sugars, 4g fiber), 14g pro.

TEST KITCHEN TIP

Avoid buying acorn squash that have too much orange coloring because they tend to be tougher and more fibrous. You can store acorn squash for up to 1 month before using.

CURRIED SQUASH & SAUSAGE

PORK & APPLE
TAMALES

PORK & APPLE TAMALES

Apple lends a hint of sweetness to this
lightly spiced tamale filling.
—*Marie Macy, Fort Collins, CO*

PREP: 45 min. + soaking • **COOK:** 45 min.
MAKES: 3 dozen

43 to 44 dried corn husks
DOUGH

3 cups masa harina
1¾ cups water
1 cup lard or shortening
1 tsp. salt

FILLING

1 lb. ground pork or beef
½ cup chopped onion
1 garlic clove, minced
1 can (10¾ oz.) tomato puree
1 tart medium apple, peeled and
chopped
½ cup chopped almonds, toasted
¼ cup minced fresh parsley

1 Tbsp. cider vinegar
1 tsp. sugar
½ tsp. ground coriander
½ tsp. coarsely ground pepper
½ tsp. chili powder
¼ tsp. ground cumin
1 cup chicken broth or water
Hot water

1. Cover dried corn husks with cold water;
soak overnight.
2. For the dough, combine masa harina
and water. Let stand, covered, 30 minutes.
Meanwhile, in another bowl, beat the lard
and salt until mixture resembles beaten
egg whites, about 6 minutes. Add the
masa harina mixture 2 Tbsp. at a time,
beating constantly.
3. For the filling, cook pork and onion,
crumbling meat, in a large skillet over
medium heat until the meat is no longer
pink. Add garlic; cook 1 minute longer.
Drain. Add next 10 ingredients. Bring

to a boil. Reduce heat; simmer, covered,
25 minutes. Cool slightly.
4. Drain the corn husks and pat dry; tear
7-8 husks to make 36 strips for tying
tamales. (To prevent husks from drying
out, cover with a damp towel until ready to
use.) On wide end of each remaining husk,
spread 2-3 Tbsp. dough to within ½ in. of
side edges; top each with 1-2 Tbsp. filling.
Fold long sides of husk over the filling,
overlapping slightly. Fold over narrow end
of husk; tie with a strip of husk to secure.
5. Place a large steamer basket in a 6-qt.
stockpot over broth; place tamales upright
in steamer. Bring to a boil; steam, covered,
adding hot water as needed, until dough
peels away from husk, about 45 minutes.
3 tamales: 380 cal., 28g fat (9g sat. fat),
42mg chol., 308mg sod., 21g carb. (3g
sugars, 4g fiber), 12g pro.

ASIAN
LONG NOODLE
SOUP

ASIAN LONG NOODLE SOUP

This flavorful soup is perfect when you want something warm and filling in a hurry. If you can't find long noodles, angel hair pasta is a good substitute.
—*Carol Emerson, Aransas Pass, TX*

- -

TAKES: 30 min. • **MAKES:** 6 servings (2 qt.)

- 6 oz. uncooked Asian lo mein noodles
- 1 pork tenderloin (¾ lb.), cut into thin strips
- 2 Tbsp. soy sauce, divided
- ⅛ tsp. pepper
- 2 Tbsp. canola oil, divided
- 1½ tsp. minced fresh gingerroot
- 1 garlic clove, minced
- 1 carton (32 oz.) chicken broth
- 1 celery rib, thinly sliced
- 1 cup fresh snow peas, halved diagonally
- 1 cup coleslaw mix
- 2 green onions, sliced diagonally
  Fresh cilantro leaves, optional

1. Cook the noodles according to package directions. Drain and rinse with cold water; drain well.

2. Meanwhile, toss pork with 1 Tbsp. soy sauce and the pepper. In a 6-qt. stockpot, heat 1 Tbsp. oil over medium-high heat; saute pork 2-3 minutes or until lightly browned. Remove from pot.

3. In same pot, heat remaining 1 Tbsp. oil over medium-high heat; saute ginger and garlic until fragrant, 20-30 seconds. Stir in broth and remaining 1 Tbsp. soy sauce; bring to a boil. Add celery and snow peas; return to a boil. Simmer, uncovered, until crisp-tender, 2-3 minutes. Stir in pork and coleslaw mix; cook just until the cabbage begins to wilt. Add the noodles; remove from heat. Top with green onions and, if desired, cilantro.

1⅓ cups: 227 cal., 7g fat (1g sat. fat), 35mg chol., 1078mg sod., 23g carb. (2g sugars, 1g fiber), 16g pro.

TEST KITCHEN TIP

You can eat this soup alone as a meal or serve it alongside spring rolls and a salad.

JAMAICAN JERK
PORK CHOPS

JAMAICAN JERK PORK CHOPS

These sweet, spicy chops can be thrown together in minutes but definitely don't taste like it. Serve it with a side of jasmine rice and you'll feel like you're on a warm, tropical vacation!
—*Allison Ulrich, Frisco, TX*

- -

TAKES: 25 min. • **MAKES:** 2 servings

- 3 Tbsp. butter, divided
- ¼ cup peach preserves
- 4 boneless thin-cut pork loin chops (2 to 3 oz. each)
- 3 tsp. Caribbean jerk seasoning
- ½ tsp. salt
- ¼ tsp. pepper
- ½ medium sweet orange pepper
- ½ medium sweet yellow pepper
- ½ medium sweet red pepper
  Hot cooked rice, optional

1. Soften 1 Tbsp. butter; mix with the peach preserves.

2. Sprinkle the chops with seasonings. In a large skillet, heat 1 Tbsp. butter over medium-high heat; brown chops 2-3 minutes per side. Remove from pan.

3. Cut peppers into thin strips. In same pan, saute peppers in remaining butter over medium-high heat until crisp-tender and lightly browned, 5-6 minutes. Add the chops to pan with peppers; top with preserves mixture. Cook, uncovered, until heated through, 30-60 seconds. If desired, serve with rice.

1 serving: 470 cal., 26g fat (14g sat. fat), 114mg chol., 1190mg sod., 32g carb. (28g sugars, 2g fiber), 28g pro.

TENDER SWEET & SOUR PORK CHOPS

My best friend gave me the recipe for these delightful pork chops years ago. It's become one of my family's favorites, and I prepare it often.
—Gina Young, Lamar, CO

TAKES: 25 min. • **MAKES:** 6 servings

- 6 boneless pork loin chops (4 oz. each)
- ¾ tsp. pepper
- ½ cup water
- ⅓ cup cider vinegar
- ¼ cup packed brown sugar
- 2 Tbsp. reduced-sodium soy sauce
- 1 Tbsp. Worcestershire sauce
- 1 Tbsp. cornstarch
- 2 Tbsp. cold water

1. Sprinkle the pork chops with pepper. In a large skillet coated with cooking spray, cook pork over medium heat until lightly browned, 4-6 minutes on each side. Remove and keep warm.

2. Add the next 5 ingredients to the skillet, stirring to loosen browned bits. Bring to a boil. Combine the cornstarch and cold water until smooth; stir into skillet. Bring to a boil; cook and stir for 2 minutes or until thickened.

3. Return chops to the pan. Reduce heat; cover and simmer until a thermometer inserted in pork reads 145°, 4-5 minutes.

1 pork chop with 3 Tbsp. sauce: 198 cal., 6g fat (2g sat. fat), 55mg chol., 265mg sod., 12g carb. (10g sugars, 0 fiber), 22g pro.
Diabetic exchanges: 3 lean meat, 1 starch.

HAM & PEA
PASTA ALFREDO

HAM & PEA PASTA ALFREDO

When I want a filling meal that even the kids enjoy, I toss ham and sugar snap peas with Romano cream sauce and pasta.
—C.R. Monachino, Kenmore, NY

TAKES: 25 min. • **MAKES:** 8 servings

- 1 pkg. (16 oz.) fettuccine
- 2 Tbsp. butter
- 1½ lbs. sliced fully cooked ham, cut into strips (about 5 cups)
- 2 cups fresh sugar snap peas
- 2 cups heavy whipping cream
- ½ cup grated Romano cheese
- ¼ tsp. pepper

1. Cook fettuccine according to package directions. Meanwhile, in a large skillet, heat butter over medium heat. Add ham and peas; cook and stir 5 minutes. Stir in the cream, cheese and pepper; bring to a boil. Reduce the heat; simmer, uncovered, 1-2 minutes or until the sauce is slightly thickened and peas are crisp-tender.

2. Drain fettuccine; add to skillet and toss to coat. Serve immediately.

1¼ cups: 582 cal., 32g fat (18g sat. fat), 151mg chol., 1032mg sod., 45g carb. (6g sugars, 3g fiber), 33g pro.

MOO SHU PORK STIR-FRY

This is a delicious recipe that I adapted to meet our family's tastes. Cutting the ingredients into small pieces makes for a very quick stir-fry.
—*Sherri Melotik, Oak Creek, WI*

PREP: 25 min. + marinating • **COOK:** 15 min.
MAKES: 4 servings

- ½ cup hoisin sauce
- 2 tsp. plus 2 Tbsp. reduced-sodium soy sauce, divided
- 2 tsp. plus 1 Tbsp. sherry or chicken broth, divided
- 4 tsp. cornstarch, divided
- 1 pork tenderloin (¾ lb.), cut into thin strips
- ½ cup chicken broth
- 1 tsp. sesame oil
- ½ tsp. sugar
- 2 tsp. plus 1 Tbsp. canola oil, divided
- 2 large eggs, lightly beaten
- 1¾ cups sliced fresh mushrooms
- 1 small carrot, shredded
- 2 cups bean sprouts
- 1 can (5 oz.) bamboo shoots
- 2 green onions, cut into 1½ in. pieces
- 1 tsp. minced fresh gingerroot
  Hot cooked rice

1. In a large bowl, mix the hoisin sauce, 2 tsp. soy sauce, 2 tsp. sherry and 1 tsp. cornstarch until smooth. Add the meat and toss to coat. Marinate meat at room temperature for 20 minutes.
2. In a small bowl, mix broth, sesame oil, sugar and remaining soy sauce, sherry and cornstarch until smooth.
3. In a large nonstick skillet, heat 2 tsp. oil over medium heat. Pour in eggs. Mixture should set immediately. Swirl pan to move the uncooked portions toward the outside. When eggs are set and no liquid remains, roll up egg. Slide onto cutting surface; cut crosswise into ¼-in. slices.
4. In same skillet, heat remaining oil over medium-high heat. Stir-fry mushrooms for 4 minutes. Add carrots, bean sprouts, bamboo shoots and onions; cook until vegetables are crisp-tender, 2-3 minutes longer. Add ginger; cook 1 minute longer. Remove from pan.
5. Add pork to skillet; stir-fry 3-4 minutes until cooked through. Stir the cornstarch mixture and add to pan. Bring to a boil; cook and stir 1-2 minutes or until sauce is thickened. Return vegetables and eggs to pan; heat through. Serve with rice.

1 cup: 334 cal., 14g fat (3g sat. fat), 142mg chol., 1134mg sod., 26g carb. (14g sugars, 3g fiber), 25g pro.

❄

KIELBASA SKILLET STEW

I grew up on a Montana ranch, and this dish reminds me of the kind we used to prepare for the hay and harvest crews. The bacon and sausage provide rich flavor to this comforting dish. When I make it, I share my country memories with my family.
—*Machelle Lewis, Henderson, NV*

PREP: 20 min. • **COOK:** 45 min.
MAKES: 8 servings

- 5 bacon strips
- 1 to 1½ lbs. smoked kielbasa or Polish sausage, thinly sliced
- 1 medium onion, chopped
- 2 cans (15½ oz. each) great northern beans, undrained
- 2 cans (8 oz. each) tomato sauce
- 1 can (4 oz.) chopped green chiles
- 2 medium carrots, thinly sliced
- ½ medium green pepper, chopped
- ½ tsp. Italian seasoning
- ½ tsp. dried thyme
- ⅛ tsp. pepper

1. In a 12-in. skillet, cook bacon until crisp; remove to paper towel to drain. Cook the sausage and onions in drippings over medium heat until onion is tender; drain.
2. Stir in remaining ingredients; bring to a boil. Reduce the heat; cover and simmer until the vegetables are tender, stirring occasionally, about 45 minutes. Crumble bacon; sprinkle over stew.
Freeze option: Freeze the cooled stew in freezer containers. To use, partially thaw in refrigerator overnight. Heat through in a saucepan, stirring occasionally; add water or broth if necessary.

1 cup: 269 cal., 18g fat (6g sat. fat), 41mg chol., 993mg sod., 15g carb. (4g sugars, 4g fiber), 12g pro.

MOO SHU
PORK STIR-FRY

HURRY-UP HAM & NOODLES

SMOKED SAUSAGE DINNER

I treat my wife to this well-seasoned, nourishing meal when she comes home from work. The V8 gives it a really unique flavor.
—Raymond Bell, Thornton, CO

TAKES: 25 min. • **MAKES:** 2 servings

½	lb. smoked sausage, sliced
⅓	cup chopped green pepper
¼	cup chopped onion
½	tsp. dried oregano
½	tsp. dried basil
1	Tbsp. olive oil
1	small garlic clove, minced
¾	cup V8 juice
1½	cups hot cooked rice
	Minced fresh oregano, optional

1. In a large skillet, saute the sausage, green pepper, onion, oregano and basil in oil until vegetables are crisp-tender. Add garlic; cook 1 minute longer.
2. Stir in V8 juice; bring to a boil. Reduce heat; simmer, uncovered, until thickened and heated through, 7-8 minutes, stirring occasionally. Serve with rice. If desired, garnish with fresh oregano.
1⅓ cups: 603 cal., 38g fat (14g sat. fat), 76mg chol., 1518mg sod., 44g carb. (7g sugars, 2g fiber), 21g pro.

TEST KITCHEN TIP
You can experiment with this recipe by using a different kind of sausage and adding your favorite veggies or by serving the mixture over potatoes instead of rice.

HURRY-UP HAM & NOODLES

This rich-tasting dish is ready to serve in almost the time it takes to cook the noodles. I've made it for luncheons and potlucks, but mostly I make it on those days when I'm in a hurry to get something on the table.
—Lucille Howell, Portland, OR

TAKES: 25 min. • **MAKES:** 4 servings

5	to 6 cups uncooked wide egg noodles
¼	cup butter, cubed
1	cup heavy whipping cream
1½	cups chopped fully cooked ham
½	cup grated Parmesan cheese
¼	cup thinly sliced green onions
¼	tsp. salt
⅛	tsp. pepper

1. Cook noodles according to package directions. Meanwhile, in a large skillet, melt butter over medium heat. Gradually whisk in cream. Bring to a boil, stirring constantly; cook and stir until thickened, about 2 minutes longer.
2. Add the ham, cheese, onions, salt and pepper; cook, uncovered, until heated through. Drain the noodles; add to ham mixture. Toss to coat; heat through.
1½ cups: 619 cal., 43g fat (25g sat. fat), 193mg chol., 1154mg sod., 38g carb. (3g sugars, 1g fiber), 22g pro.

SMOKED SAUSAGE DINNER

SWEET-AND-SOUR PORK

SWEET-AND-SOUR PORK

When my sister went to the university, I used to visit her on weekends. She often made this wonderful tangy pork dish. Now, every time I make it for my family, it reminds me of those special visits. Everyone who tries it loves it.
—*Cherry Williams, St. Albert, AB*

- -

TAKES: 25 min. • **MAKES:** 4 servings

- 1   can (14 oz.) pineapple tidbits
- 2   Tbsp. cornstarch
- 2   Tbsp. brown sugar
- ¾   tsp. salt
- ¼   tsp. ground ginger
- ¼   tsp. pepper
- ⅓   cup water
- ⅓   cup ketchup
- 2   Tbsp. white vinegar
- 2   Tbsp. reduced-sodium soy sauce
- 1   lb. pork tenderloin, cut into 1½x¼-in. strips
- 1   medium onion, chopped
- 2   Tbsp. canola oil
- 1   green pepper, cut into thin strips
    Hot cooked rice
    Sesame seeds, optional

1. Drain the pineapple, reserving juice; set aside. In a small bowl, combine the cornstarch, brown sugar, salt, ginger and pepper. Stir in the water, ketchup, vinegar, soy sauce and reserved juice until smooth.
2. In a large skillet or wok, stir-fry pork and onion in oil for 4-8 minutes or until tender. Stir pineapple juice mixture; add to skillet. Bring to a boil; cook and stir for 1-2 minutes or until thickened.
3. Add the green pepper and reserved pineapple. Reduce heat; cover and cook for 5 minutes. Serve with rice and, if desired, sesame seeds.
1 serving: 333 cal., 11g fat (2g sat. fat), 63mg chol., 1190mg sod., 35g carb. (24g sugars, 2g fiber), 25g pro.

APRICOT HAM STEAK

APRICOT HAM STEAK

Ham is a versatile main menu item that's a standby with all country cooks. One of the best and easiest ways to serve ham slices is topped off with a slightly sweet glaze, like this apricot version.
—*Scott Woodward, Shullsburg, WI*

- -

TAKES: 10 min. • **MAKES:** 4 servings

- 2   Tbsp. butter, divided
- 4   fully cooked boneless ham steaks (5 oz. each)
- ½   cup apricot preserves
- 1   Tbsp. cider vinegar
- ¼   tsp. ground ginger
    Dash salt

1. In a large skillet, heat 1 Tbsp. butter over medium heat. Cook ham on both sides until lightly browned and heated through. Remove from pan; keep warm.
2. Add remaining 1 Tbsp. butter and remaining ingredients to pan; cook and stir over medium heat until blended and heated through. Serve over ham.
1 ham steak: 299 cal., 11g fat (5g sat. fat), 88mg chol., 1899mg sod., 26g carb. (17g sugars, 0 fiber), 26g pro.
Grilled Apricot Ham Steaks: Melt 1 Tbsp. butter and brush over ham steaks. Grill, covered, over medium heat until lightly browned, 3-5 minutes on each side. Serve as directed.

Fish & Seafood

SWEET & TANGY SHRIMP

SWEET & TANGY SHRIMP

With its delightfully sweet-tangy flavor, this easy entree is destined to become a hit with your gang! My husband and I adapted this from a recipe in a magazine, and we just love it.
—*Kathleen Davis, North Bend, WA*

TAKES: 30 min. • **MAKES:** 4 servings

- ½ cup ketchup
- 2 Tbsp. sugar
- 2 Tbsp. cider vinegar
- 2 Tbsp. reduced-sodium soy sauce
- 1 tsp. sesame oil
- ¼ tsp. crushed red pepper flakes
- 1½ lbs. uncooked medium shrimp, peeled and deveined
- 1 Tbsp. minced fresh gingerroot
- 1 Tbsp. canola oil
- 3 garlic cloves, minced
- 2 green onions, sliced
- 1 tsp. sesame seeds, toasted
  Hot cooked rice, optional

1. In a bowl, combine first 6 ingredients; set aside. In a large nonstick skillet or wok, stir-fry the shrimp and ginger in oil until shrimp turn pink. Add garlic; cook 1 minute longer.

2. Add ketchup mixture; cook and stir until heated through, 2-3 minutes. Sprinkle with onions and sesame seeds. If desired, serve with rice.

¾ cup: 241 cal., 7g fat (1g sat. fat), 252mg chol., 954mg sod., 17g carb. (10g sugars, 1g fiber), 28g pro.

"I made this for my daughter and son-in-law, and we all loved it. It went nicely with rice. I may try adding some pineapple next time."
—MUFFBEAR74, TASTEOFHOME.COM

PINE NUT-CRUSTED
TILAPIA

SEARED SCALLOPS WITH CHEDDAR-ONION GRITS

My holiday guests always love shrimp and grits, but one year when I wanted to shake things up, I added a little something new. These pan scallops are crisp and tender and contrast well with the creamy grits.
—*Janice Elder, Charlotte, NC*

PREP: 20 min. • **COOK:** 35 min.
MAKES: 4 servings

- 2 Tbsp. butter
- 3 medium onions, chopped
- ½ tsp. salt
- 1 garlic clove, minced
- 2 cans (14½ oz. each) reduced-sodium chicken broth
- ¾ cup quick-cooking grits
- 1 cup shredded sharp cheddar cheese
- ½ cup sour cream
- 12 sea scallops (about 1½ lbs.)
- ½ tsp. Cajun seasoning
- ¼ cup yellow cornmeal
- 2 Tbsp. canola oil
  Minced fresh parsley

1. In a large saucepan, heat butter over medium heat. Add onions and salt; cook and stir 8-10 minutes or until softened. Reduce heat to medium-low; cook for 15-20 minutes or until golden brown, stirring occasionally. Add garlic; cook 1 minute longer.
2. Add broth to onion mixture; bring to a boil. Slowly stir in grits. Reduce heat to medium-low; cook, covered, until thickened, about 5 minutes, stirring occasionally. Stir in cheese and sour cream until cheese is melted. Remove from heat; keep warm.
3. Meanwhile, pat scallops dry with paper towels. Sprinkle with Cajun seasoning. Press flat sides into cornmeal. In a large skillet, heat oil over medium-high heat. Add scallops; cook on each side until golden brown and firm, 2-3 minutes.
4. Serve with grits; sprinkle with parsley.
3 scallops with 1¼ cups grits: 464 cal., 29g fat (13g sat. fat), 69mg chol., 1251mg sod., 37g carb. (6g sugars, 3g fiber), 17g pro.

PINE NUT-CRUSTED TILAPIA

This golden-brown fish has a tender texture, nutty coating and hint of sweet honey. It's fast to fix and can be served for a special family meal or when you want to impress guests.
—*Taste of Home Test Kitchen*

TAKES: 25 min. • **MAKES:** 4 servings

- ½ cup pine nuts, ground
- ¼ cup all-purpose flour
- ¼ tsp. dill weed
- ¼ tsp. lemon-pepper seasoning
- 1 large egg
- 3 Tbsp. lemon juice
- 1 tsp. honey
- 4 tilapia fillets (6 oz. each)
- 2 Tbsp. butter
  Additional honey, optional

1. In a shallow bowl, combine the pine nuts, flour, dill and lemon pepper. In another shallow bowl, combine the egg, lemon juice and honey. Dip fillets in egg mixture; coat with nut mixture.
2. In a large nonstick skillet, cook fish in butter over medium heat until fillets just begin to flake easily with a fork, 4-5 minutes on each side. If desired, drizzle with additional honey.
1 serving: 237 cal., 16g fat (5g sat. fat), 89mg chol., 119mg sod., 11g carb. (3g sugars, 1g fiber), 14g pro.

DID YOU KNOW?

Also know as pignolia or pinon, the pine nut is a small seed produced by some pine tree varieties. They have a soft texture and a buttery taste and are often toasted to enhance their flavor.

NEW YEAR'S OYSTER STEW

Oyster stew is quite popular along the coast of Ireland, where oysters are served to celebrate many festivals. Immigrants brought the recipe with them to the Atlantic and Gulf coasts of the U.S.
—*Christa Scott, Santa Fe, NM*

- -

PREP: 15 min. • **COOK:** 40 min.
MAKES: 12 servings (3 qt.)

- 3 medium leeks (white portion only), chopped
- ¼ cup butter, cubed
- 2 medium potatoes, peeled and diced
- 2 cups hot water
- 3 tsp. chicken bouillon granules
- 2 cups whole milk
- 2 cups half-and-half cream
- 4 cans (16 oz. each) oysters, drained
- ¼ tsp. cayenne pepper
  Salt and pepper to taste
  Minced fresh parsley

1. In a Dutch oven, saute the leeks in butter for 10 minutes or until tender. Add the potatoes, water and bouillon; cover and simmer for 20 minutes or until the potatoes are tender. Cool.
2. Transfer mixture to a blender. Cover and process until blended. Return to the pan; stir in the milk, cream, oysters, cayenne, salt and pepper. Cook on low until heated through (do not boil). Garnish with parsley.
1 cup: 251 cal., 13g fat (7g sat. fat), 117mg chol., 448mg sod., 17g carb. (5g sugars, 1g fiber), 14g pro.

COLORFUL SHRIMP PAD THAI

Bright fresh veggie flavors, a splash of tart lime juice, the crunch of peanuts and a hint of heat make this healthy, beautiful shrimp stir-fry a real standout!
—*Taste of Home Test Kitchen*

- -

PREP: 30 min. • **COOK:** 15 min.
MAKES: 6 servings

- 6 oz. uncooked thick rice noodles
- ¼ cup rice vinegar
- 3 Tbsp. reduced-sodium soy sauce
- 2 Tbsp. sugar
- 2 Tbsp. fish sauce or additional reduced-sodium soy sauce
- 1 Tbsp. lime juice
- 2 tsp. Thai chili sauce
- 1 tsp. sesame oil
- ¼ tsp. crushed red pepper flakes

STIR-FRY

- 1½ lbs. uncooked medium shrimp, peeled and deveined
- 3 tsp. sesame oil, divided
- 2 cups fresh snow peas
- 2 medium carrots, grated
- 2 garlic cloves, minced
- 2 large eggs, lightly beaten
- 2 cups bean sprouts
- 2 green onions, chopped
- ¼ cup minced fresh cilantro
- ¼ cup unsalted dry roasted peanuts, chopped

1. Cook noodles according to package directions. Meanwhile, in a small bowl, combine the vinegar, soy sauce, sugar, fish sauce, lime juice, chili sauce, oil and pepper flakes until blended; set aside.
2. In a large nonstick skillet or wok, stir-fry the shrimp in 2 tsp. oil until they turn pink; remove and keep warm. Stir-fry snow peas and carrots in the remaining oil 1-2 minutes. Add the garlic, cook until vegetables are crisp-tender, about 1 minute longer. Add eggs; cook and stir until set.
3. Drain noodles; add to vegetable mixture. Stir vinegar mixture and add to the skillet. Bring to a boil. Add shrimp, bean sprouts and green onions; heat through. Sprinkle with cilantro and peanuts.
1 cup: 352 cal., 10g fat (2g sat. fat), 208mg chol., 955mg sod., 38g carb. (10g sugars, 4g fiber), 28g pro.

HOISIN SHRIMP & BROCCOLI

Get out the chopsticks! This Asian-inspired dinner is a healthier alternative to takeout and is so easy to prepare. The sesame oil, ginger and soy sauce add a rich flavor that enhances the taste of fresh broccoli.
—*Mary Kisinger, Calgary, AB*

- -

TAKES: 30 min. • **MAKES:** 4 servings

- 1 Tbsp. cornstarch
- ⅓ cup reduced-sodium chicken broth
- 4½ tsp. reduced-sodium soy sauce
- 4½ tsp. hoisin sauce
- 1 tsp. sesame oil
- 3 cups fresh broccoli florets
- 1 Tbsp. canola oil
- 4 green onions, chopped
- 3 garlic cloves, minced
- 1 tsp. minced fresh gingerroot
- 1 lb. uncooked medium shrimp, peeled and deveined
- 2 cups hot cooked rice
  Additional chopped green onions, optional

1. In a small bowl, combine cornstarch and broth until smooth. Stir in soy sauce, hoisin sauce and sesame oil; set aside.
2. In a large nonstick skillet or wok, stir-fry broccoli in oil until crisp-tender. Add the onions, garlic and ginger; stir-fry until vegetables are tender, 3-4 minutes. Add the shrimp; stir-fry until they turn pink, 4-5 minutes longer.
3. Stir the cornstarch mixture and add to the pan. Bring to a boil; cook and stir until thickened, about 2 minutes. Serve with rice. If desired, garnish servings with additional green onions.
1 serving: 289 cal., 7g fat (1g sat. fat), 138mg chol., 524mg sod., 33g carb. (3g sugars, 2g fiber), 23g pro. **Diabetic exchanges:** 3 lean meat, 1½ starch, 1 vegetable, 1 fat.

HOISIN SHRIMP
& BROCCOLI

SKILLET SHRIMP JAMBALAYA

Spice up this shrimp and rice dish to your taste by increasing the amount of Creole seasoning and cayenne pepper. You can add a few drops of hot pepper sauce, too.
—Taste of Home *Test Kitchen*

PREP: 15 min. • **COOK:** 30 min.
MAKES: 6 servings

- ¼ cup butter, cubed
- 1 cup chopped onion
- ½ cup chopped celery
- ½ cup chopped green pepper
- 3 cups vegetable broth
- 1½ cups uncooked long grain rice
- 2 tsp. Creole seasoning
- ½ tsp. Worcestershire sauce
- ⅛ to ¼ tsp. cayenne pepper
- 2 cans (14½ oz. each) diced tomatoes, drained
- 1 lb. cooked medium shrimp, peeled and deveined
- 1½ cups frozen peas

1. Heat a large skillet over medium-high heat; add butter. Saute onion, celery and green pepper until tender, 2-3 minutes. Add the broth, rice, Creole seasoning, Worcestershire sauce and cayenne.
2. Bring to a boil. Reduce the heat to low; cover and cook until the rice is tender, 15-20 minutes. Stir in tomatoes, shrimp and peas; heat through.
Note: If you don't have Creole seasoning in your cupboard, you can make your own using ¼ tsp. each salt, garlic powder and paprika; and a pinch each of dried thyme, ground cumin and cayenne pepper.
1½ cups: 397 cal., 10g fat (5g sat. fat), 135mg chol., 1141mg sod., 54g carb. (10g sugars, 5g fiber), 23g pro.

CREAMY TOMATO SHRIMP WITH PENNE

People love this creamy pasta and think it's complicated, but jarred sauces make it so quick to prepare. It feels special enough for festive occasions.
—Cassandra Gourley, Williams, AZ

TAKES: 20 min. • **MAKES:** 4 servings

- 2 cups uncooked penne pasta
- 2 Tbsp. olive oil
- 1 lb. uncooked medium shrimp, peeled and deveined
- 1 tsp. minced garlic
- ½ tsp. crushed red pepper flakes
- 1½ cups pasta sauce
- 1 carton (10 oz.) refrigerated Alfredo sauce
- 2 Tbsp. butter
- ¼ tsp. salt
- ⅛ tsp. pepper
- 2 Tbsp. minced fresh parsley

1. Cook the pasta according to package directions. Meanwhile, in a large skillet, heat oil over medium heat. Add shrimp, garlic and pepper flakes; cook and stir until shrimp turn pink, 3-5 minutes. Stir in pasta sauce, Alfredo sauce, butter, salt and pepper; heat through.
2. Drain pasta; serve with shrimp mixture. Sprinkle with parsley.
1 serving: 554 cal., 30g fat (13g sat. fat), 188mg chol., 1097mg sod., 42g carb. (11g sugars, 4g fiber), 30g pro.

CREAMY TOMATO SHRIMP WITH PENNE

SHRIMP PANZANELLA SALAD

CATFISH WITH BROWN BUTTER-PECAN SAUCE

My husband is from the Midwest and grew up eating fried catfish. This dish is one of his favorites. The rich, toasty pecans and tangy citrus are a perfect complement to any fish.
—*Trisha Kruse, Eagle, ID*

- -

TAKES: 25 min. • **MAKES:** 4 servings

- ⅓ cup all-purpose flour
- ½ tsp. salt
- ½ tsp. cayenne pepper
- ¼ tsp. pepper
- 4 catfish fillets (6 oz. each)
- 6 Tbsp. butter, divided
- ¾ cup chopped pecans
- 2 tsp. grated lemon zest
- 2 tsp. lemon juice
  Lemon wedges

1. In a shallow dish, combine the flour, salt, cayenne and pepper. Add catfish, 1 fillet at a time, and turn to coat. In a large skillet, heat 2 Tbsp. butter over medium-high heat, add fish. Cook until fillets just begin to flake easily with a fork, 2-4 minutes on each side. Remove fish to a serving platter and keep warm.

2. In the same skillet, melt the remaining butter. Add pecans and cook over medium heat until toasted, 2-3 minutes. Stir in the lemon zest and juice. Serve with fish and lemon wedges.

1 serving: 574 cal., 46g fat (15g sat. fat), 125mg chol., 507mg sod., 12g carb. (1g sugars, 3g fiber), 30g pro.

SHRIMP PANZANELLA SALAD

These days, I'm only cooking for two. After working in the garden, I can dash indoors and have this shrimp and bread salad on the table pronto.
—*Kallee Krong-McCreery, Escondido, CA*

- -

TAKES: 20 min. • **MAKES:** 2 servings

- 1 cup cubed (¾ in.) French bread
- 1 tsp. olive oil
- ⅛ tsp. garlic salt
- 1 tsp. butter
- ½ lb. uncooked shrimp (31-40 per lb.), peeled and deveined
- 1 garlic clove, minced
- 3 cups fresh baby spinach
- ½ medium ripe avocado, peeled and cubed
- 1 medium tomato, chopped
- 2 Tbsp. Italian salad dressing
- 1 Tbsp. grated Parmesan cheese

1. In a large nonstick skillet, toss bread cubes with oil and garlic salt. Cook over medium heat until the bread is toasted, 3-4 minutes, stirring frequently. Remove from the pan.

2. In the same skillet, heat the butter over medium heat. Add the shrimp and garlic; cook and stir until the shrimp turn pink, 2-3 minutes. Remove from heat.

3. In a large bowl, combine spinach, avocado, tomato, toasted bread and shrimp; drizzle with dressing and toss gently to coat. Sprinkle with cheese; serve immediately.

1 serving: 306 cal., 16g fat (3g sat. fat), 145mg chol., 567mg sod., 19g carb. (4g sugars, 5g fiber), 23g pro. **Diabetic exchanges:** 3 lean meat, 2 vegetable, 1 fat, ½ starch.

TEST KITCHEN TIP

To increase fiber in this salad, substitute cubed bread from a crusty whole wheat dinner roll.

CORNMEAL-CRUSTED
CATFISH

CORNMEAL-CRUSTED CATFISH

To help the breading adhere to the fish, pat the fillets dry and coat lightly with flour before dipping in the egg and dredging in the cornmeal coating. Let stand for 5 to10 minutes before frying.
—Taste of Home *Test Kitchen*

TAKES: 30 min. • **MAKES:** 4 servings

- 1 large egg, lightly beaten
- 2 Tbsp. lemon juice
- ½ cup all-purpose flour
- ¼ cup yellow cornmeal
- 1 tsp. Cajun seasoning
- ½ tsp. garlic powder
- ½ tsp. salt
- 4 catfish fillets (6 oz. each)
- 3 Tbsp. canola oil

1. In a shallow bowl, combine the egg and lemon juice. In another shallow bowl, combine the flour, cornmeal, Cajun seasoning, garlic powder and salt. Dip catfish into egg mixture, then coat with cornmeal mixture.

2. In a large skillet, heat oil over medium heat. Fry the fish, 2 at a time, just until fillets begin to flake easily with a fork, 5-6 minutes on each side.

1 serving: 430 cal., 25g fat (5g sat. fat), 133mg chol., 568mg sod., 20g carb. (1g sugars, 1g fiber), 30g pro.

CRAWFISH FETTUCCINE

CRAWFISH FETTUCCINE

I enjoy cooking Cajun dishes, especially those with seafood. Served alongside a green salad and garlic bread, this dish is great for family gatherings. The recipe can easily be doubled to serve a larger group. If you'd like it less spicy, remove the seeds from the jalapeno before chopping it.
—Carolyn Lejeune, Welsh, LA

PREP: 30 min.
COOK: 30 min.
MAKES: 8 servings

- 1 large onion, chopped
- 1 medium sweet red pepper, chopped
- ⅔ cup sliced green onions
- 1 celery rib, chopped
- 1¼ cups butter, cubed
- 1 garlic clove, minced
- ¼ cup all-purpose flour
- 8 oz. Velveeta, cubed
- 1 cup half-and-half cream
- 1 Tbsp. chopped jalapeno pepper
- ½ tsp. salt
- 8 oz. uncooked fettuccine
- 1½ lbs. frozen cooked crawfish tails, thawed or cooked medium shrimp, peeled and deveined

1. In a Dutch oven or large skillet, saute the onion, red pepper, green onions and celery in butter until the vegetables are crisp-tender, about 5 minutes. Add garlic; cook 1 minute longer. Stir in flour until blended; cook and stir 2 minutes. Add cheese, cream, jalapeno and salt; cook and stir until mixture is thickened and cheese is melted, about 10 minutes.

2. Meanwhile, cook fettuccine according to package directions; drain. Stir fettuccine and crawfish into the vegetable mixture. Cook, uncovered, over medium heat until the mixture is heated through, about 10 minutes, stirring occasionally.

Note: Wear disposable gloves when cutting hot peppers; the oils can burn skin. Avoid touching your face.

1 cup: 590 cal., 41g fat (25g sat. fat), 236mg chol., 853mg sod., 30g carb. (5g sugars, 2g fiber), 26g pro.

SALMON TARRAGON

As graduate students with two young children, my husband and I are always on the lookout for quick and healthy meals. Tarragon and peas complement the salmon in this main course and, best of all, it's on the table in minutes.
—*Shannon Beck, Laredo, TX*

TAKES: 30 min. • **MAKES:** 4 servings

- 4   salmon fillets (4 oz. each)
- 1   Tbsp. butter
- ½   cup chopped green onions
- 3   Tbsp. all-purpose flour
- 1½   cups fat-free milk
- 1   cup frozen peas, thawed
- ¾   cup fat-free sour cream
- 1   tsp. dried tarragon
- ½   tsp. salt
- ¼   tsp. white pepper
- ⅛   tsp. ground turmeric
- ⅛   tsp. cayenne pepper

1. In a large skillet, bring 1 in. water to a boil. Carefully add salmon. Reduce heat; cover and simmer until fillets just begin to flake easily with a fork, 5-10 minutes.
2. Meanwhile, in a large saucepan, heat the butter; cook and stir the onions until tender, 5-10 minutes. Stir in flour until blended; gradually add milk. Bring to a boil over medium heat; cook and stir until thickened, 1-2 minutes. Reduce heat to low. Stir in the peas, sour cream and seasonings; heat until warmed through. Serve over salmon.

3 oz. cooked salmon: 373 cal., 16g fat (4g sat. fat), 84mg chol., 519mg sod., 24g carb. (10g sugars, 2g fiber), 32g pro. **Diabetic exchanges:** 3 lean meat, 1½ starch, 1½ fat, 1 vegetable.

TEQUILA LIME SHRIMP ZOODLES

This tangy shrimp dish is a great way to cut carbs without sacrificing flavor. If you don't have a spiralizer, you can use thinly julienned zucchini to get a similar effect.
—*Brigette Schroeder, Yorkville, IL*

TAKES: 30 min. • **MAKES:** 4 servings

- 3   Tbsp. butter, divided
- 1   shallot, minced
- 2   garlic cloves, minced
- ¼   cup tequila
- 1½   tsp. grated lime zest
- 2   Tbsp. lime juice
- 1   Tbsp. olive oil
- 1   lb. uncooked shrimp (31-40 per lb.), peeled and deveined
- 2   medium zucchini, spiralized (about 6 cups)
- ½   tsp. salt
- ¼   tsp. pepper
- ¼   cup minced fresh parsley
      Additional grated lime zest

1. In a large cast-iron or other heavy skillet, heat 2 Tbsp. butter over medium heat. Add the shallot and garlic; cook 1-2 minutes. Remove from heat; stir in tequila, lime zest and lime juice. Cook over medium heat until liquid is almost evaporated, 2-3 minutes.
2. Add olive oil and remaining butter; stir in shrimp and zucchini. Sprinkle with salt and pepper. Cook and stir until shrimp begin to turn pink and zucchini is crisp-tender, 4-5 minutes. Sprinkle with parsley and additional lime zest.

1¼ cups: 246 cal., 14g fat (6g sat. fat), 161mg chol., 510mg sod., 7g carb. (3g sugars, 1g fiber), 20g pro. **Diabetic exchanges:** 3 lean meat, 3 fat, 1 vegetable.

TEQUILA LIME SHRIMP ZOODLES

BLOCK ISLAND LITTLENECKS
WITH CHORIZO

BLOCK ISLAND LITTLENECKS
WITH CHORIZO

Every summer, my family digs clams on
the shores of Block Island, Rhode Island.
This dish highlights the fresh sweet and
salty clam flavor while the chorizo adds a
little kick. Fresh Swiss chard greens from
our garden and corn and cannellini beans
round out the flavor profile. The best part,
though, is dipping crusty bread into the
delicious broth!
—*Pamela Gelsomini, Wrentham, MA*

- -

PREP: 20 min. • **COOK:** 25 min.
MAKES: 8 servings (4 qt.)

- 3   lbs. fresh littleneck clams
- 1   bunch Swiss chard, stems removed
  and chopped (about 4 cups)
- ½   lb. fully cooked Spanish chorizo links,
  chopped
- 1   can (15 oz.) cannellini beans, rinsed
  and drained
- 1   medium onion, chopped
- 1   cup fresh or frozen corn
- 4   garlic cloves, minced
- 1   tsp. salt
- 1   tsp. pepper
- 1   bottle (12 oz.) beer
- ⅓   cup olive oil
  Grilled French bread baguette
  slices

1. Place clams in a stockpot; top with the
next 8 ingredients. Add beer and oil; bring
to a boil. Reduce heat; simmer, covered,
for 10 minutes.
2. Stir; cook, covered, until the clams open,
5–7 minutes longer. Discard the unopened
clams. Ladle into bowls; serve with bread.
2 cups: 265 cal., 17g fat (4g sat. fat), 28mg
chol., 729mg sod., 16g carb. (3g sugars, 4g
fiber), 12g pro.

TEST KITCHEN TIP
Make this recipe your own! Use
kielbasa in place of the chorizo,
spinach instead of kale and other
beans (like black beans or butter
beans) for the white kidney beans.
Or try serving this over pasta.

QUICK MOROCCAN
SHRIMP SKILLET

QUICK MOROCCAN SHRIMP SKILLET

When my niece was attending West Point, she was sent to Morocco for five months. I threw her a going-away party complete with Moroccan decorations, costumes and cuisine, including this saucy shrimp dish. Whenever I make it now, I think of her and smile.
—*Barbara Lento, Houston, PA*

TAKES: 25 min. • **MAKES:** 4 servings

- 1 Tbsp. canola oil
- 1 small onion, chopped
- ¼ cup pine nuts
- 1 lb. uncooked shrimp (16-20 per lb.), peeled and deveined
- 1 cup uncooked pearl (Israeli) couscous
- 2 Tbsp. lemon juice
- 3 tsp. Moroccan seasoning (ras el hanout)
- 1 tsp. garlic salt
- 2 cups hot water
   Minced fresh parsley, optional

1. In a large skillet, heat oil over medium-high heat; saute onion and pine nuts until the onion is tender, 2-3 minutes. Stir in the shrimp, couscous, lemon juice, seasoning, garlic salt and water; bring just to a boil. Reduce the heat; simmer, covered, until the shrimp turn pink, 4-6 minutes.
2. Remove from heat; let stand 5 minutes. If desired, top with parsley.
1 cup: 335 cal., 11g fat (1g sat. fat), 138mg chol., 626mg sod., 34g carb. (1g sugars, 1g fiber), 24g pro.

TEST KITCHEN TIP

Letting the mixture stand before serving helps the pasta absorb more liquid. But it's still a saucy dish, so serve it in a shallow bowl.

EASY SHRIMP STIR-FRY

I love shrimp, and I'm always looking for new ways to fix it. This medley features peanuts and a hint of ginger.
—*Josie Smith, Winamac, IN*

TAKES: 30 min. • **MAKES:** 4 servings

- 2 Tbsp. cornstarch
- ¾ cup cold water
- 2 Tbsp. reduced-sodium soy sauce
- 1 tsp. garlic powder
- ½ tsp. ground ginger
- 2 Tbsp. olive oil
- 2 cups fresh broccoli florets
- 1 medium sweet red pepper, julienned
- 3 green onions, chopped
- 1 lb. uncooked medium shrimp, peeled and deveined
- 1 cup frozen stir-fry vegetable blend, thawed
- 3 garlic cloves, minced
- ¼ cup chopped peanuts

1. In a small bowl, combine cornstarch and water until smooth. Stir in soy sauce, garlic powder and ginger; set aside.
2. Heat a large nonstick skillet or wok over medium-high heat. Add the oil; stir-fry broccoli 2 minutes. Add red pepper and onions; stir-fry until the vegetables are crisp-tender, 2-3 minutes longer. Add shrimp, vegetable blend and garlic; cook 3 minutes more.
3. Stir in the cornstarch mixture; add the peanuts. Bring to a boil; cook and stir until thickened, about 2 minutes.
1 cup: 273 cal., 13g fat (2g sat. fat), 129mg chol., 593mg sod., 18g carb. (4g sugars, 4g fiber), 23g pro. **Diabetic exchanges:** 3 lean meat, 2 vegetable, 1 fat, ½ starch.

EASY SHRIMP
STIR-FRY

SEAFOOD IN TOMATO SAUCE

We live near the Chesapeake Bay and reap its bountiful seafood harvest. I serve this to company often—to rave reviews. I hope you enjoy it as much as my family does!
—*Jeffrey MacCord, New Castle, DE*

PREP: 20 min. • **COOK:** 50 min.
MAKES: 4 servings

- 1¾ cups sliced fresh mushrooms
- 1 garlic clove, minced
- 3 Tbsp. canola oil, divided
- 1 can (14½ oz.) diced tomatoes, drained
- 1½ tsp. dried oregano
- 1 tsp. sugar
- 1 tsp. dried thyme
  Salt and pepper to taste
- ½ lb. lump crabmeat or imitation crabmeat
- ½ lb. bay scallops
- ½ lb. uncooked small shrimp, peeled and deveined
- 1 cup cooked long grain rice
- ¾ cup shredded Parmesan cheese

1. Preheat the oven to 350°. In a large saucepan, saute mushrooms and garlic in 1 Tbsp. oil 3-4 minutes. Add tomatoes, oregano, sugar, thyme, salt and pepper.
2. Bring to a boil. Reduce heat; cook and simmer for 30 minutes. Uncover; cook 10 minutes longer. Remove from the heat; stir in crab.
3. Meanwhile, in a large skillet, cook the scallops and shrimp in remaining oil until shrimp turn pink and scallops are opaque.
4. Divide rice among 4 individual baking dishes. Top with shrimp and scallops. Spoon tomato mixture over rice and sprinkle with Parmesan cheese. Bake until heated through and the cheese is melted, about 10 minutes.
1 serving: 399 cal., 17g fat (4g sat. fat), 171mg chol., 834mg sod., 21g carb. (5g sugars, 2g fiber), 39g pro.

ASIAN SALMON TACOS

ASIAN SALMON TACOS

This Asian/Mexican fusion dish is ready in minutes! If the salmon begins to stick, add 2 to 3 tablespoons of water to the pan.
—*Marisa Raponi, Vaughan, ON*

TAKES: 20 min. • **MAKES:** 4 servings

- 1 lb. salmon fillet, skin removed, cut into 1-in. cubes
- 2 Tbsp. hoisin sauce
- 1 Tbsp. olive oil
  Shredded lettuce
- 8 corn tortillas (6 in.), warmed
- 1½ tsp. black sesame seeds
  Mango salsa, optional

1. Toss the salmon with hoisin sauce. In a large nonstick skillet, heat oil over medium-high heat. Cook the salmon for 3-5 minutes or until it begins to flake easily with a fork, turning gently to brown all sides.
2. Serve salmon and lettuce in tortillas; sprinkle with sesame seeds. If desired, top with salsa.
2 tacos: 335 cal., 16g fat (3g sat. fat), 57mg chol., 208mg sod., 25g carb. (3g sugars, 3g fiber), 22g pro. **Diabetic exchanges:** 3 lean meat, 2 starch, 1 fat.

"I loved these. The flavor was perfect and it came together in a snap. I love that it is just one more way to serve up something delicious to my family. My 14-year-old also thought this was delicious! You can never have too many ways to have salmon!"
—PEAPOD0114, TASTEOFHOME.COM

SEAFOOD MEDLEY WITH LINGUINE

Who can resist a savory blend of seafood and pasta? This dish teeming with scallops, shrimp, linguine and tomatoes is nutritious and rich in flavor.
—*Charlene Chambers, Ormond Beach, FL*

PREP: 35 min. • **COOK:** 5 min.
MAKES: 8 servings

- 1 large onion, chopped
- 2 Tbsp. butter
- 1 Tbsp. olive oil
- 3 garlic cloves, minced
- 1 cup white wine or chicken broth
- 1 can (28 oz.) diced fire-roasted tomatoes
- 1 Tbsp. minced fresh rosemary or 1 tsp. dried rosemary, crushed
- 1 tsp. sugar
- 1 tsp. minced fresh oregano or ¼ tsp. dried oregano
- ¼ tsp. salt
- ¼ tsp. pepper
- 1 pkg. (16 oz.) linguine
- 1 lb. sea scallops
- 9 oz. uncooked large shrimp, peeled and deveined
- 2 Tbsp. minced fresh parsley Shredded Parmesan cheese, optional

1. In a large skillet, saute onion in butter and oil until tender. Add the garlic; cook 1 minute longer. Add wine. Bring to a boil; cook until liquid is reduced to ½ cup. Add tomatoes, rosemary, sugar, oregano, salt and pepper. Bring to a boil over medium heat. Reduce heat; simmer, uncovered, for 15 minutes.

2. Meanwhile, cook linguine according to package directions. Add scallops and shrimp to tomato mixture; cook until shrimp turn pink and scallops are firm and opaque, 4-5 minutes. Stir in parsley.

3. Drain the linguine. Serve the seafood mixture with linguine. If desired, sprinkle with cheese.

¾ cup: 374 cal., 7g fat (2g sat. fat), 74mg chol., 372mg sod., 51g carb. (7g sugars, 4g fiber), 23g pro.

CREAMED SALMON ON TOAST

When our children were small and we were busy outside, we'd come in to enjoy this quick meal. We still make it when we don't feel like fussing in the kitchen.
—*Elsie Bloom, Courtenay, BC*

TAKES: 30 min. • **MAKES:** 6 servings

- 3 Tbsp. butter
- 3 Tbsp. all-purpose flour
- 2 Tbsp. chopped green onions
- 2 cups 2% milk
- 1 can (14¾ oz.) salmon, drained, skin and bones removed
- ½ tsp. salt
- ⅛ tsp. pepper
- 6 slices bread, toasted

In a saucepan, melt butter over medium heat. Stir in flour until smooth; add onions. Gradually stir in the milk. Bring to a boil; cook and stir for until thickened, about 2 minutes. Reduce the heat. Stir in the salmon, salt and pepper. Cook until heated through, 10-12 minutes. Serve over toast.

¾ cup: 296 cal., 14g fat (6g sat. fat), 79mg chol., 680mg sod., 19g carb. (5g sugars, 1g fiber), 21g pro.

SEAFOOD MEDLEY WITH LINGUINE

TRADITIONAL
SHEPHERD'S PIE
PAGE 163

Oven Entrees

The family will come eagerly to the table when you serve these cozy dishes fresh from the oven. Heartwarming pastas, homey potpies, savory meat loaves and extra-special casseroles are some of the 80 best-loved entrees you'll discover in this section.

Beef & Ground Beef

SHEET PAN
STEAK DINNER

SHEET-PAN STEAK DINNER

Asparagus and steak is a classic combination for a delicious dinner. In our house, any meal that can be put in the oven while we get a few more things done for the day is a win! Cooking them together makes for easy prep and cleanup.
—*Estelle Forrest, Springfield, OR*

- -

PREP: 15 min. • **BAKE:** 25 min.
MAKES: 4 servings

  1 tsp. minced fresh rosemary
  ½ tsp. each salt, pepper, paprika
      and garlic powder
  1½ lbs. beef flank steak
  1 lb. fresh asparagus, trimmed
  2 Tbsp. avocado oil
  2 Tbsp. butter, melted
  1 garlic clove, minced

1. Preheat oven to 400°. In small bowl, combine rosemary and spices; set aside.
2. Place steak on 1 side of a 15x10x1-in. baking pan; place asparagus on remaining side in a single layer. Brush steak with oil and sprinkle with seasoning mix. Combine butter and garlic, pour over asparagus.
3. Cover with foil; bake until the meat reaches desired doneness (for medium-rare, a thermometer should read 135°, medium, 140°; medium-well, 145°), 25-30 minutes. Let the steak stand 5-10 minutes before slicing. Serve with asparagus.

5 oz. cooked beef with 8 asparagus spears: 380 cal., 25g fat (10g sat. fat), 96mg chol., 448mg sod., 3g carb. (1g sugars, 1g fiber), 34g pro.

CORNED BEEF HASH RUSTIC PIE

---

a stem. Brush dough trimmings with milk. Bake until the crust and cheese are golden brown, 35-40 minutes.

1 piece: 356 cal., 23g fat (14g sat. fat), 72mg chol., 827mg sod., 27g carb. (1g sugars, 1g fiber), 12g pro.

❄️

SPINACH MEAT ROLL

We love the spinach, ham and cheese swirled in every slice.
—*Gail Buss, New Bern, NC*

PREP: 15 min. • **BAKE:** 1¼ hours
MAKES: 8 servings

- 2   large eggs
- ¾   cup seasoned bread crumbs
- ⅓   cup ketchup
- ¼   cup 2% milk
- 1   tsp. salt, divided
- ¼   tsp. pepper
- ¼   tsp. dried oregano
- 2   lbs. ground beef
- 1   pkg. (10 oz.) frozen leaf spinach, thawed and squeezed dry
- ½   lb. thinly sliced fully cooked ham
- 2   cups shredded mozzarella cheese, divided

1. Preheat oven to 350°. In a bowl, lightly beat the eggs; add bread crumbs, ketchup, milk, ½ tsp. salt, pepper and oregano. Add beef and mix lightly but thoroughly .
2. On a large piece of heavy-duty foil, pat beef mixture into a 12x10-in. rectangle. Cover with the spinach to within ½-in. of edges. Sprinkle with remaining salt. Top with ham and 1½ cups cheese. Roll up jelly-roll style, starting with a short side and peeling foil away while rolling. Seal seam and ends; place with seam side down in a greased 15x10x1-in. baking pan.
3. Bake, uncovered, for 1 hour and 10 minutes. Top with the remaining cheese; bake until cheese is melted, about 5 minutes longer.
Freeze option: Securely wrap and freeze cooled meat roll in foil. To use, partially thaw in refrigerator overnight. Unwrap meat roll; reheat on a greased 15x10x1-in. baking pan in a preheated 350° oven until heated through and a thermometer inserted in center reads 165°.
1 piece: 414 cal., 23g fat (10g sat. fat), 161mg chol., 1029mg sod., 14g carb. (2g sugars, 2g fiber), 37g pro.

CORNED BEEF HASH RUSTIC PIE

This suppertime pie has all the yummies: homemade crust, seasoned potatoes and lots and lots of corned beef and cheese.
—*Colleen Delawder, Herndon, VA*

PREP: 25 min. + chilling • **BAKE:** 55 min.
MAKES: 8 servings

- 1¾   cups all-purpose flour
- 1   tsp. kosher salt
- 1   tsp. sugar
- ½   cup plus 2 Tbsp. cold unsalted butter, cubed
- 2   to 4 Tbsp. cold lager beer or beef broth

POTATOES
- 2   medium red potatoes, cut into ¼-in. cubes
- ½   tsp. kosher salt
- 3   green onions, chopped
- 2   Tbsp. unsalted butter, cubed
- 1   Tbsp. stone-ground Dijon mustard
- ½   tsp. pepper

RUSTIC PIE
- ½   lb. thinly sliced deli corned beef
- ¼   lb. sliced provolone cheese
- 1   Tbsp. cold whole milk or heavy whipping cream

1. Whisk flour, salt and sugar; cut in butter until mixture resembles small peas. Gradually add beer, tossing with a fork until dough holds together when pressed. Shape into a disk; wrap and refrigerate 1 hour or overnight.

2. Meanwhile, place potatoes and salt in a small saucepan; add water to cover. Bring to a boil. Reduce heat; simmer, uncovered, until potatoes are tender, 6-8 minutes. Drain. Return to saucepan; add the green onions, butter, mustard and pepper. Cook over medium heat, stirring frequently, until potatoes are tender and browned, 6-8 minutes. Remove from heat; cool.
3. Roll dough between 2 pieces of waxed paper to a ⅛-in.-thick, 12-in.-diameter circle. Remove top piece of waxed paper; place a 9-in. pie plate upside down over crust. Lifting with bottom waxed paper, carefully invert crust into pan. Remove waxed paper. Trim crust to ½ in. beyond rim of plate; flute the edge. Refrigerate 30 minutes.
4. Preheat oven to 400°. Prick bottom and side of crust with a fork; line with a double thickness of foil. Fill with pie weights, dried beans or uncooked rice. Bake on a lower oven rack until edge is light golden brown, 15-20 minutes. Remove foil and weights; bake until bottom is golden brown, 3-6 minutes longer. Cool slightly.
5. To assemble the rustic pie, layer half the corned beef, half the cheese and three-fourths of potato mixture in baked crust. Repeat corned beef and cheese layers; sprinkle with remaining potato mixture. Reroll dough trimmings; use a heart-shaped cookie cutter to make shamrock petals and a knife to cut out

TACO CRESCENT BAKE

A friend shared the recipe with me, and I've prepared it monthly ever since. The crust is made from refrigerated crescent roll dough. While the beef is browning, I simply press the dough into a baking dish. Guests always comment on the crust, the zesty filling and the crunchy topping.
—Patricia Eckard, Singers Glen, VA

PREP: 25 min. • **BAKE:** 25 min.
MAKES: 8 servings

- 1 tube (8 oz.) refrigerated crescent rolls
- 2 cups crushed corn chips, divided
- 1½ lbs. ground beef
- 1 can (15 oz.) tomato sauce
- 1 envelope taco seasoning
- 1 cup sour cream
- 1 cup shredded cheddar cheese
  Optional: Cubed avocado, chopped tomatoes, shredded lettuce and cilantro

1. Preheat oven to 350°. Unroll crescent dough into a rectangle; press onto bottom and 1 in. up the sides of a greased 13x9-in. baking dish. Seal seams and perforations. Sprinkle with 1 cup chips; set aside.
2. In a large skillet, cook beef over medium heat until no longer pink; drain. Stir in the tomato sauce and taco seasoning; bring to a boil. Reduce heat; simmer, uncovered, for 5 minutes. Spoon over chips. Top with sour cream, cheese and remaining chips.
3. Bake, uncovered, until crust is lightly browned, 25-30 minutes. Garnish with optional toppings if desired.
1 piece: 497 cal., 27g fat (10g sat. fat), 74mg chol., 1183mg sod., 41g carb. (5g sugars, 3g fiber), 24g pro.

CHEESE-FILLED MEAT LOAF

Swirled with a filling of rich sour cream and flavorful cheese and olives, my mother's meat loaf is something special. It's a timeless centerpiece for Sunday dinner or even a festive occasion.
—Susan Hansen, Auburn, AL

PREP: 35 min. • **BAKE:** 65 min. + standing
MAKES: 8 servings

- ½ cup 2% milk
- 2 large eggs, lightly beaten
- 1 Tbsp. Worcestershire sauce
- 1 cup crushed cornflakes
- ½ cup finely chopped onion
- 3 Tbsp. finely chopped celery
- 1 tsp. salt
- ½ tsp. ground mustard
- ½ tsp. rubbed sage
- ¼ tsp. pepper
- 1½ lbs. ground beef
- 1 cup sour cream
- 1 cup finely shredded cheddar cheese
- ½ cup sliced pimiento-stuffed olives
  Mashed potatoes, optional

1. Preheat oven to 350°. In a large bowl, combine the first 10 ingredients. Crumble beef over the mixture and mix lightly but thoroughly. On a large piece of heavy-duty foil, pat the beef mixture into a 14x10-in. rectangle. Spread sour cream to within ½ in. of edges. Sprinkle with the cheese and olives.
2. Roll up, jelly-roll style, starting with a short side and peeling away the foil while rolling. Seal seam and ends. Place seam side down in a greased 13x9-in. baking dish.
3. Bake, uncovered, until the meat is no longer pink and a thermometer reads 160°, 65-75 minutes. Let stand 10 minutes before slicing. If desired, serve with mashed potatoes.
1 piece: 486 cal., 30g fat (15g sat. fat), 194mg chol., 988mg sod., 18g carb. (5g sugars, 0 fiber), 32g pro.

CHEESE-FILLED MEAT LOAF

BURGER SLIDERS
WITH SECRET SAUCE

CONFETTI SPAGHETTI

It's not uncommon for folks to go back for second helpings of this hearty main dish when I share it at church carry-in suppers. The combination of ground beef, noodles, cheese and a zippy tomato sauce is a real people-pleaser.

—*Katherine Moss, Gaffney, SC*

PREP: 20 min. • **BAKE:** 35 min.
MAKES: 12 servings

- 1   pkg. (16 oz.) spaghetti
- 1½   lbs. ground beef
- 1   medium green pepper, chopped
- 1   medium onion, chopped
- 1   can (14½ oz.) diced tomatoes, undrained
- 1   can (8 oz.) tomato sauce
- 1   Tbsp. brown sugar
- 1   tsp. salt
- 1   tsp. chili powder
- ½   tsp. pepper
- ¼   tsp. garlic powder
- ⅛   tsp. cayenne pepper
- ¾   cup shredded cheddar cheese

1. Preheat oven to 350°. Cook spaghetti according to the package directions. Meanwhile, in a large skillet, cook beef, green pepper and onion over medium heat until meat is no longer pink; drain. Stir in next 8 ingredients. Drain spaghetti; add to beef mixture.

2. Transfer to a greased 13x9-in. baking dish. Cover and bake 30 minutes. Uncover; sprinkle with cheese. Bake until cheese is melted, about 5 minutes longer.

Freeze option: Freeze cooled spaghetti mixture in freezer containers. To use, partially thaw in refrigerator overnight. Heat through in a covered saucepan over low heat, stirring gently; add water if necessary.

1 cup: 259 cal., 10g fat (4g sat. fat), 42mg chol., 424mg sod., 27g carb. (4g sugars, 2g fiber), 16g pro.

TEST KITCHEN TIP

If you're shredding your own cheese, try spraying your grater with a bit of olive oil or cooking spray to prevent the cheese from sticking.

BURGER SLIDERS WITH SECRET SAUCE

These sliders are super easy to put together and are always a hit! I love that they are fast food without having to go to a restaurant. Take them to a party, make them for dinner or serve them on game day. The meat can also be made ahead of time in preparation for your gathering.

—*April Lee Wiencek, Chicago, IL*

TAKES: 30 min. • **MAKES:** 12 sliders

- 2   lbs. ground beef
- 2   large eggs, beaten
- ¾   cup minced onion, divided
- 2   tsp. garlic powder
- 1   tsp. salt
- 1   tsp. pepper
- 1   pkg. (17 oz.) dinner rolls
- ½   cup Thousand Island salad dressing, divided
- 10   slices American cheese
- 12   sliced dill pickles
- 1½   cups shredded iceberg lettuce
- 1   Tbsp. butter, melted
- 1   Tbsp. sesame seeds, toasted

1. Preheat oven to 350°. In a large bowl, mix the beef, eggs, ½ cup minced onion, garlic powder, salt and pepper lightly but thoroughly. Place meat mixture on a large parchment-lined baking sheet; shape into two 6x8-in. rectangles, each about ½ in. thick. Bake until a thermometer reads 160°, 15-20 minutes.

2. Meanwhile, without separating rolls, cut the bread in half horizontally. Spread ¼ cup of dressing evenly over bottom halves of rolls.

3. Blot meat with paper towels to remove the excess fat; top meat with cheese and return to oven. Bake until the cheese has just melted, 2-3 minutes. Place meat on bottom halves of rolls; spread with remaining ¼ cup dressing. Layer with pickles, remaining ¼ cup minced onion and shredded lettuce; replace with top halves of rolls. Brush butter on top of rolls and sprinkle with sesame seeds; cut into sandwiches. Serve immediately.

1 slider: 397 cal., 21g fat (8g sat. fat), 105mg chol., 785mg sod., 26g carb. (6g sugars, 2g fiber), 22g pro.

BROILED SIRLOIN

Serve this succulent beef with fluffy mashed potatoes, fresh greens and crusty bread. It's a meal fit for company!
—*Sue Ross, Casa Grande, AZ*

PREP: 10 min. + marinating
BROIL: 15 min. • **MAKES:** 10 servings

- 3 lbs. beef top sirloin or round steaks (about 1 in. thick)
- 1 medium onion, chopped
- ½ cup lemon juice
- ¼ cup canola oil
- 1 tsp. garlic salt
- 1 tsp. dried thyme
- 1 tsp. dried oregano
- ½ tsp. celery salt
- ½ tsp. pepper
- 2 Tbsp. butter, melted

1. With a meat fork, pierce holes in both sides of steaks. Place in a shallow dish. Add the onion, lemon juice, oil, garlic salt, thyme, oregano, celery salt and pepper. Turn to coat; cover and refrigerate for 6 hours or overnight.

2. Preheat broiler. Drain steak and discard marinade; place steaks on a broiler pan. Broil 6 in. from the heat 6-8 minutes. Brush with butter and turn. Broil until meat reaches desired doneness (for medium-rare, a thermometer should read 135°; medium, 140°; medium-well, 145°), about 6 minutes longer.

4 oz. cooked beef: 247 cal., 13g fat (4g sat. fat), 61mg chol., 313mg sod., 2g carb. (1g sugars, 0 fiber), 29g pro. **Diabetic exchanges:** 4 lean meat, ½ fat.

FIESTA BEEF & CHEESE SKILLET COBBLER

FIESTA BEEF & CHEESE SKILLET COBBLER

I tweaked my beefy skillet cobbler until it achieved the wow factor. It's now a family tradition. Top it off with lettuce, avocado, cherry tomatoes and sour cream.
—*Gloria Bradley, Naperville, IL*

PREP: 40 min. • **BAKE:** 20 min. + standing
MAKES: 8 servings

- 1 lb. ground beef
- 1 can (15 oz.) black beans, rinsed and drained
- 1 can (14½ oz.) diced tomatoes with mild green chiles
- 1 can (10 oz.) enchilada sauce
- 1 tsp. ground cumin
- 4 Tbsp. chopped fresh cilantro or parsley, divided
- 1½ cups biscuit/baking mix
- 1½ cups shredded Colby-Monterey Jack cheese, divided
- 4 bacon strips, cooked and crumbled
- ⅔ cup 2% milk
- 1 large egg, lightly beaten
  Sour cream, optional

1. Preheat oven to 400°. In a 10-in. cast-iron or other ovenproof skillet, cook beef over medium heat until no longer pink, breaking into crumbles, 5-7 minutes; drain. Stir in black beans, tomatoes, enchilada sauce and cumin; bring to a boil. Reduce heat; simmer, uncovered, about 20 minutes to allow flavors to blend, stirring occasionally. Stir in 2 Tbsp. cilantro.

2. In a bowl, combine baking mix, ½ cup cheese, bacon and remaining cilantro. Add milk and beaten egg; stir just until a soft dough is formed. Spoon over beef mixture.

3. Bake, uncovered, until golden brown, 13-15 minutes. Sprinkle with remaining cheese; bake until the cheese is melted, 2-3 minutes longer. Let stand 10 minutes before serving. If desired, serve with sour cream.

1 serving: 373 cal., 18g fat (9g sat. fat), 83mg chol., 949mg sod., 30g carb. (4g sugars, 4g fiber), 23g pro.

OVEN-FRIED RANCH STEAK

I've made this recipe with chicken instead of beef, and the results were equally good. The combination of ranch salad dressing and Cajun seasoning also is great as a dip for fresh veggies.
—*LaDonna Reed, Ponca City, OK*

PREP: 10 min. + marinating • **BAKE:** 20 min.
MAKES: 2 servings

- 1 cup ranch salad dressing
- 1 tsp. Cajun seasoning
- ¾ lb. beef top sirloin steak
- ⅓ cup cornmeal
- ⅓ cup dry bread crumbs
- ½ tsp. garlic powder

1. In a shallow dish, combine salad dressing and seasoning; add beef and turn to coat. Cover and refrigerate for at least 8 hours or overnight. Drain steak and discard marinade. Using a rubber spatula, remove excess ranch coating from steak.

2. Place 15x10x1-in. baking sheet into oven; preheat oven to 375°. In a shallow plate, combine cornmeal, bread crumbs and garlic powder. Coat both sides of beef in cornmeal mixture.

3. Carefully remove baking sheet from oven; grease. Quickly place steak on baking sheet and return to the oven. Bake until the bottom is golden brown, 8-10 minutes. Carefully flip steak; bake until a meat reaches desired doneness (for medium-rare, a thermometer should read 135°; medium, 140°; medium-well, 145°), 8-10 minutes longer.

1 serving: 472 cal., 17g fat (4g sat. fat), 77mg chol., 468mg sod., 36g carb. (3g sugars, 2g fiber), 41g pro.

TACO PIZZA SQUARES

Everyone will come running the minute you take this fun twist on pizza out of the oven. I top a convenient refrigerated pizza dough with leftover taco meat, tomatoes and cheese, bringing a full-flavored fiesta to the table. Try it with salsa on the side.
—*Sarah Vovos, Middleton, WI*

TAKES: 25 min. • **MAKES:** 10 servings

- 1 tube (13.8 oz.) refrigerated pizza crust
- 1 can (8 oz.) pizza sauce
- 2 cups seasoned taco meat
- 2 medium tomatoes, seeded and chopped
- 2 cups shredded mozzarella cheese
  Optional: Shredded lettuce and sour cream

Unroll pizza dough and place in a 15x10x1-in. baking pan. Spread with pizza sauce; sprinkle with the taco meat, tomatoes and cheese. Bake at 400° until crust is golden brown, 15-20 minutes. Top with shredded lettuce and sour cream if desired.

1 piece: 259 cal., 11g fat (5g sat. fat), 40mg chol., 660mg sod., 23g carb. (4g sugars, 2g fiber), 17g pro.

"My kids just love this pizza. They also loved helping put it together. Very quick, easy and tasty!"
—NELSONA99, TASTEOFHOME.COM

OVEN-FRIED RANCH STEAK

MEATBALL HASH BROWN BAKE

FRITO PIE

Frito pie is legendary in the Southwest for being spicy, salty and fabulously cheesy . Here's my take on this crunchy classic.

—*Jan Moon, Alamogordo, NM*

- -

TAKES: 30 min. • **MAKES:** 6 servings

- 1 lb. ground beef
- 1 medium onion, chopped
- 2 cans (15 oz. each) Ranch Style beans (pinto beans in seasoned tomato sauce)
- 1 pkg. (9¼ oz.) Frito corn chips
- 2 cans (10 oz. each) enchilada sauce
- 2 cups shredded cheddar cheese
  Thinly sliced green onions, optional

1. Preheat oven to 350°. In a large skillet, cook beef and onion over medium heat 6-8 minutes or until beef is no longer pink and onion is tender, crumbling meat; drain. Stir in beans; heat mixture through.
2. Reserve 1 cup corn chips for topping. Place remaining corn chips in a greased 13x9-in. baking dish. Layer with meat mixture, enchilada sauce and cheese; top with reserved chips.
3. Bake, uncovered, 15-20 minutes or until cheese is melted. If desired, sprinkle with green onions.
1 serving: 731 cal., 41g fat (14g sat. fat), 84mg chol., 1733mg sod., 54g carb. (6g sugars, 8g fiber), 34g pro.

DID YOU KNOW?

This casserole is inspired by the Walking Taco, a favorite that involves dumping taco fixings into a bag of Fritos. It's believed to have been invented at a New Mexico Woolworth's drugstore in 1960.

MEATBALL HASH BROWN BAKE

For a seniors potluck at church, I wanted to create a recipe that would incorporate a meat dish and side dish in one. This casserole proved to be a crowd-pleaser, and many people asked for my recipe.

—*Joann Fritzler, Belen, NM*

- -

PREP: 25 min. • **BAKE:** 55 min.
MAKES: 8 servings

- 1 can (10¾ oz.) condensed cream of chicken soup, undiluted
- 1 large onion, chopped
- 1 cup shredded cheddar cheese
- 1 cup sour cream
- 1½ tsp. pepper, divided
- 1 tsp. salt, divided
- 1 pkg. (30 oz.) frozen shredded hash brown potatoes, thawed and patted dry
- 2 large eggs, lightly beaten
- ¾ cup crushed saltines (20-25 crackers)
- 6 to 8 garlic cloves, minced
- 1 lb. lean ground beef (90% lean)

1. Preheat oven to 350°. Mix the first 4 ingredients, 1 tsp. pepper and ½ tsp. salt; stir in potatoes. Spread evenly in a greased 13x9-in. baking dish.
2. In a large bowl, combine eggs, cracker crumbs, garlic and the remaining ½ tsp. pepper and ½ tsp. salt. Add ground beef; mix lightly but thoroughly. Shape into 1-in. balls.
3. In large skillet, brown meatballs over medium-high heat. Place over potato mixture, pressing in lightly.
4. Bake, covered, 45 minutes. Uncover; bake until the meatballs are cooked through and the potatoes are tender, 10-15 minutes longer.
1 serving: 387 cal., 20g fat (9g sat. fat), 106mg chol., 808mg sod., 32g carb. (4g sugars, 3g fiber), 21g pro.

FRITO PIE

REUBEN-STYLE PIZZA

This homemade pie has all the goodness of a classic Reuben sandwich in a form that will feed a crowd. It has a cheesy sauce, and it smells so wonderful coming out of the oven.
—*Tracy Miller, Wakeman, OH*

PREP: 20 min. • **BAKE:** 15 min.
MAKES: 6 servings

1 tube (13.8 oz.) refrigerated pizza crust
4 oz. cream cheese, softened
1 can (10¾ oz.) condensed cheddar cheese soup, undiluted
¼ cup Thousand Island salad dressing
2 cups cubed pumpernickel bread
2 Tbsp. butter, melted
½ lb. sliced deli corned beef, coarsely chopped
2 cups sauerkraut, rinsed and well drained
1½ cups shredded Swiss cheese

1. Preheat oven to 425°. Unroll and press the dough onto the bottom of a greased 15x10x1-in. baking pan. Bake 6-8 minutes or until edges are lightly browned.
2. Meanwhile, in a small bowl, beat the cream cheese, soup and salad dressing until blended. In another bowl, toss bread cubes with melted butter.
3. Spread cream cheese mixture over crust; top with corned beef, sauerkraut and cheese. Sprinkle with bread cubes. Bake 12-15 minutes or until crust is golden and cheese is melted.
1 piece: 539 cal., 28g fat (14g sat. fat), 84mg chol., 1939mg sod., 48g carb. (7g sugars, 4g fiber), 24g pro.

❄ MUFFIN-CUP CHEDDAR BEEF PIES

My kids love these beef rolls so much that I always make extra since they heat up so quickly. I give them their choice of dipping sauces—spaghetti sauce or ranch dressing are the top picks.
—*Kimberly Farmer, Wichita, KS*

PREP: 25 min. + standing • **BAKE:** 20 min.
MAKES: 20 beef pies

2 loaves (1 lb. each) frozen bread dough
2 lbs. ground beef
1 can (8 oz.) mushroom stems and pieces, drained
1¼ cups shredded cheddar cheese
1½ tsp. Italian seasoning
1 tsp. garlic powder
½ tsp. salt
¼ tsp. pepper
Spaghetti sauce, warmed

1. Let dough stand at room temperature until softened, about 30 minutes. Preheat the oven to 350°. Meanwhile, in a Dutch oven, cook the beef over medium heat until no longer pink, crumbling the meat, 12-15 minutes; drain. Stir in mushrooms, cheese and seasonings.
2. Divide each loaf into 10 portions; roll each portion into a 4-in. circle. Top each circle with ¼ cup filling; bring edge of dough up over filling and pinch to seal.
3. Place meat pies in greased muffin cups, seam side down. Bake until golden brown, 20-25 minutes. Serve with spaghetti sauce.
Freeze option: Freeze cooled pies in a freezer container. To use, reheat beef pies on greased baking sheets in a preheated 350° oven until heated through.
2 beef pies: 482 cal., 19g fat (7g sat. fat), 71mg chol., 850mg sod., 45g carb. (4g sugars, 4g fiber), 29g pro.

MUFFIN-CUP
CHEDDAR
BEEF PIES

SATURDAY AFTERNOON
OVEN POT ROAST

MEAT LOAF STUFFED ZUCCHINI

When someone challenged me to find a different way to serve zucchini, I thought of adding it to my meat loaf. Then I decided to reverse the process—and put the meat into the zucchini!
—*Ruth Fluckiger, Tolland, CT*

- -

PREP: 15 min. • **BAKE:** 30 min.
MAKES: 2 servings

- 2 medium zucchini
- ½ lb. ground beef or bulk Italian sausage
- ¼ cup chopped onion
- 1 garlic clove, minced
- ⅔ cup seasoned bread crumbs
- ⅓ cup 2% milk
- ⅛ tsp. dill weed
- 1 cup spaghetti sauce
- ½ cup shredded cheddar cheese

1. Preheat oven to 325°. Cut zucchini in half lengthwise. Scoop out pulp, leaving a ¼-in. shell. Chop pulp; set pulp and shells aside.
2. In a large skillet, cook beef, onion and garlic over medium heat until no longer pink; drain. Add pulp, bread crumbs, milk and dill. Spoon into zucchini shells.
3. Place in a greased 2-qt. baking dish. Top with spaghetti sauce; sprinkle with cheese. Cover and bake until zucchini is tender, about 30 minutes.
2 zucchini halves: 586 cal., 26g fat (12g sat. fat), 94mg chol., 1465mg sod., 50g carb. (16g sugars, 6g fiber), 38g pro.

TEST KITCHEN TIP
Ripe zucchini should be firm, not soft, and a little bit more flexible than a cucumber.

❄ SATURDAY AFTERNOON OVEN POT ROAST

This pot roast will be a welcome sight and will leave your house smelling heavenly. If the cooking liquid evaporates quickly, add more broth to the Dutch oven.
—*Colleen Delawder, Herndon, VA*

- -

PREP: 40 min. • **BAKE:** 3 hours
MAKES: 8 servings

- 1 boneless beef chuck roast (2½ lbs.)
- 1 tsp. salt
- ½ tsp. pepper
- 1 Tbsp. olive oil
- 1 Tbsp. butter
- 4 cups sliced sweet onion
- 1 can (6 oz.) tomato paste
- 4 garlic cloves, minced
- 1 tsp. dried thyme
- ½ tsp. celery seed
- ½ cup dry red wine
- 1 carton (32 oz.) reduced-sodium beef broth
- 6 medium carrots, cut into 1½ in. pieces
- ½ lb. medium fresh mushrooms, quartered

1. Preheat oven to 325°. Sprinkle roast with salt and pepper.
2. In a Dutch oven, heat oil and butter over medium-high heat; brown the roast on all sides. Remove from pot. Add onion to the same pot; cook and stir over medium heat until tender, 8-10 minutes. Add the tomato paste, garlic, thyme and celery seed; cook and stir 1 minute longer.
3. Add wine, stirring to loosen browned bits from pot; stir in broth. Return roast to pot. Arrange carrots and mushrooms around the roast; bring to a boil. Bake, covered, until the meat is fork-tender, 2½-3 hours. If desired, skim fat and thicken cooking juices for gravy.
Freeze option: Freeze cooled beef and vegetable mixture in freezer containers. To use, partially thaw in refrigerator overnight. Microwave, covered, on high in a microwave-safe dish until heated through, stirring gently.
4 oz. cooked beef with ½ cup vegetables and ¼ cup gravy: 339 cal., 17g fat (6g sat. fat), 98mg chol., 621mg sod., 14g carb. (7g sugars, 2g fiber), 32g pro.

TRADITIONAL SHEPHERD'S PIE

TRADITIONAL SHEPHERD'S PIE

Instead of using a pastry crust, this pie has a savory crust made with mashed potatoes. The bacon flavor in the filling is fabulous! Serve with a tossed salad or green vegetable. Add dessert and you'll have a complete meal that's sure to please your family.
—*Chris Eschweiler, Dallas, TX*

PREP: 30 min. • **BAKE:** 30 min.
MAKES: 8 servings

- 1   lb. ground beef
- 3   bacon strips, diced
- 1   small onion, chopped
- 2   garlic cloves, minced
- ¼   tsp. dried oregano
- ½   cup tomato sauce
- 1   can (4¼ oz.) chopped ripe olives, drained
- 5½ cups hot mashed potatoes (prepared without milk and butter)
- 2   large eggs, lightly beaten
- 2   Tbsp. butter, softened
- 1   Tbsp. minced fresh cilantro
- ¼   tsp. salt
      Additional butter, melted

1. Preheat oven to 375°. In a large skillet, cook beef over medium heat until no longer pink; drain and set aside. In the same skillet, cook bacon, onion, garlic and oregano until bacon is crisp; drain. Stir in the tomato sauce, olives and beef. Simmer, uncovered, until heated through, about 10 minutes.
2. Meanwhile, combine the mashed potatoes, eggs, butter, cilantro and salt. Spread half of the potato mixture onto the bottom and up the side of a greased 9-in. pie plate. Layer with beef mixture and remaining potato mixture.
3. Bake 20 minutes. Brush the pie with melted butter. Bake until the top is golden brown, about 10 minutes longer. If desired, garnish with additional cilantro.
1 piece: 288 cal., 13g fat (5g sat. fat), 100mg chol., 354mg sod., 23g carb. (1g sugars, 5g fiber), 16g pro.

BUTTERMILK NOODLE BAKE

BUTTERMILK NOODLE BAKE

I enjoyed Mom's old-fashioned casserole as a child and made it often for my own family to enjoy.
—*Alice Fraser, Meridale, NY*

PREP: 25 min. • **BAKE:** 45 min.
MAKES: 6 servings

- 1½ lbs. ground beef
- 1   large onion, finely chopped
- ¼   cup butter
- ¼   cup all-purpose flour
- 2½ tsp. salt
      Dash pepper
- 2   cups buttermilk
- 1   can (4 oz.) mushroom stems and pieces, undrained
- ⅓   cup ketchup
- 1   Tbsp. Worcestershire sauce
- 8   oz. medium egg noodles, cooked and drained
      Chopped fresh parsley, optional

1. Preheat oven to 350°. In a large skillet, cook beef and onion over medium heat until meat is no longer pink; drain.

2. In a large saucepan, melt butter. Stir in flour, salt and pepper until smooth. Gradually add the buttermilk. Stir in the mushrooms, ketchup and Worcestershire sauce. Bring to a boil; cook and stir until thickened, about 2 minutes. Add noodles and beef mixture; mix well.
3. Transfer to a greased 2½-qt. baking dish. Bake, uncovered, until heated through, about 45 minutes. If desired, sprinkle with parsley.
1 cup: 471 cal., 20g fat (10g sat. fat), 111mg chol., 1535mg sod., 42g carb. (10g sugars, 2g fiber), 29g pro.

TEST KITCHEN TIP

You don't need to run to the store if you find you're out of buttermilk. Make your own! For every 1 cup of buttermilk, place 1 Tbsp. of lemon juice or vinegar in a glass measuring cup. Add enough milk to measure 1 cup. Let stand for 5 minutes before using.

SPAGHETTI SQUASH BOATS

With a bounty of fresh ingredients, this recipe makes a fun summer dish. Spaghetti squash has an interesting texture that's delightfully different.
—*Vickey Lorenger, Detroit, MI*

PREP: 1 hour • **BAKE:** 20 min.
MAKES: 2 servings

- 1   medium spaghetti squash (2 to 2½ lbs.)
- ¼   lb. ground beef (90% lean)
- ½   cup chopped onion
- ½   cup chopped green pepper
- ½   cup sliced fresh mushrooms
- 1   garlic clove, minced
- ½   tsp. dried basil
- ½   tsp. dried oregano
- ¼   tsp. salt
- ⅛   tsp. pepper
- 1   can (14½ oz.) diced tomatoes, drained
- ⅓   cup shredded part-skim mozzarella cheese

1. Preheat oven to 375°. Cut squash in half lengthwise; scoop out seeds. Place squash, cut side down, in a baking dish. Fill dish with hot water to a depth of ½ in. Bake, uncovered, for 30-40 minutes or until tender. Reduce oven setting to 350°.
2. When cool enough to handle, scoop out squash, separating strands with a fork; set shells and squash aside.
3. In a skillet, cook the beef, onion and green pepper over medium heat until meat is no longer pink; drain. Add the mushrooms, garlic, basil, oregano, salt and pepper; cook and stir 2 minutes. Add tomatoes; cook and stir 2 minutes more. Stir in squash.
4. Cook, uncovered, until liquid has evaporated, about 10 minutes. Fill shells; place in shallow baking dish.
5. Bake, uncovered, for 15 minutes. Sprinkle with cheese; bake until the cheese is melted, about 5 minutes longer.
1 serving: 306cal., 9g fat (3g sat. fat), 39mg chol., 738mg sod., 39g carb. (12g sugars, 9g fiber), 21g pro.

PAN BURRITOS

PAN BURRITOS

Our family loves Mexican food, so this satisfying casserole is a favorite. It is nice to be able to get the taste of burritos and cut any serving size you want.
—*Joyce Kent, Grand Rapids, MI*

PREP: 35 min. • **BAKE:** 35 min. + standing
MAKES: 10 servings

- 2   pkg. (1½ oz. each) enchilada sauce mix
- 3   cups water
- 1   can (12 oz.) tomato paste
- 1   garlic clove, minced
- ¼   tsp. pepper
    Salt to taste
- 2   lbs. ground beef
- 9   large flour tortillas (9 in.)
- 4   cups shredded cheddar cheese or Mexican cheese blend
- 1   can (16 oz.) refried beans, warmed
    Optional: Taco sauce, sour cream, chile peppers, chopped onion and guacamole

1. In a saucepan, combine the first 6 ingredients; simmer 15-20 minutes.
2. In a skillet, brown and crumble the beef. Drain; stir in a third of the sauce. Spread another third on the bottom of a greased 13x9-in. baking pan or dish.
3. Place 3 tortillas over sauce, tearing to fit bottom of pan. Spoon half of the meat mixture over tortillas; sprinkle with 1½ cups cheese. Add 3 more tortillas. Spread refried beans over tortillas; top with remaining meat. Sprinkle with 1½ cups of cheese. Layer remaining tortillas; top with the remaining sauce. Sprinkle with remaining cheese.
4. Bake, uncovered, at 350° for 35-40 minutes. Let stand 10 minutes before cutting. Serve with optional ingredients as desired.
1 piece: 646 cal., 32g fat (15g sat. fat), 101mg chol., 1379mg sod., 52g carb. (7g sugars, 5g fiber), 36g pro.

MUSHROOM-STUFFED FLANK STEAK ROLL

My daughter and her family, who live in Hong Kong, love to make my flank steak because it reminds them of home. The classic combination of yummy beef and mushrooms, topped with a rich sauce, make this a lovely meal for company.
—*Ethel Klyasheff, Granite City, IL*

PREP: 25 min. + marinating
BAKE: 1¼ hours + standing
MAKES: 6 servings

- 1   beef flank steak (about 1½ lbs.)
- ½   cup lemon juice
- ½   cup soy sauce
- ½   cup honey
- 2   tsp. ground mustard
- 1   tsp. pepper
- ½   tsp. grated lemon zest, optional

MUSHROOM FILLING
- 1   lb. sliced fresh mushrooms
- 1   medium onion, finely chopped
- ¼   cup butter, cubed
- ½   cup minced fresh parsley
- 2   Tbsp. cornstarch
- 2   cups beef broth

1. Cut steak horizontally from a long side to within ½ in. of opposite side. Open steak so it lies flat; cover with waxed paper. Flatten to ¼-in. thickness.

2. In a small bowl, combine the lemon juice, soy sauce, honey, mustard, pepper and, if desired, lemon zest. Pour half of marinade into a large shallow dish; add the beef and turn to coat. Cover and refrigerate overnight. Cover and refrigerate remaining marinade.

3. In a large skillet, saute mushrooms and onion in butter until tender. Remove from the heat; stir in parsley. Drain steak and discard marinade. Open steak; spoon filling over the steak to within ½ in. of edges. Roll up tightly jelly-roll style, starting with a long side. Tie with kitchen string. Place in a greased shallow roasting pan. Pour reserved marinade over steak.

4. Cover and bake at 350° for 45 minutes. Uncover; baste with pan drippings. Bake 30 minutes longer or until meat reaches desired doneness (for medium-rare, a thermometer should read 135°, medium, 140°, medium-well, 145°). Remove and keep warm. Meanwhile, transfer cooking juices to a saucepan; skim fat. Bring cooking juices to a boil. Mix cornstarch and broth until smooth. Stir into cooking juices. Bring to a boil; cook and stir for 1-2 minutes or until thickened. Slice steak and serve with sauce.

4 oz. cooked beef with stuffing: 358 cal., 16g fat (8g sat. fat), 74mg chol., 1345mg sod., 26g carb. (21g sugars, 2g fiber), 28g pro.

COCOA-CRUSTED BEEF TENDERLOIN

My family and I have cooking competitions with secret ingredients and a 30-minute time limit. This tenderloin recipe earned me a sweet victory.
—*Gina Myers, Spokane, WA*

TAKES: 30 min. • **MAKES:** 4 servings

- 4   beef tenderloin steaks (1½ in. thick and 6 oz. each)
- ½   tsp. salt
- ½   tsp. coarsely ground pepper
- 3   Tbsp. baking cocoa
- 3   Tbsp. finely ground coffee

1. Preheat broiler. Sprinkle steaks with salt and pepper. In a shallow bowl, mix cocoa and coffee. Dip the steaks in cocoa mixture to coat all sides; shake off excess.

2. Place the steaks on a rack of a broiler pan. Broil 3-4 in. from heat 9-11 minutes on each side or until the meat reaches desired doneness (for medium-rare, a thermometer should read 135°; medium, 140°; medium-well, 145°).

1 steak: 252 cal., 10g fat (4g sat. fat), 75mg chol., 296mg sod., 1g carb. (0 sugars, 0 fiber), 37g pro. **Diabetic exchanges:** 5 lean meat.

MUSHROOM-STUFFED FLANK STEAK ROLL

Poultry

CHICKEN & CHEDDAR
BISCUIT CASSEROLE

CHICKEN & CHEDDAR BISCUIT CASSEROLE

I always get rave reviews when I bring this casserole to my son's Cub Scout meetings. This is the perfect comfort meal after a long day.
—Sarah Phillips, East Lansing, MI

PREP: 40 min. • BAKE: 35 min.
MAKES: 12 servings

⅓ cup butter, cubed
1 large onion, chopped
2 celery ribs, chopped
2 medium carrots, chopped
2 garlic cloves, minced
½ cup all-purpose flour
1 tsp. salt
½ tsp. pepper
4 cups chicken broth or stock
5 cups cubed cooked chicken
3 cups biscuit/baking mix
¾ cup 2% milk
1 cup shredded cheddar cheese
1 cup roasted sweet red peppers, drained and chopped

1. Preheat oven to 425°. In a 6-qt. stockpot, heat butter over medium-high heat. Add onion, celery and carrots; cook and stir 3-5 minutes or until tender. Add garlic; cook and stir 1 minute longer. Stir in flour, salt and pepper until blended; gradually whisk in broth. Bring to a boil, stirring constantly; cook and stir over medium heat 4-6 minutes or until thickened. Add the chicken.
2. Transfer mixture to a greased 13x9-in. baking dish. Bake, uncovered, 20 minutes. Meanwhile, in a large bowl, combine the biscuit mix and milk just until moistened. Turn onto a lightly floured surface; knead gently 8-10 times. Roll the dough into a 12x8-in. rectangle. Sprinkle with cheese and peppers. Roll dough up jelly-roll style, starting with a long side; pinch seam to seal. Cut crosswise into 1-in.-thick slices. Place slices on top of hot chicken mixture. Bake, uncovered, 15-20 minutes or until biscuits are golden brown.
1 serving: 357 cal., 16g fat (7g sat. fat), 78mg chol., 1081mg sod., 29g carb. (4g sugars, 2g fiber), 23g pro.

**CHICKEN POTPIE GALETTE
WITH CHEDDAR-THYME CRUST**

4. Preheat oven to 400°. On a floured sheet of parchment, roll dough into a 12-in. circle. Transfer to a baking sheet. Spoon filling over crust to within 2 in. of edge. Fold crust edge over filling, pleating as you go, leaving center uncovered. Bake on a lower oven rack until crust is golden brown and filling is bubbly, 30-35 minutes. Cool 15 minutes before slicing. Sprinkle with parsley.

1 piece: 342 cal., 21g fat (12g sat. fat), 81mg chol., 594mg sod., 22g carb. (2g sugars, 2g fiber), 16g pro.

CHICKEN & CHIPS

My husband, Chad, is always ready to try a new recipe, so I surprised him with this creamy chicken casserole sprinkled with crushed tortilla chips. He loves the flavor, and I like that it's the perfect size for our small family.
—Kendra Schneider, Grifton, NC

PREP: 10 min. • **BAKE:** 25 min.
MAKES: 6 servings

- 1 can (10¾ oz.) condensed cream of chicken soup, undiluted
- 1 cup sour cream
- 2 Tbsp. taco sauce
- ¼ cup chopped green chiles
- 3 cups cubed cooked chicken
- 12 slices process American cheese
- 4 cups crushed tortilla chips

1. Preheat oven to 350°. In a large bowl, combine the soup, sour cream, taco sauce and chiles. In an ungreased shallow 2-qt. baking dish, layer half of the chicken, soup mixture, cheese and tortilla chips. Repeat the layers.

2. Bake, uncovered, until the mixture is bubbly, 25-30 minutes.

1 serving: 575 cal., 32g fat (15g sat. fat), 120mg chol., 1186mg sod., 36g carb. (4g sugars, 2g fiber), 33g pro.

"I used a combination of pepper jack and cheddar cheese. Excellent—even better than expected. I will be adding this to my recipe file."
—TJTRAILS, TASTEOFHOME.COM

CHICKEN POTPIE GALETTE WITH CHEDDAR-THYME CRUST

This gorgeous galette takes traditional chicken potpie and gives it a fun open-faced spin. The rich filling and flaky cheddar-flecked crust make it taste so homey. It's lovely for fall and winter dinners, but you can enjoy it anytime.
—Elisabeth Larsen, Pleasant Grove, UT

PREP: 45 min. + chilling
BAKE: 30 min. + cooling
MAKES: 8 servings

- 1¼ cups all-purpose flour
- ½ cup shredded sharp cheddar cheese
- 2 Tbsp. minced fresh thyme
- ¼ tsp. salt
- ½ cup cold butter, cubed
- ¼ cup ice water

FILLING
- 3 Tbsp. butter
- 2 large carrots, sliced
- 1 celery rib, diced
- 1 small onion, diced
- 8 oz. sliced fresh mushrooms
- 3 cups julienned Swiss chard
- 3 garlic cloves, minced
- 1 cup chicken broth
- 3 Tbsp. all-purpose flour
- ½ tsp. salt
- ¼ tsp. pepper
- 2 cups shredded cooked chicken
- ½ tsp. minced fresh oregano
- 2 Tbsp. minced fresh parsley

1. Combine flour, cheese, thyme and salt; cut in butter until crumbly. Gradually add ice water, tossing with a fork until dough holds together when pressed. Shape into a disk; refrigerate 1 hour.

2. For filling, melt the butter in a large saucepan over medium-high heat. Add carrots, celery and onion; cook and stir until slightly softened, 5-7 minutes. Add mushrooms; cook 3 minutes longer. Add Swiss chard and garlic; cook until chard is wilted, 2-3 minutes.

3. Whisk together broth, flour, salt and pepper; slowly pour over vegetables, stirring constantly. Cook until thickened, 2-3 minutes. Stir in chicken and oregano.

EASY ARROZ CON POLLO

My children really look forward to dinner when they know I'm serving this—and it's easy to make!
—Debbie Harris, Tucson, AZ

PREP: 10 min. • **BAKE:** 55 min.
MAKES: 6 servings

- 1¾ cups uncooked instant rice
- 6 boneless skinless chicken breast halves (4 oz. each)
- ½ tsp. garlic salt
- ¼ tsp. pepper
- 1 can (14½ oz.) chicken broth
- 1 cup picante sauce
- 1 can (8 oz.) tomato sauce
- ½ cup chopped onion
- ½ cup chopped green pepper
- ½ cup shredded Monterey Jack cheese
- ½ cup shredded cheddar cheese

1. Preheat the oven to 350°. Spread the rice in a greased 13x9-in. baking dish. Sprinkle both sides of chicken with garlic salt and pepper; place over rice. In a large bowl, combine the broth, picante sauce, tomato sauce, onion and green pepper; pour over the chicken.

2. Cover and bake until a thermometer reads 165°, 50-55 minutes. Sprinkle with cheeses. Bake, uncovered, until cheese is melted, about 5 minutes more.

1 serving: 334 cal., 9g fat (4g sat. fat), 80mg chol., 1055mg sod., 30g carb. (3g sugars, 2g fiber), 31g pro.

🍎 BAKED ORANGE CHICKEN

This is a very quick, elegant recipe. It can easily be doubled or tripled for company. I like to serve mine with baked potatoes.
—Pamela Siple, Punxsutawney, PA

PREP: 5 min. + marinating
BAKE: 25 min. • **MAKES:** 2 servings

- ½ cup orange juice
- 1 Tbsp. reduced-sodium soy sauce
- 2 boneless skinless chicken breast halves (4 oz. each)
- 2 Tbsp. orange marmalade

1. In a small bowl, combine the orange juice and soy sauce. Pour ¼ cup marinade into a shallow dish; add the chicken and turn to coat. Cover and refrigerate at least 1 hour. Cover and refrigerate the remaining marinade.

2. Drain chicken and discard marinade. Place the chicken and reserved marinade in an 8-in. square baking dish coated with cooking spray. Spoon marmalade over chicken. Bake, uncovered, at 350° for 25-30 minutes or until chicken juices run clear.

1 chicken breast half: 189 cal., 3g fat (1g sat. fat), 63mg chol., 224mg sod., 17g carb. (15g sugars, 0 fiber), 23g pro.

EASY ARROZ CON POLLO

BAKED CHICKEN
PARMIGIANA

✳ CHICKEN & MUSHROOM SPANAKOPITAS

I love to make these spanakopitas; they're so easy, but look like a lot of work! Not only do they make a tasty entree, but they're great for hearty appetizers as well.
—*Teena Petrus, Johnstown, PA*

PREP: 30 min. • **BAKE:** 20 min.
MAKES: 6 servings

- 4 cups fully cooked frozen grilled chicken breast strips
- 1 Tbsp. olive oil
- 1 cup sliced fresh mushrooms
- 2 garlic cloves, minced
- 1 tsp. minced fresh mint
- ½ tsp. each minced fresh sage and thyme
- 1 pkg. (10 oz.) frozen chopped spinach, thawed and squeezed dry
- 1 cup crumbled feta cheese
- 36 sheets phyllo dough (14x9-in. size) Butter-flavored cooking spray Refrigerated tzatziki sauce, optional

1. Preheat oven to 350°. Prepare chicken according to package directions; coarsely chop. In a skillet, heat oil over medium-high heat. Add mushrooms; cook and stir until tender. Add garlic; cook 1 minute longer. Transfer to a bowl; stir in herbs, spinach, cheese and chicken.

2. Layer 6 sheets of phyllo dough on a work surface, spritzing each with cooking spray. (Cover remaining phyllo with waxed paper and a damp towel.) Cut the stack of 6 lengthwise in half. Place ⅓ cup filling on 1 end of each strip. Fold a corner of dough over filling, forming a triangle. Fold the triangle up, continuing to fold like a flag. Spritz end with cooking spray and seal. Repeat with remaining ingredients.

3. Spritz triangles with cooking spray; place on baking sheets. Bake until golden brown, about 20 minutes. If desired, serve with tzatziki.

Freeze option: Freeze cooled spanakopitas in a freezer container. To use, reheat on a greased baking sheet in a preheated 350° oven until heated through.

2 spanakopitas: 371 cal., 14g fat (3g sat. fat), 57mg chol., 751mg sod., 42g carb. (3g sugars, 4g fiber), 23g pro.

BAKED CHICKEN PARMIGIANA

Spaghetti sauce mix is the secret to the flavorful breading in this dish. It's always a quick and easy dinner on busy nights, particularly with a no-fuss green salad or some garlic bread.
—*Trisha Lange, Appleton, WI*

PREP: 10 min. • **BAKE:** 45 min.
MAKES: 4 servings

- ½ cup seasoned bread crumbs
- ¼ cup grated Parmesan cheese
- 3 Tbsp. spaghetti sauce mix
- 1½ tsp. garlic powder
- 4 boneless skinless chicken breast halves (6 oz. each)
- ½ cup Italian salad dressing
- ½ cup meatless spaghetti sauce
- ¼ cup shredded part-skim mozzarella cheese

1. Preheat oven to 350°. In a shallow bowl, combine the first 4 ingredients. Dip the chicken in salad dressing, then coat with crumb mixture. Place in a greased 13x9-in. baking dish.

2. Bake, uncovered, until chicken juices run clear, 40-45 minutes. Drizzle with the spaghetti sauce and sprinkle with mozzarella cheese. Bake until cheese is melted, 5-7 minutes.

1 chicken breast half: 342 cal., 10g fat (3g sat. fat), 103mg chol., 1048mg sod., 18g carb. (5g sugars, 1g fiber), 40g pro.

TEST KITCHEN TIP

You can prepare this Italian staple ahead of time. Simply assemble and bake the breaded chicken as directed. Once cool, cover the dish and keep it in your refrigerator until you are ready to serve. At that time, put the chicken back in the oven to heat through and crisp up before topping the chicken with the sauce and cheese.

FAST CHICKEN DIVAN

FAST CHICKEN DIVAN

Frozen broccoli and leftover chicken get a simple—but elegant—treatment in this meal-in-one dish. It's easy to dress up chicken with a saucy blend of cream soup and mayonnaise. I top it all off with a golden, cheesy crumb topping.
—*Bertille Cooper, CA, MD*

PREP: 5 min. • **BAKE:** 30 min. + standing
MAKES: 6 servings

- 8 cups frozen broccoli florets or chopped broccoli
- 2 cans (10¾ oz. each) condensed cream of chicken soup, undiluted
- 1 cup mayonnaise
- 1 tsp. lemon juice
- 3 cups cubed cooked chicken
- 1 cup shredded sharp cheddar cheese
- ¾ cup dry bread crumbs
- 3 Tbsp. butter, melted
- 1 Tbsp. sliced pimientos, optional

1. Preheat oven to 325°. In a large saucepan, cook the broccoli in boiling water for 1 minute; drain. Set aside.
2. In a large bowl, combine the soup, mayonnaise and lemon juice; add the broccoli and chicken. Gently stir to combine; transfer mixture to a greased 11x7-in. baking dish. Sprinkle with cheese. Combine bread crumbs and butter; sprinkle over top.
3. Bake, uncovered, until bubbly and golden brown, about 30 minutes. Let stand for 10 minutes before serving. If desired, garnish with pimientos.
1 cup: 629 cal., 49g fat (14g sat. fat), 115mg chol., 944mg sod., 16g carb. (1g sugars, 2g fiber), 28g pro.

MISO BUTTER ROASTED CHICKEN

MISO BUTTER ROASTED CHICKEN

I love this recipe because the prep work is done in the beginning. Look for a prepared spatchcocked chicken in your grocery store or ask your butcher to do it for you—then you'll just have to chop the veggies. Once it's in the oven, there's ample time to set the table and talk.
—*Stefanie Schaldenbrand, Los Angeles, CA*

PREP: 25 min.
BAKE: 1½ hours + standing
MAKES: 6 servings

- 1 lb. medium fresh mushrooms
- 1 lb. baby red potatoes
- 1 lb. fresh Brussels sprouts, halved
- 6 garlic cloves, minced
- 1 Tbsp. olive oil
- 1½ tsp. minced fresh thyme or ½ tsp. dried thyme
- ½ tsp. salt
- ½ tsp. pepper
- 1 roasting chicken (5 to 6 lbs.)
- ¼ cup butter, softened
- ¼ cup white miso paste
  Addition fresh thyme, optional

1. Preheat oven to 425°. Mix mushrooms, potatoes, Brussels sprouts and garlic; drizzle with oil. Sprinkle with the thyme, salt and pepper; toss to coat. Place in a shallow roasting pan.
2. Place chicken on a work surface, breast side down and tail end facing you. Using kitchen shears, cut along each side of backbone; discard backbone. Turn chicken over so the breast side is up; flatten by pressing down firmly on breastbone until it cracks. Place the chicken on a rack over vegetables. Twist and tuck wings under to secure in place. Combine the butter and miso paste; spread over skin (mixture will be thick).
3. Roast until a thermometer inserted in thickest part of thigh reads 170°-175°, 1½-1¾ hours, covering loosely with foil after 45 minutes of cooking. (The miso mixture on the chicken will appear very dark while roasting.)
4. Remove chicken from oven; tent with foil. Let stand 15 minutes before carving. If desired, skim fat and thicken pan drippings for gravy. Serve with chicken. Top with additional fresh thyme if desired.
1 serving: 653 cal., 37g fat (13g sat. fat), 170mg chol., 912mg sod., 25g carb. (3g sugars, 4g fiber), 54g pro.

TEST KITCHEN TIP

It's easy to amp up the flavor in this dish. Toss the vegetables with grated Parmesan cheese and lemon zest once they are finished roasting, or add a dash or 2 of red chili flakes to the chicken or the vegetables.

CHICKEN CHILES RELLENOS STRATA

This versatile bake can be made as an entree, a brunch option or a potluck dish. It's one of the easiest meals to assemble on a busy weeknight.
—Kallee Krong-McCreery, Escondido, CA

PREP: 20 min. + chilling
BAKE: 35 min. + standing
MAKES: 10 servings

- 6 cups cubed French bread (about 6 oz.)
- 2 cans (4 oz. each) chopped green chiles
- 2 cups shredded Monterey Jack cheese
- 2 cups shredded cooked chicken
- 12 large eggs
- 1½ cups 2% milk
- 2 tsp. baking powder
- 1 tsp. garlic salt
- 1 cup shredded cheddar cheese
  Salsa

1. In a greased 13x9-in. baking dish, layer half each of the following: bread cubes, chiles, Monterey Jack cheese and chicken. Repeat layers.
2. In a large bowl, whisk eggs, milk, baking powder and garlic salt until blended. Pour over layers. Sprinkle with cheddar cheese. Refrigerate, covered, overnight.
3. Preheat oven to 350°. Remove strata from refrigerator while oven heats. Bake, uncovered, 35-40 minutes or until puffed and golden at edges. Let stand 10 minutes before serving. Serve with salsa.

1 piece: 338 cal., 20g fat (9g sat. fat), 282mg chol., 820mg sod., 13g carb. (3g sugars, 1g fiber), 27g pro.

❄ CREAMY CHICKEN & MUSHROOM RICE CASSEROLE

Gravy, chicken soup and sour cream make this rich and hearty dish one you'll want to curl up with. Be prepared to make it often, as it fills 'em up fast and tastes fantastic!
—Nancy Foust, Stoneboro, PA

PREP: 20 min. • BAKE: 50 min.
MAKES: 9 servings

- 3 cups shredded cooked chicken
- 2⅔ cups chicken gravy
- 2 cups uncooked instant rice
- 1 can (10¾ oz.) condensed cream of chicken soup, undiluted
- 1 cup sour cream
- 1 can (8 oz.) mushroom stems and pieces, drained
- 1 medium onion, chopped
- ⅔ cup chopped celery
- ⅔ cup water
- ¼ cup chopped pitted green olives
- ¼ cup chopped ripe olives
- 2 tsp. dried parsley flakes
- ⅛ tsp. pepper
  Chopped green onions, optional

1. Preheat oven to 375°. In a large bowl, combine first 13 ingredients. Transfer to a greased 13x9-in. baking dish.
2. Cover and bake 30 minutes. Uncover and stir; bake until bubbly and rice and vegetables are tender, 20-25 minutes. If desired, top with chopped green onions.

Freeze option: Freeze cooled casserole mixture in freezer containers. To use, partially thaw in refrigerator overnight. Heat in a saucepan, stirring occasionally; add water if necessary.

1⅓ cups: 305 cal., 12g fat (5g sat. fat), 68mg chol., 790mg sod., 28g carb. (3g sugars, 2g fiber), 19g pro. Diabetic exchanges: 2 starch, 2 lean meat, 1 fat.

CREAMY CHICKEN & MUSHROOM RICE CASSEROLE

BAKED CHIMICHANGAS

DRESSED-UP CORNISH HEN

When my husband and I dine alone, this is one of our favorite main courses. Add a green vegetable or baked potatoes, and you have a wonderful meal.
—*Dixie Terry, Goreville, IL*

PREP: 15 min. + marinating
BAKE: 50 min. • **MAKES:** 2 servings

1 Cornish game hen (20 to 24 oz.)
¼ cup olive oil
2 Tbsp. lemon juice
2 tsp. ground cumin
2 tsp. Worcestershire sauce
1 tsp. dried thyme
½ tsp. salt
½ tsp. hot pepper sauce

1. Place Cornish hen in a large resealable container. In a small bowl, combine the remaining ingredients. Pour half of the marinade over hen; seal the container and refrigerate for 8 hours or overnight, turning several times. Refrigerate the remaining marinade for basting.
2. Preheat oven to 400°. Drain hen and discard marinade. Place hen, skin side up, in a greased 9-in. square baking dish.
3. Bake, uncovered, 30 minutes. Baste with reserved marinade. Bake until a thermometer inserted in thickest part of thigh reads 170°-175°, 20-30 minutes longer. Let stand 15 minutes before cutting in half to serve.
½ hen: 561 cal., 47g fat (10g sat. fat), 175mg chol., 650mg sod., 3g carb. (1g sugars, 1g fiber), 30g pro.

TEST KITCHEN TIP

For the perfect Cornish hen, consider rotating the pan once during baking. This helps ensure even cooking.

BAKED CHIMICHANGAS

My baked chimichanga recipe is healthier than a deep-fried version, but it's just as delicious. You can omit the chiles for less heat if you'd like.
—*Angela Oelschlaeger, Tonganoxie, KS*

TAKES: 30 min. • **MAKES:** 6 servings

2½ cups shredded cooked chicken breast
1 cup salsa
1 small onion, chopped
¾ tsp. ground cumin
½ tsp. dried oregano
6 flour tortillas (10 in.), warmed
¾ cup shredded reduced-fat cheddar cheese
1 cup reduced-sodium chicken broth
2 tsp. chicken bouillon granules
⅛ tsp. pepper
¼ cup all-purpose flour
1 cup fat-free half-and-half
1 can (4 oz.) chopped green chiles

1. Preheat oven to 425°. In a nonstick skillet, simmer the chicken, salsa, onion, cumin and oregano until the ingredients are heated through and most of the liquid has evaporated.
2. Place ½ cup chicken mixture down the center of each tortilla; top with 2 Tbsp. cheese. Fold sides and ends over filling and roll up.
3. Place seam side down in a 13x9-in. baking dish coated with cooking spray. Bake, uncovered, until lightly browned, about 15 minutes.
4. Meanwhile, in a small saucepan, combine the broth, bouillon and pepper. Cook until bouillon is dissolved. In a small bowl, combine the flour and half-and-half until smooth; gradually stir into the broth. Bring to a boil; cook and stir for 2 minutes or until thickened. Stir in chiles; cook until heated through. Serve with chimichangas.
1 chimichanga: 427 cal., 11g fat (4g sat. fat), 55mg chol., 1306mg sod., 49g carb. (7g sugars, 3g fiber), 30g pro.

HORSERADISH-CRUSTED
TURKEY TENDERLOINS

JALAPENO POPPER
CHICKEN CASSEROLE

This comforting supper is like a jalapeno popper in casserole form. It's rich and cheesy, and it has just a bit of heat.
—*Kerry Whitaker, Carthage, TX*

PREP: 20 min. • **BAKE:** 20 min.
MAKES: 8 servings

- 1 pkg. (32 oz.) frozen Tater Tots
- 2 pkg. (8 oz. each) cream cheese, softened
- 1 cup sour cream
- 6 jalapeno peppers, seeded and finely chopped
- 1½ tsp. garlic salt
- ½ tsp. pepper
- 4 cups rotisserie chicken, shredded
- 2 cups shredded Mexican cheese blend
- 1 lb. bacon strips, cooked and crumbled
- 6 green onions, chopped
   Optional: Additional sour cream and jalapeno slices

1. Preheat oven to 425°. Arrange Tater Tots in an ungreased 13x9-in. baking dish. Bake, uncovered, 15 minutes.
2. Meanwhile, in a large bowl, combine cream cheese, sour cream, jalapenos, garlic salt and pepper. Stir in half each of the chicken, Mexican cheese blend, bacon and green onions. Arrange chicken over Tater tots. Top with cream cheese mixture. Sprinkle with remaining Mexican cheese blend, green onions and bacon. Cover and bake until heated through, 20-25 minutes. If desired, top with additional sour cream and jalapeno slices.
1 piece: 701 cal., 53g fat (24g sat. fat), 116mg chol., 1648mg sod., 33g carb. (5g sugars, 3g fiber), 22g pro.

TEST KITCHEN TIP

You can make this recipe a little more keto-friendly by using cauliflower Tater Tots and adding sliced avocado on top of the baked casserole.

🍎 HORSERADISH-CRUSTED
TURKEY TENDERLOINS

Looking for a low-carb entree ideal for company? Consider this simple option. It won a local recipe contest and was featured on a restaurant's menu. The creamy sauce adds a flavorful punch.
—*Ellen Cross, Hubbardsville, NY*

PREP: 20 min. • **BAKE:** 15 min.
MAKES: 4 servings

- 2 Tbsp. reduced-fat mayonnaise
- 2 Tbsp. prepared horseradish
- ½ cup soft bread crumbs
- 1 green onion, chopped
- 2 Tbsp. minced fresh parsley
- 1 lb. turkey breast tenderloins

SAUCE
- ¼ cup reduced-fat mayonnaise
- ¼ cup fat-free plain yogurt
- 2 Tbsp. fat-free milk
- 1 Tbsp. prepared horseradish
- 1 Tbsp. Dijon mustard
- ¼ tsp. paprika

1. Preheat oven to 425°. Mix mayonnaise and horseradish. In a shallow bowl, toss the bread crumbs with green onion and parsley. Spread the tenderloins with the mayonnaise mixture; dip in crumb mixture to coat. Place tenderloins in a greased 15x10x1-in. pan.
2. Bake until a thermometer reads 165°, 12-15 minutes. Let stand 5 minutes before slicing.
3. Mix the sauce ingredients. Serve with the tenderloins.
Note: To make soft bread crumbs, tear bread into pieces and place in a food processor or blender. Cover and pulse until crumbs form. A slice of bread yields ½-¾ cup crumbs.
1 serving: 230 cal., 9g fat (1g sat. fat), 53mg chol., 386mg sod., 8g carb. (3g sugars, 1g fiber), 30g pro. **Diabetic exchanges:** 3 lean meat, 2 fat, ½ starch.

JALAPENO POPPER
CHICKEN CASSEROLE

SOUR CREAM & DILL
CHICKEN

FLAKY CHICKEN WELLINGTON

This cozy chicken Wellington takes a classic recipe and makes it super easy! I like to cook the chicken a day or so ahead of time to make it even simpler to throw together on busy nights.
—*Kerry Dingwall, Wilmington, NC*

- -

PREP: 30 min. • **BAKE:** 15 min.
MAKES: 6 servings

- 2 cups cubed cooked chicken
- 1 pkg. (10 oz.) frozen chopped spinach, thawed and squeezed dry
- 3 hard-boiled large eggs, chopped
- ½ cup finely chopped dill pickles
- ⅓ cup finely chopped celery
- 2 tubes (8 oz. each) refrigerated crescent rolls
- 2 tsp. prepared mustard, divided
- 1 cup sour cream
- 2 Tbsp. dill pickle juice

1. Preheat oven to 350°. In a large bowl, combine the first 5 ingredients. Unroll 1 tube of crescent dough into 1 long rectangle; press perforations to seal.
2. Spread half the mustard over dough; top with half of chicken mixture to within ¼ in. of the edges. Roll up jelly-roll style, starting with a long side; pinch seam to seal. Place cut side down on a parchment-lined baking sheet. Cut slits in top. Repeat with remaining crescent dough, mustard and chicken mixture.
3. Bake the pastries until golden brown, 15-20 minutes. Meanwhile, combine sour cream and pickle juice; serve with the pastries.

Freeze option: Cover and freeze unbaked pastries on a parchment-lined baking sheet until firm. Transfer to a freezer container; return to freezer. To use, bake pastries on a parchment-lined baking sheet in a preheated 350° oven until golden brown, 30-35 minutes. Prepare the sauce as directed.

⅓ pastry with about 3 Tbsp. sauce: 495 cal., 28g fat (6g sat. fat), 144mg chol., 830mg sod., 37g carb. (10g sugars, 2g fiber), 25g pro.

SOUR CREAM & DILL CHICKEN

This one is an updated version of the Sunday dinner my mother used to prepare. Today, it's the latest favorite with my family.
—*Rebekah Brown, Three Hills, AB*

- -

PREP: 10 min. • **BAKE:** 1 hour
MAKES: 4 servings

- 8 chicken drumsticks, skin removed
  Pepper to taste
- 1 can (10½ oz.) condensed cream of mushroom soup, undiluted
- 1 envelope onion soup mix
- 1 cup sour cream
- 1 Tbsp. lemon juice
- 1 Tbsp. fresh dill, chopped or 1 tsp. dill weed
- 1 can (4 oz.) mushroom stems and pieces, drained
  Paprika
  Cooked wide egg noodles, optional

1. Place the chicken in a single layer in a 13x9-in. baking dish. Sprinkle with pepper. Combine the soup, soup mix, sour cream, lemon juice, dill and mushrooms; pour over chicken. Sprinkle with paprika.
2. Bake, uncovered, at 350° until chicken is tender, about 1 hour. If desired, serve the drumsticks over egg noodles and sprinkle with additional dill.

2 drumsticks: 359 cal., 21g fat (9g sat. fat), 98mg chol., 1346mg sod., 13g carb. (3g sugars, 2g fiber), 29g pro.

FLAKY CHICKEN WELLINGTON

GREEK CHICKEN
SHEET-PAN DINNER

GREEK CHICKEN SHEET-PAN DINNER

I love roasted vegetables and keeping things simple. One bowl, one sheet pan, that's it. This dish works well with boneless cuts of chicken, too, and you can add other veggies. I serve it with a cucumber salad.
—*Sara Martin, Whitefish, MT*

PREP: 10 min. • **BAKE:** 30 min.
MAKES: 4 servings

- 4 bone-in chicken thighs, skin removed
- ½ cup Greek vinaigrette
- 8 small red potatoes, quartered
- 1 medium sweet red pepper, cut into ½-in. strips
- 1 can (14 oz.) water-packed artichoke hearts, drained and halved
- ¾ cup pitted ripe olives, drained
- 1 small red onion, cut into 8 wedges
- ¼ tsp. pepper
- ⅓ cup crumbled feta cheese

1. Preheat the oven to 375°. Spray a 15x10x1-in. baking pan with cooking spray; set aside.
2. In a large bowl, combine the first 7 ingredients; toss to coat. Place chicken and vegetables in a single layer on baking pan; sprinkle with the pepper. Bake until a thermometer inserted in chicken reads 170°-175° and vegetables are tender, 30-35 minutes.
3. If desired, preheat broiler. Broil chicken and vegetables 3-4 in. from heat until lightly browned, 2-3 minutes. Remove from oven, cool slightly. Sprinkle with the feta cheese.
1 serving: 481 cal., 24g fat (5g sat. fat), 92mg chol., 924mg sod., 31g carb. (3g sugars, 4g fiber), 31g pro.

MOM'S ROAST CHICKEN

MOM'S ROAST CHICKEN

This is the best way to cook a whole chicken that roasts up super juicy with crisp, golden skin. It's simply seasoned, but packs so much flavor.
—*James Schend, Pleasant Prairie, WI*

PREP: 15 min. + chilling
BAKE: 35 min. + standing
MAKES: 6 servings

- 1 broiler/fryer chicken (4 to 5 lbs.)
- 2 tsp. kosher salt
- 1 tsp. coarsely ground pepper
- 2 tsp. olive oil
  Optional: Minced fresh thyme or rosemary

1. Rub outside of the chicken with salt and pepper. Transfer chicken to a rack on a rimmed baking sheet. Refrigerate, uncovered, overnight.
2. Preheat oven to 450°. Remove chicken from refrigerator while oven heats. Heat a 12-in. cast-iron or ovenproof skillet in the oven for 15 minutes.

3. Place chicken on a work surface, neck side down. Cut through skin where legs connect to body. Press thighs down so joints pop and legs lie flat.
4. Carefully place chicken, breast side up, into hot skillet; press legs down so they lie flat on bottom of pan. Brush with oil. Roast until a thermometer inserted in thickest part of thigh reads 170°-175°, 35-40 minutes. Remove chicken from oven; let stand 10 minutes before carving. If desired, top with herbs before serving.
5 oz. cooked chicken: 405 cal., 24g fat (6g sat. fat), 139mg chol., 760mg sod., 0 carb. (0 sugars, 0 fiber), 44g pro.

TEST KITCHEN TIP
Not a fan of thyme or rosemary? Feel free to leave them out or replace them with the fresh herbs you and your family like best.

HAM STUFFED PRETZEL-CRUSTED CHICKEN

Buttery pretzels, mustard and deli ham fancy up this scrumptious chicken recipe. The combination's always a hit with my fussy family!

—*Marie McCarthy, Cobleskill, NY*

PREP: 10 min. • **BAKE:** 40 min.
MAKES: 4 servings

- 4 boneless skinless chicken breast halves (6 oz. each)
- ¼ cup honey mustard
- 8 thin slices deli ham
- 1 Tbsp. butter, melted
- ½ cup crushed pretzels

1. Preheat oven to 350°. Cut a horizontal slit in 1 side of each chicken breast half to within ½ in. of the opposite side. Spread honey mustard inside each pocket; stuff with 2 ham slices.

2. Place in a greased 13x9-in. baking dish. Brush with melted butter; sprinkle with the pretzels. Bake, uncovered, until a thermometer inserted in chicken reads 165°, 40-45 minutes.

1 stuffed chicken breast half: 330 cal., 11g fat (4g sat. fat), 118mg chol., 787mg sod., 16g carb. (5g sugars, 1g fiber), 41g pro.

TEST KITCHEN TIP
Amp up this dish by tucking a slice of Swiss or provolone cheese into the pocket of each chicken breast.

TURKEY LATTICE PIE

With its pretty lattice crust, this cheesy baked dish is as appealing as it is tasty. It's easy to make, too, since it uses ready-to-go crescent roll dough.

—*Lorraine Naig, Emmetsburg, IA*

PREP: 20 min. • **BAKE:** 20 min.
MAKES: 12 servings

- 3 tubes (8 oz. each) refrigerated crescent rolls
- 4 cups cubed cooked turkey
- 1½ cups shredded cheddar or Swiss cheese
- 3 cups frozen chopped broccoli, thawed and drained
- 1 can (10¾ oz.) condensed cream of chicken soup, undiluted
- 1⅓ cups 2% milk
- 2 Tbsp. Dijon mustard
- 1 Tbsp. dried minced onion
- ½ tsp. salt
    Dash pepper
- 1 large egg, lightly beaten

1. Preheat oven to 375°. Unroll 2 tubes of crescent roll dough; separate dough into rectangles. Place rectangles in an ungreased 15x10x1-in. baking pan. Press onto the bottom and ¼ in. up the sides of pan to form a crust, sealing seams and perforations. Bake 5-7 minutes or until light golden brown.

2. Meanwhile, in a large bowl, combine the turkey, cheese, broccoli, soup, milk, mustard, onion, salt and pepper. Spoon over crust.

3. Unroll the remaining dough; divide into 2 rectangles. Seal perforations. Cut each rectangle lengthwise into 1-in. strips. Using strips, make a lattice design on top of turkey mixture. Brush with egg. Bake 17-22 minutes or until top crust is golden brown and filling is bubbly.

1 serving: 396 cal., 20g fat (4g sat. fat), 81mg chol., 934mg sod., 30g carb. (8g sugars, 2g fiber), 24g pro.

TURKEY LATTICE PIE

TANDOORI CHICKEN

SNEAKY TURKEY MEATBALLS

Like most kids, mine refuse to eat certain veggies. In order to get healthy foods into their diets, I have to be sneaky sometimes. The veggies in this recipe keep the meatballs moist while providing nutrients—and I'm happy to say my kids love 'em.
—*Courtney Stultz, Weir, KS*

PREP: 15 min. • **BAKE:** 20 min.
MAKES: 6 servings

- ¼ head cauliflower, broken into florets
- ½ cup finely shredded cabbage
- 1 Tbsp. potato starch or cornstarch
- 1 Tbsp. balsamic vinegar
- 1 tsp. sea salt
- 1 tsp. dried basil
- ½ tsp. pepper
- 1 lb. ground turkey
   Optional: Barbecue sauce and fresh basil leaves

1. Preheat the oven to 400°. Place the cauliflower in a food processor; pulse until finely chopped. Transfer to a large bowl. Add the cabbage, potato starch, vinegar, salt, basil and pepper.
2. Add turkey; mix lightly but thoroughly. With an ice cream scoop or with wet hands, shape into 1½-in. balls. Place the meatballs on a greased rack in a 15x10x1-in. baking pan. Bake meatballs 20-24 minutes or until cooked through. If desired, toss with barbecue sauce and top with basil.
Freeze option: Freeze cooled meatball mixture in freezer containers. To use, partially thaw in refrigerator overnight. Heat through in a covered saucepan, stirring and add water if necessary. Serve as directed.
2 meatballs: 125 cal., 6g fat (1g sat. fat), 50mg chol., 370mg sod., 4g carb. (1g sugars, 1g fiber), 15g pro. **Diabetic exchanges:** 2 medium-fat meat.

TANDOORI CHICKEN

A hand-mixed spice rub makes ordinary chicken worthy of a special occasion. Plus, it takes awhile to marinate, so you can do other things while the spicy yogurt sauce works its magic.
—*Dena Leigh, Oldsmar, FL*

PREP: 15 min. + marinating
BAKE: 20 min. • **MAKES:** 6 pieces

- 1½ cups plain Greek yogurt
- 3 chipotle peppers in adobo sauce, minced
- 1 Tbsp. minced fresh gingerroot
- 1 Tbsp. minced garlic
- 1 tsp. paprika
- 1 tsp. cinnamon
- 1 tsp. salt
- ¾ tsp. fennel seed
- ¾ tsp. ground fenugreek
- ½ tsp. ground turmeric
- ½ tsp. ground coriander
- ¼ tsp. ground cloves
- ¼ tsp. pepper
- 6 bone-in chicken thighs (about 2 lbs.)

HONEY-LIME SAUCE

- 2 Tbsp. water
- 2 tsp. honey
- 3 Tbsp. lime juice
- 1 Tbsp. chopped fresh cilantro

1. Whisk together the first 13 ingredients until blended. Pour 1 cup marinade into a shallow dish. Add chicken; turn to coat. Refrigerate, covered, at least 3 hours or overnight. Cover and refrigerate the remaining marinade.
2. Preheat oven to 375°. Drain chicken, discarding marinade. Bake chicken in a greased 15x10x1-in. baking pan until a thermometer reads 170°, 20-25 minutes.
3. Meanwhile, to make sauce, simmer reserved marinade, water and honey in a small saucepan over medium-low heat. Remove from heat; stir in lime juice and cilantro. Serve chicken topped with sauce.
1 piece: 310 cal., 20g fat (7g sat. fat), 96mg chol., 548mg sod., 7g carb. (5g sugars, 1g fiber), 25g pro.

PUFF PASTRY CHICKEN BUNDLES

Inside these golden puff pastry packages, the chicken breasts rolled with spinach, herbed cream cheese and walnuts are a savory surprise. I like to serve this elegant entree when we have guests over for dinner or are celebrating a holiday or special occasion.
—*Brad Moritz, Limerick, PA*

PREP: 30 min. • **BAKE:** 20 min.
MAKES: 8 servings

- 8 boneless skinless chicken breast halves (about 6 oz. each)
- 1 tsp. salt
- ½ tsp. pepper
- 40 large spinach leaves
- 1 carton (8 oz.) spreadable chive and onion cream cheese
- ½ cup chopped walnuts, toasted
- 2 sheets frozen puff pastry, thawed
- 1 large egg
- ½ tsp. cold water

1. Preheat oven to 400°. Cut a lengthwise slit in each chicken breast half to within ½ in. of the other side; open meat so it lies flat. Cover with waxed paper; pound with a meat mallet to ⅛-in. thickness. Remove the paper. Sprinkle with salt and pepper.
2. Place 5 spinach leaves on each chicken breast half. Spoon a scant 2 Tbsp. of cream cheese down the center of each chicken breast half; sprinkle with 1 Tbsp. walnuts. Roll up chicken; tuck in ends.
3. Unfold puff pastry; cut into 8 portions. Roll each into a 7-in. square. Place chicken on 1 half of each square; fold other half of pastry over chicken. Crimp edges with fork. Combine egg and cold water; brush over edges of pastry.
4. Bake on a greased 15x10x1-in. baking sheet until a thermometer reads 165°, 20-25 minutes.
1 bundle: 624 cal., 32g fat (10g sat. fat), 136mg chol., 742mg sod., 39g carb. (1g sugars, 6g fiber), 44g pro.

SAUSAGE-TOPPED WHITE PIZZA

SAUSAGE-TOPPED WHITE PIZZA

I love cooking, and I learned from Nana and Mom. Pizza is easily one of my favorite dishes to prepare. I switched up this recipe to make it my own.
—*Tracy Brown, River Edge, NJ*

TAKES: 30 min. • **MAKES:** 6 servings

- 2 hot Italian turkey sausage links, casings removed
- 1 cup reduced-fat ricotta cheese
- ¼ tsp. garlic powder
- 1 prebaked 12-in. thin, whole wheat pizza crust
- 1 medium sweet red pepper, julienned
- 1 small onion, halved and thinly sliced
- ½ tsp. Italian seasoning
- ¼ tsp. freshly ground pepper
- ¼ tsp. crushed red pepper flakes, optional
- ½ cup shredded part-skim mozzarella cheese
- 2 cups arugula or baby spinach

1. Preheat oven to 450°. In a large skillet, cook and crumble sausage over medium-high heat until meat is no longer pink, 4-6 minutes. Mix the ricotta cheese and garlic powder.
2. Place the crust on a baking sheet; spread with ricotta cheese mixture. Top with the sausage, red pepper and onion; sprinkle with seasonings, then with mozzarella cheese.
3. Bake on a lower oven rack until edge is lightly browned and cheese is melted, 8-10 minutes. Top with arugula.
1 piece: 242 cal., 8g fat (4g sat. fat), 30mg chol., 504mg sod., 28g carb. (5g sugars, 4g fiber), 16g pro. **Diabetic exchanges:** 2 starch, 2 medium-fat meat.

❄ SPINACH-FILLED TURKEY ROLL

This attractive ground turkey loaf is truly something special, but you won't have to fuss a lot. The tasty entree features a swirl of spinach filling that's flavored with mushrooms, celery and green onions.

—*Louise Tomb, Harrison Valley, PA*

- -

PREP: 15 min. • **BAKE:** 1 hour
MAKES: 8 servings

- ¾ lb. fresh mushrooms, sliced
- ½ cup chopped green onions
- ⅓ cup finely chopped celery
- 2 Tbsp. butter
- 2 pkg. (10 oz. each) frozen chopped spinach, drained and squeezed dry
- ⅛ tsp. salt
- 2 large eggs, beaten
- 4 slices day-old whole wheat bread, crumbled
- 2 Tbsp. dried minced onion
- 4 tsp. herb and garlic onion soup mix
- ¼ tsp. pepper
- 2 lbs. lean ground turkey

1. Preheat oven to 350°. In a large skillet, saute the mushrooms, green onions and celery in butter until tender. Stir in spinach and salt; heat through. Remove from the heat; cool. In a large bowl, combine the eggs, bread, minced onion, soup mix and pepper. Crumble the turkey over mixture; mix lightly but thoroughly.

2. On a large piece of heavy-duty foil, pat turkey mixture into a 16x10-in. rectangle. Spread spinach mixture to within 1 in. of edges. Roll up, starting with a short side; seal seams and ends.

3. Place seam side down in a 13x9-in. baking dish coated with cooking spray. Bake, covered, 50 minutes. Uncover; bake until a thermometer reads 165°, about 10 minutes longer. Let stand for 5 minutes before cutting.

Freeze option: Securely wrap and freeze cooled turkey roll in foil. To use, partially thaw in refrigerator overnight. Unwrap turkey roll; reheat on a greased 15x10x1-in. baking pan in a preheated 350° oven until heated through and a thermometer inserted in the center reads 165°.

1 piece: 297 cal., 15g fat (5g sat. fat), 150mg chol., 470mg sod., 16g carb. (0 sugars, 4g fiber), 26g pro. **Diabetic exchanges:** 3 lean meat, 1 starch, 1 fat.

**THAI PEANUT
CHICKEN CASSEROLE**

THAI PEANUT CHICKEN CASSEROLE

I used traditional pizza sauce and toppings in this recipe for years. After becoming a fan of Thai peanut chicken pizza, I decided to use those flavors instead. Serve the pizza with stir-fried vegetables or a salad topped with sesame dressing for an easy, delicious meal.

—*Katherine Wollgast, Troy, MO*

- -

PREP: 30 min. • **BAKE:** 40 min.
MAKES: 10 servings

- 2 tubes (12 oz. each) refrigerated buttermilk biscuits
- 3 cups shredded cooked chicken
- 1 cup sliced fresh mushrooms
- 1 bottle (11½ oz.) Thai peanut sauce, divided
- 2 cups shredded mozzarella cheese, divided
- ½ cup chopped sweet red pepper
- ½ cup shredded carrot
- 4 green onions, sliced
- ¼ cup honey-roasted peanuts, coarsely chopped

1. Preheat oven to 350°. Cut each biscuit into 4 pieces. Place in a greased 13x9-in. baking pan.

2. In a large bowl, combine chicken, mushrooms and 1 cup peanut sauce; spread over biscuits. Top with 1 cup cheese, red pepper, carrot and green onions. Sprinkle with remaining cheese.

3. Bake until topping is set, cheese is melted and biscuits have cooked all the way through, about 40 minutes. Sprinkle with peanuts and serve with remaining peanut sauce.

1 serving: 490 cal., 25g fat (8g sat. fat), 55mg chol., 1013mg sod., 43g carb. (13g sugars, 1g fiber), 26g pro.

TEST KITCHEN TIP
This dish needs to bake until the centers of the biscuits are no longer doughy. Near the end of baking, cut into a biscuit in the center of the dish to confirm it is cooked through.

SMOTHERED TURKEY CUTLETS

Why have turkey just for Thanksgiving? This is an easy recipe that makes it feel like the holidays any day of the week.

—*Lisa Keys, Kennet Square, PA*

PREP: 30 min. • **BAKE:** 5 min.
MAKES: 4 servings

 1 cup mild chunky salsa
 ¼ cup dried cranberries
 1 Tbsp. chopped fresh cilantro
 1 cup orange sections, cut into
   1-in. pieces
 2 Tbsp. all-purpose flour
 1 tsp. ground cumin
 1 large egg
 1 Tbsp. water
 1 cup panko bread crumbs
 ¼ cup grated Parmesan cheese
 4 turkey breast cutlets (2½ oz. each)
 ½ tsp. pepper
 ⅛ tsp. salt
 2 Tbsp. olive oil, divided
 ½ cup shredded sharp cheddar cheese
 ½ medium ripe avocado, cubed
   Additional chopped cilantro
   Reduced-fat sour cream, optional

1. Preheat oven to 350°. Mix the salsa, cranberries and cilantro; gently stir in the oranges. In a shallow bowl, mix the flour and cumin. In another shallow bowl, whisk together the egg and water. In a third bowl, toss the bread crumbs with Parmesan cheese.
2. Sprinkle cutlets with pepper and salt; coat lightly with flour mixture, shaking off excess. Dip in egg mixture, then in crumb mixture, patting firmly.
3. In a large skillet, heat 1 Tbsp. oil over medium heat; add 2 cutlets and cook until golden brown, 1-2 minutes per side. Transfer to a foil-lined baking sheet. Repeat with remaining oil and turkey.
4. Sprinkle cutlets with cheddar cheese; bake until cheese is melted and turkey is no longer pink, 4-6 minutes. Top with the avocado, salsa mixture, additional cilantro and, if desired, sour cream.
1 serving: 401 cal., 19g fat (5g sat. fat), 106mg chol., 638mg sod., 31g carb. (12g sugars, 4g fiber), 26g pro.

❄ CHEESY CHICKEN LASAGNA

When my nephews were younger, I would make their favorite meal for their birthdays. This is what they usually asked for. The cheese makes it easier for kids to eat their vegetables.

—*Janet Lorton, Effingham, IL*

PREP: 20 min. • **BAKE:** 35 min. + standing
MAKES: 12 servings

 9 uncooked lasagna noodles
 2 cans (10¾ oz. each) condensed
   cream of chicken soup, undiluted
 ⅔ cup 2% milk
 2½ cups frozen mixed vegetables
 2 cups cubed cooked chicken
 18 slices American cheese

1. Cook noodles according to package directions. Preheat oven to 350°.
2. In a large saucepan, combine the soup and milk. Cook and stir over low heat until blended. Remove from the heat; stir in the vegetables and chicken.
3. In a greased 13x9-in. baking dish, layer 3 noodles, a third of the soup mixture and 6 cheese slices. Repeat the layers twice.
4. Bake, covered, 30 minutes. Uncover; bake until bubbly, 5-10 minutes longer. Let stand for 15 minutes before cutting.
Freeze option: Cover and freeze the unbaked lasagna. To use, partially thaw in refrigerator overnight. Remove from refrigerator 30 minutes before baking. Bake lasagna as directed, increasing time as necessary to heat through and for a thermometer to read 165°.
1 piece: 261 cal., 11g fat (6g sat. fat), 45mg chol., 613mg sod., 24g carb. (4g sugars, 2g fiber), 17g pro.

SMOTHERED
TURKEY
CUTLETS

SPICED TURKEY
WITH SWISS CHARD

SPICED TURKEY WITH SWISS CHARD

I love turkey in any way, shape or form. I feel the same about Swiss chard or any leafy greens, so I decided to combine the two in this tasty, healthy meal. To complete the dinner, serve with dinner rolls or make extra spice rub and toss it with oil and new potatoes, then roast them in the oven along with the turkey tenderloins.
—*Susan Bickta, Kutztown, PA*

- -

PREP: 25 min. + chilling
BAKE: 20 min. + standing
MAKES: 4 servings

- ¾ tsp. smoked paprika
- ½ tsp. dried parsley flakes
- ½ tsp. kosher salt
- ½ tsp. freshly ground pepper
- ¼ tsp. onion powder
  Pinch cayenne pepper
- 1 pkg. (20 oz.) turkey breast tenderloins
- 1 Tbsp. olive oil

SWISS CHARD

- 1 Tbsp. butter
- 1 large bunch Swiss chard, trimmed and chopped
- ¾ cup reduced-sodium chicken broth
- ⅛ tsp. freshly ground pepper
  Minced fresh parsley, optional

1. Preheat oven to 375°. Mix the first 6 ingredients; rub over tenderloins. Refrigerate, covered, 30 minutes.
2. In a large ovenproof skillet, heat the oil over medium-high heat, brown the tenderloins on all sides. Transfer skillet to oven; roast turkey until a thermometer reads 165°, 20-25 minutes. Remove from pan; tent with foil. Let stand 10 minutes before slicing.
3. In same skillet, heat the butter over medium-high heat; saute chard 5 minutes. Stir in broth and pepper. Reduce heat to medium; cook, covered, until tender, about 5 minutes, stirring occasionally. Serve with turkey. If desired, sprinkle the turkey with parsley.
3 oz. cooked turkey and ½ cup chard: 228 cal., 8g fat (2g sat. fat), 64mg chol., 633mg sod., 4g carb. (1g sugars, 2g fiber), 37g pro.

FOUR-CHEESE TURKEY PASTA BAKE

Leftover turkey combines with penne and cheeses to make a classic comfort food. The pasta bake works with chicken, shrimp or beef, too.
—*Mary Cokenour, Monticello, UT*

- -

PREP: 30 min. • **BAKE:** 35 min.
MAKES: 6 servings

- 8 oz. uncooked penne
- 1 small onion, chopped
- 2 Tbsp. butter
- 4 garlic cloves, minced
- 1 can (10¾ oz.) condensed cream of mushroom soup, undiluted
- 1 pkg. (8 oz.) cream cheese, softened and cubed
- 1 cup heavy whipping cream
- 1 cup 2% milk
- 1 jar (4½ oz.) sliced mushrooms, drained
- ½ cup shredded part-skim mozzarella cheese
- ½ cup shredded Parmesan cheese
- ½ cup shredded Swiss cheese
- ¼ tsp. ground nutmeg
- ¼ tsp. coarsely ground pepper
- 2 cups cubed cooked turkey breast

TOPPING

- ½ cup seasoned bread crumbs
- 3 Tbsp. butter, melted

1. Cook penne according to package directions. Preheat oven to 350°.
2. Meanwhile, in a large skillet, saute the onion in butter until tender. Add the garlic; cook 2 minutes longer. Add soup, cream cheese, cream and milk; cook and stir just until cream cheese is melted. Stir in the mushrooms, cheeses and spices; cook just until cheeses are melted. Add turkey and penne; heat through.
3. Transfer to a greased 2½ qt. baking dish. In a small bowl, combine topping ingredients; sprinkle over the pasta mixture. Bake, covered, 25 minutes. Uncover; bake until bubbly and golden brown, 10-15 minutes longer.
1¼ cups: 752 cal., 48g fat (28g sat. fat), 185mg chol., 1026mg sod., 46g carb. (6g sugars, 3g fiber), 34g pro.

SPICED TURKEY WITH
SWISS CHARD

Pork

**SAUSAGE, PEAR &
SWEET POTATO
SHEET-PAN DINNER**

SAUSAGE, PEAR & SWEET POTATO SHEET-PAN DINNER

This delicious, foolproof weeknight dinner is naturally gluten-free, uses one pan and is on your table with so little work! The recipe is also easily adaptable to whatever seasonal fruits and veggies you have on hand.

—*Melissa Erdelac, Valparaiso, IN*

- -

PREP: 15 min. • **BAKE:** 45 min.
MAKES: 5 servings

  2 large sweet potatoes, peeled and cut
      into ½-in. cubes
  1 large sweet onion, cut into wedges
  2 Tbsp. olive oil
  1 Tbsp. brown sugar
  ½ tsp. salt
  ½ tsp. ground allspice
  ¼ tsp. ground cinnamon
  ⅛ tsp. pepper
  3 small pears, quartered
  1 pkg. (19 oz.) Italian sausage links

1. Preheat oven to 425°. Place the sweet potatoes and onion in 15x10x1-in. baking pan; drizzle with oil. Sprinkle with brown sugar and seasonings; toss to coat. Bake for 15 minutes. Gently stir in pears; top with sausages.
2. Bake 20 minutes longer, stirring once. Increase the oven temperature to 450°. Bake until sausages are golden brown and a thermometer inserted in sausage reads at least 160°, 8-10 minutes longer, turning once.

1 serving: 533 cal., 29g fat (8g sat. fat), 58mg chol., 912mg sod., 56g carb. (28g sugars, 8g fiber), 15g pro.

CARNE ADOVADA SOPES

I call this "dude food"—my husband and son would eat this weekly. The tender cubed pork is great with homemade sopes.
—*Johnna Johnson, Scottsdale, AZ*

PREP: 25 min. + marinating
COOK: 2 hours • **MAKES:** 12 servings

- 3 cups chicken broth, divided
- ¾ cup chili powder
- 2 Tbsp. red wine vinegar
- 1 Tbsp. chopped fresh cilantro
- 1 Tbsp. honey
- 2 tsp. ground cumin
- 2 tsp. dried oregano
- 1 tsp. salt
- 1 tsp. ground cinnamon
- 1 boneless pork shoulder butt roast (3 to 4 lbs.), cut into ¾-in. cubes
- 5 Tbsp. canola oil, divided
- 2 large onions, chopped
- 6 garlic cloves, minced
- 1 can (10 oz.) diced tomatoes and green chiles, undrained

SOPES

- 3 cups masa harina
- ½ tsp. salt
- 2 cups water
- 3 Tbsp. canola oil
  Optional toppings: Hot refried beans, shredded lettuce, chopped tomatoes, shredded cheddar cheese, guacamole and/or sour cream

1. In a large shallow dish, combine 1 cup broth, chili powder, vinegar, cilantro, honey and seasonings. Add the pork; turn to coat. Refrigerate for 4 hours or overnight.

2. In an ovenproof Dutch oven, brown pork in 4 Tbsp. oil in batches. Remove and keep warm. In the same pan, saute onions in remaining oil until tender. Add garlic; cook 2 minutes longer.

3. Return pork to pan; add the remaining broth and tomatoes. Bring to a boil. Cover and bake at 350° until the meat is tender, 1½-1¾ hours. With a slotted spoon, remove the meat to a large bowl. Skim the fat from cooking liquid. Bring to a boil over high heat; cook until sauce is slightly thickened and reduced to about 2 cups, stirring occasionally. Return meat to the pan; set aside and keep warm.

4. For sopes, in a large bowl, combine the masa harina and salt; stir in water. Knead until smooth, adding additional water, 1 tsp. at a time, if necessary. Divide into 12 portions, about ¼ cup each. Roll each to form a ball; flatten to 4-in. patty. Cover with a damp towel.

5. Heat a large ungreased skillet over medium heat until hot. Cook the sopes in batches until lightly browned, about 1 minute on each side. Remove from the pan. Immediately pinch edge to form a ½-in. rim; set aside.

6. To serve, in same skillet, cook sopes in hot oil in batches over medium-high heat until golden brown and slightly crisp, 15-30 seconds on each side. Drain on paper towels. Using a slotted spoon, place the pork on sopes; serve with the toppings of your choice.

1 sope with ½ cup pork mixture: 423 cal., 23g fat (5g sat. fat), 68mg chol., 787mg sod., 32g carb. (4g sugars, 6g fiber), 24g pro.

TEST KITCHEN TIP

Masa harina is dried corn dough used to make tortillas. Look for packages in the ethnic aisle of your grocery store.

CARNE ADOVADA SOPES

EASY HAM HASH

HOT DOG CASSEROLE

When our children were small and I was busy trying to get all those extra things done that are part of a mom's normal schedule, I would make this quick hot dish. Kids love it!
—*JoAnn Gunio, Franklin, NC*

PREP: 10 min. • **BAKE:** 70 min.
MAKES: 8 servings

- 3 Tbsp. butter
- 2 Tbsp. all-purpose flour
- 1 to 1½ tsp. salt
- ¼ to ½ tsp. pepper
- 1½ cups 2% milk
- 5 medium red potatoes, thinly sliced
- 1 pkg. (1 lb.) hot dogs, halved lengthwise and cut into ½-in. slices
- 1 medium onion, chopped
- ⅓ cup shredded cheddar cheese
  Chopped green onions, optional

1. Preheat the oven to 350°. In a small saucepan, melt butter. Stir in the flour, salt and pepper until smooth. Gradually add milk. Bring to a boil; cook and stir 2 minutes or until thickened and bubbly.
2. In a greased 2½-qt. baking dish, layer with a third of the potatoes, half of the hot dogs and half of the onion. Repeat layers. Top with remaining potatoes. Pour white sauce over all.
3. Bake, covered, 1 hour. Uncover; sprinkle with cheese. Bake until the potatoes are tender, 10-15 minutes longer. If desired, garnish with green onions.
1 cup: 330 cal., 24g fat (11g sat. fat), 52mg chol., 967mg sod., 18g carb. (4g sugars, 2g fiber), 11g pro.

TEST KITCHEN TIP

To switch things up in this casserole, try replacing the cheddar cheese with American or Velveeta cheese. Or swap the red potatoes for Tater Tots. You could also use Italian sausage or bratwurst instead of hot dogs.

EASY HAM HASH

As the oldest of six children, I learned to cook early in life. Now my files are bulging with a variety of recipes. This delicious casserole remains an old standby.
—*Esther Johnson Danielson, Greenville, TX*

PREP: 10 min. • **BAKE:** 35 min.
MAKES: 6 servings

- 1 lb. finely ground fully cooked ham
- 1 large onion, finely chopped
- 3 medium potatoes, peeled and cooked
- 2 Tbsp. butter, melted
- 2 Tbsp. grated Parmesan cheese
- 1 Tbsp. prepared mustard
- 2 tsp. Worcestershire sauce
- 1 tsp. prepared horseradish
- ¼ tsp. pepper
- 1 cup shredded cheddar cheese
- ½ cup shredded Monterey Jack cheese

1. Preheat oven to 350°. In a large bowl, combine ham and onion. Shred potatoes and add to ham mixture. Stir in the butter, Parmesan, mustard, Worcestershire sauce, horseradish and pepper.
2. Spoon into a greased 11x7-in. baking dish, pressing down firmly. Combine shredded cheeses; sprinkle over top. Bake, uncovered, until bubbly and cheese is melted, 35-40 minutes.
1 cup: 426 cal., 27g fat (14g sat. fat), 82mg chol., 1260mg sod., 23g carb. (3g sugars, 2g fiber), 24g pro.

HOT DOG
CASSEROLE

POTATO HAM OMELET PIE

As a holiday kickoff, my family gets together in early December for a hearty brunch before going out to cut our Christmas trees. This flavorful breakfast pie, assembled in layers, is always a big hit and warms us up through and through.
—Shelly Rynearson, Oconomowoc, WI

PREP: 45 min.
BAKE: 30 min. + standing
MAKES: 8 servings

- 1 pkg. (17¼ oz.) frozen puff pastry, thawed
- ¼ cup butter, cubed
- 3 cups sliced red potatoes
- 1 cup thinly sliced onion
- ¼ tsp. salt
- ¼ tsp. pepper

OMELETS
- 6 large eggs, lightly beaten
- ¼ cup minced fresh parsley
- 2 Tbsp. water
  Dash each salt and pepper
- 2 Tbsp. butter

FILLING
- 2 cups shredded cheddar cheese
- 1½ cups cubed fully cooked ham
- 1 large egg, lightly beaten
- 1 Tbsp. water

1. Preheat the oven to 375°. On a lightly floured surface, roll each puff pastry sheet into a 12-in. square. Place 1 square in a 10-in. quiche dish; set dish and remaining pastry aside.

2. In a large skillet, melt the butter over medium heat. Add potatoes, onion, salt and pepper; cover and cook until potatoes are tender and golden brown, stirring occasionally, 10-12 minutes. Set aside.

3. In a large bowl, beat the eggs, parsley, water, salt and pepper. In a 10-in. skillet, melt 1 Tbsp. butter over medium heat; add half of the egg mixture. As eggs set, lift edges, letting uncooked portion flow underneath. Continue cooking until set. Slide omelet onto a baking sheet. Repeat with remaining butter and egg mixture to make a second omelet.

4. Sprinkle 1 cup cheese over prepared pastry. Top with 1 omelet and half of the potato mixture. Layer with ham and the remaining potato mixture, cheese, omelet and puff pastry. Trim pastry to fit dish; seal and flute edge.

5. In a small bowl, combine the egg and water; brush over the pastry. Bake until golden brown, 30-35 minutes. Let stand 10 minutes before cutting.

1 piece: 628 cal., 40g fat (17g sat. fat), 253mg chol., 946mg sod., 47g carb. (2g sugars, 6g fiber), 22g pro.

❄️
BREADSTICK PIZZA

Make any Monday a fun day with this tasty, hassle-free homemade pizza featuring convenient refrigerated breadsticks as the no-fuss crust. Feeding kids? Slice pieces into small strips and let them dip each strip into marinara sauce. They'll love it!
—Mary Hankins, Kansas City, MO

PREP: 25 min. • BAKE: 20 min.
MAKES: 12 servings

- 2 tubes (11 oz. each) refrigerated breadsticks
- ½ lb. sliced fresh mushrooms
- 2 medium green peppers, chopped
- 1 medium onion, chopped
- 1½ tsp. Italian seasoning, divided
- 4 tsp. olive oil, divided
- 1½ cups shredded cheddar cheese, divided
- 5 oz. Canadian bacon, chopped
- 1½ cups shredded part-skim mozzarella cheese
  Marinara sauce

1. Unroll breadsticks into a greased 15x10x1-in. baking pan. Press onto the bottom and up the sides of pan; pinch the seams to seal. Bake at 350° until set, 6-8 minutes.

2. Meanwhile, in a large skillet, cook and stir the mushrooms, peppers, onion and 1 tsp. Italian seasoning in 2 tsp. oil until crisp-tender; drain.

3. Brush crust with remaining 2 tsp. oil. Sprinkle with ¾ cup cheddar cheese; top with vegetable mixture and Canadian bacon. Combine mozzarella cheese and remaining ¾ cup cheddar cheese; sprinkle over top. Sprinkle with remaining ½ tsp. Italian seasoning.

4. Bake until cheese is melted and crust is golden brown, 20-25 minutes. Serve with marinara sauce.

Freeze option: Bake the crust as directed, add the toppings and cool. Securely wrap and freeze unbaked pizza. To use, unwrap the pizza and bake as directed, increasing time as necessary.

1 piece: 267 cal., 11g fat (6g sat. fat), 27mg chol., 638mg sod., 29g carb. (5g sugars, 2g fiber), 13g pro.

BREADSTICK PIZZA

PORK CHOP CASSEROLE

HAM & ASPARAGUS CASSEROLE

I love to try out new recipes on my family. I'm always looking for ways to incorporate some of my favorite vegetables in with my main dishes, and this one was a success!
—*Rachel Kowasic, Valrico, FL*

- -

PREP: 25 min. • **BAKE:** 25 min.
MAKES: 4 servings

- 3¾ cups uncooked yolk-free whole wheat noodles
- 2½ cups cut fresh asparagus (1-in. pieces)
- 1 medium onion, chopped
- 1 Tbsp. reduced-fat butter
- ¼ cup all-purpose flour
- ½ tsp. dried thyme
- ⅛ tsp. pepper
- 1 cup fat-free milk
- 1 cup reduced-sodium chicken broth
- 1 Tbsp. lemon juice
- 1½ cups cubed fully cooked lean ham
- ¼ cup minced fresh parsley
- ⅓ cup french-fried onions
- 2 Tbsp. shredded Parmesan cheese

1. Cook noodles according to package directions. Preheat the oven to 350°. Meanwhile, in a saucepan, bring 2 cups of water to a boil. Add asparagus. Cover and cook until crisp-tender, 3-5 minutes. Drain and set aside.

2. In a large skillet, saute the chopped onion in butter until tender. Combine the flour, thyme and pepper; gradually whisk in milk and broth until smooth. Add milk mixture to the skillet. Bring to a boil; cook and stir until thickened, 1-2 minutes. Remove from the heat; stir in lemon juice.

3. Drain noodles; add ham, parsley, sauce and asparagus. Transfer to a 13x9-in. baking dish coated with cooking spray. Top with fried onions and cheese.

4. Cover and bake for 20 minutes or until bubbly. Uncover; bake until golden brown, 5-10 minutes longer.

Note: This recipe was tested with Land O'Lakes light stick butter.

1½ cups: 343 cal., 8g fat (3g sat. fat), 27mg chol., 946mg sod., 50g carb. (8g sugars, 7g fiber), 22g pro.

PORK CHOP CASSEROLE

One bite of these tender pork chops smothered in this creamy sauce and we could taste the care Mother put into her cooking. She was happy to share the recipe with guests who requested it after they tried this delicious dish at our house.
—*Nancy Duty, Jacksonville, FL*

- -

PREP: 25 min. • **BAKE:** 55 min.
MAKES: 6 servings

- ¾ cup all-purpose flour
- 1 tsp. salt
- ½ tsp. pepper
- 6 bone-in pork loin chops (¾-in. thick and 8 oz. each)
- 2 Tbsp. canola oil
- 1 can (10¾ oz.) condensed cream of mushroom soup, undiluted
- 1 cup sour cream, divided
- ⅔ cup chicken broth
- ½ tsp. ground ginger
- ¼ tsp. dried rosemary, crushed
- 1 can (2.8 oz.) french-fried onions, divided

1. Preheat oven to 350°. In a shallow bowl, combine flour, salt and pepper. Add pork chops, 1 at a time, and turn to coat.

2. In a large skillet, brown pork chops in oil on both sides. Arrange in a single layer in an ungreased 13x9-in. baking dish. In a large bowl, combine soup, ½ cup sour cream, broth, ginger and rosemary; pour over chops. Sprinkle with half the onions.

3. Cover and bake 45-50 minutes or until tender. Stir remaining sour cream into sauce. Sprinkle with remaining onions. Bake, uncovered, until the onions are browned, about 10 minutes longer.

1 pork chop: 628 cal., 40g fat (14g sat. fat), 123mg chol., 1074mg sod., 23g carb. (2g sugars, 1g fiber), 40g pro.

"Didn't have rosemary and ginger on hand so substituted a small amount of garlic. Very delicious recipe!"
—VBCOOKS, TASTEOFHOME.COM

SAUSAGE & 'SHROOM
DUTCH OVEN PIZZA

SAUSAGE & 'SHROOM DUTCH OVEN PIZZA

We created this pizza when we were experimenting with different ways to use a Dutch oven. We couldn't believe how well it turned out. You can use your favorite pizza toppings if desired.
—Taste of Home *Test Kitchen*

PREP: 10 min. • **COOK:** 20 min.
MAKES: 6 servings

- 1   lb. frozen pizza dough, thawed
- 1   Tbsp. olive oil
- 1   cup marinara sauce
- 1   cup shredded Italian cheese blend
- 8   oz. bulk spicy pork sausage, cooked and drained
- ⅓   cup chopped onion
- ½   cup sliced fresh mushrooms
      Optional: Minced fresh basil, red pepper flakes and grated Parmesan cheese

1. Preheat oven to 450°. Place a 10-in. Dutch oven on bottom rack in oven to heat through, 2-3 minutes.
2. Roll dough on a lightly floured surface into a 12-in. circle. Fold an 18-in. piece of foil lengthwise into thirds, making a sling. Remove pan from oven; place dough on sling and gently lower dough into pan. Using a wooden spoon, move dough into place and up the side, leaving sling in pan. Brush dough with oil; spread with marinara sauce. Top evenly with cheese, sausage, onion and mushrooms.
3. Bake until the crust is lightly browned and crisp, about 20 minutes. Cool slightly. Using sling, remove from Dutch oven. Serve with basil, red pepper flakes and grated Parmesan cheese as desired.
1 piece: 385 cal., 18g fat (6g sat. fat), 35mg chol., 750mg sod., 39g carb. (4g sugars, 2g fiber), 16g pro.

RANCH PORK ROAST

RANCH PORK ROAST

This simple pork roast with a mild rub is perfect for new cooks. The leftover meat is tender and flavorful enough to be used in countless recipes.
—Taste of Home *Test Kitchen*

PREP: 10 min. • **BAKE:** 50 min. + standing
MAKES: 8 servings

- 1   boneless pork loin roast (2½ lbs.)
- 2   Tbsp. olive oil
- 1   Tbsp. ranch salad dressing mix
- 2   tsp. Dijon mustard
- 1   garlic clove, minced
- ½   tsp. pepper

1. Preheat oven to 350°. If desired, tie the pork with kitchen string at 2-in. intervals to help roast hold its shape. Combine the next 5 ingredients; rub over roast. Place on a rack in a shallow roasting pan. Pour 1 cup water into pan.
2. Bake, uncovered, until a thermometer reads 145°, 50-55 minutes. Let stand for 10-15 minutes before slicing.
Freeze option: Freeze the cooled sliced pork in freezer containers. To use, partially thaw in the refrigerator overnight. Heat through in a covered saucepan, gently stirring occasionally; add broth or water if necessary.
4 oz. cooked pork: 212 cal., 10g fat (3g sat. fat), 70mg chol., 248mg sod., 2g carb. (0 sugars, 0 fiber), 27g pro. **Diabetic exchanges:** 4 lean meat, ½ fat.

HAM-STUFFED MANICOTTI

Here's a fun and different use for ham. It's unexpected combined with the manicotti, yet delicious. The creamy cheese sauce makes this casserole perfect for chilly days. I'm always asked for the recipe whenever I serve it to guests.
—*Dorothy Anderson, Ottawa, KS*

PREP: 20 min. • **BAKE:** 30 min.
MAKES: 8 servings

- 8   manicotti shells
- ½   cup chopped onion
- 1   Tbsp. canola oil
- 3   cups (1 lb.) ground fully cooked ham
- 1   can (4 oz.) sliced mushrooms, drained
- 1   cup shredded Swiss cheese, divided
- 3   Tbsp. grated Parmesan cheese
- ¼   to ½ cup chopped green pepper
- 3   Tbsp. butter
- 3   Tbsp. all-purpose flour
- 2   cups 2% milk
-     Paprika
-     Chopped fresh parsley

1. Cook manicotti according to package directions; set aside. Preheat oven to 350°. In a large skillet, saute onion in oil until tender. Remove from the heat. Add the ham, mushrooms, half of Swiss and the Parmesan; set aside.

2. In a small saucepan, saute the green pepper in butter until tender; stir in flour until combined. Add milk; cook and stir until thickened, about 2 minutes. Stir a fourth of the sauce into ham mixture.

3. Stuff each shell with about ⅓ cup of filling. Place in a greased 11x7-in. baking dish. Top with remaining sauce; sprinkle with paprika.

4. Cover and bake until heated through, about 30 minutes. Sprinkle with parsley and the remaining Swiss cheese before serving.

Note: Recipe can easily be doubled for a larger group.

1 stuffed shell: 604 cal., 40g fat (15g sat. fat), 114mg chol., 2333mg sod., 20g carb. (4g sugars, 1g fiber), 41g pro.

OKTOBERFEST CASSEROLE

❄ OKTOBERFEST CASSEROLE

In northeastern Ohio, we love German flavors. This delicious casserole is a trifecta mashup of my favorite dishes. It combines the flavors of classic cheesy hash brown casserole with bratwursts and sauerkraut, and pretzels and beer cheese. It takes less than 10 minutes to mix and uses only one bowl. It's sure to please everyone.
—*Sarah Markley, Ashland, OH*

PREP: 15 min.
BAKE: 1½ hours + standing
MAKES: 12 servings

- 2   cans (10½ oz. each) condensed cheddar cheese soup, undiluted
- 1   cup beer or chicken broth
- 1   cup sour cream
- 1   pkg. (32 oz.) frozen cubed hash brown potatoes, thawed
- 1   can (14 oz.) sauerkraut, rinsed and well drained
- 2   cups shredded cheddar cheese
- 1   pkg. (14 oz.) fully cooked bratwurst links, chopped
- 2   cups pretzel pieces

1. Preheat oven to 350°. In a large bowl, whisk soup, beer and sour cream until combined. Stir in potatoes, sauerkraut, cheese and chopped bratwurst. Transfer to a greased 13x9-in. baking dish. Cover and bake for 45 minutes.

2. Uncover; bake 30 minutes. Top with pretzel pieces. Bake until bubbly and heated through, 12-15 minutes longer. Let stand 10 minutes before serving.

Freeze option: Freeze the cooled potato mixture in freezer containers. To use, partially thaw in refrigerator overnight. Heat through in a saucepan, stirring occasionally; add broth or water if necessary.

1 serving: 356 cal., 21g fat (10g sat. fat), 49mg chol., 884mg sod., 29g carb. (4g sugars, 3g fiber), 13g pro.

TEST KITCHEN TIP
To add a little more variety, you can substitute any flavor of brats or pretzel pieces in this casserole.

HASH BROWN MAPLE SAUSAGE CASSEROLE

This craveworthy casserole has a golden hash-brown crust that's topped with sausage and veggies. My favorite part is the surprise layer of gooey Gruyere.
—*Anuja Argade, Foster City, CA*

PREP: 15 min. • **BAKE:** 45 min. + standing
MAKES: 8 servings

- 1 lb. maple pork sausage
- ½ cup cubed peeled sweet potato
- 2 Tbsp. olive oil
- 1 pkg. (30 oz.) frozen shredded hash brown potatoes, thawed
- 1½ cups shredded Gruyere or cheddar cheese
- 2 cups coarsely chopped fresh kale (tough stems removed)
- ¾ cup fresh or frozen corn
- 5 large eggs, lightly beaten
- 2 cups half-and-half cream
- 1 tsp. salt
- ½ tsp. pepper
  Maple syrup, optional

1. Preheat oven to 375°. In a large skillet, cook sausage and sweet potato over medium-high heat until sausage is no longer pink, 5-7 minutes, breaking up sausage into crumbles. Remove with a slotted spoon; drain on paper towels.
2. Meanwhile, coat bottom of a 12-in. cast-iron or other ovenproof skillet with oil. Reserve ½ cup hash browns for the topping; add remaining potatoes to skillet, pressing firmly with a spatula to form an even layer.
3. Layer with cheese, kale and corn; top with sausage mixture and reserved hash browns. In a bowl, whisk eggs, cream, salt and pepper until blended; pour over top.
4. Bake, uncovered, for 45-55 minutes or until the edges are golden brown and egg portion is set. Cover loosely with foil during the last 10 minutes if needed to prevent overbrowning. Let stand for 20 minutes before serving. If desired, serve with syrup.
1¼ cups: 487 cal., 32g fat (13g sat. fat), 200mg chol., 899mg sod., 27g carb. (5g sugars, 2g fiber), 22g pro.

❄ GLAZED HAM BALLS

Over the years, I have found this recipe ideal for using leftovers from a baked ham. The pleasantly soft ham balls are glazed with a thick sauce that's slightly sweet with a hint of cloves.
—*Esther Leitch, Fredericksburg, VA*

PREP: 20 min. • **BAKE:** 35 min.
MAKES: 10 servings

- 3 large eggs
- 1 cup 2% milk
- 1¼ cups quick-cooking oats
- 2½ lbs. ground fully cooked ham

SAUCE
- 1 cup plus 2 Tbsp. packed brown sugar
- 3 Tbsp. cornstarch
- ½ tsp. ground cloves, optional
- 1¾ cups pineapple juice
- ½ cup light corn syrup
- 3 Tbsp. cider vinegar
- 4½ tsp. Dijon mustard

1. Preheat the oven to 350°. In a bowl, combine the eggs, milk, oats and ham; mix lightly but thoroughly. Shape into 1½-in. balls. Place in greased 15x10x1-in. baking pan.
2. In a saucepan, combine the brown sugar, cornstarch and cloves, if desired. Stir in the pineapple juice, corn syrup, vinegar and mustard until smooth. Bring to a boil over medium heat; cook and stir 2 minutes. Pour over ham balls.
3. Bake, uncovered, for 35-40 minutes or until browned.
Freeze option: Freeze the cooled ham balls mixture in freezer containers. To use, partially thaw in refrigerator overnight. Heat through in a covered saucepan, stirring occasionally; add water if necessary.
1 serving: 531 cal., 24g fat (9g sat. fat), 131mg chol., 1574mg sod., 53g carb. (40g sugars, 1g fiber), 25g pro.

HASH BROWN MAPLE SAUSAGE CASSEROLE

SAUSAGE BREAD
SANDWICHES

SAUSAGE-STUFFED SHELLS

I wanted to make manicotti one day but was out of the noodles. So I came up with this recipe, using jumbo shells instead. They were much easier to work with.
—*Lori Daniels, Beverly, WV*

PREP: 25 min. • BAKE: 20 min.
MAKES: 2 servings

- ⅓ lb. bulk Italian sausage
- 1 can (8 oz.) tomato sauce
- ¼ cup tomato paste
- 2 Tbsp. water
- 1 tsp. brown sugar
- ½ tsp. Italian seasoning
- ⅓ cup 4% cottage cheese
- ¾ cup shredded part-skim mozzarella cheese, divided
- 2 Tbsp. beaten egg
- ½ tsp. minced fresh parsley
- 6 jumbo pasta shells, cooked and drained
  Grated Parmesan cheese, optional

1. Preheat the oven to 350°. In a small saucepan, cook sausage over medium heat until no longer pink; drain. Set half of the sausage aside for the filling. Add the tomato sauce, tomato paste, water, brown sugar and seasoning to the sausage in the pan. Bring to a boil. Reduce heat; simmer, uncovered, for 15 minutes, stirring occasionally.
2. In a small bowl, combine the cottage cheese, ½ cup mozzarella cheese, egg, parsley and reserved sausage. Stuff into shells. Spread ¼ cup meat sauce in an ungreased 1-qt. shallow baking dish. Place stuffed shells in dish; drizzle with remaining meat sauce.
3. Sprinkle with remaining mozzarella cheese and, if desired, Parmesan cheese. Bake, uncovered, until filling reaches 160°, 20-25 minutes. If desired, garnish with additional parsley.

3 stuffed shells: 437 cal., 14g fat (7g sat. fat), 67mg chol., 1371mg sod., 40g carb. (13g sugars, 4g fiber), 36g pro.

❄ SAUSAGE BREAD SANDWICHES

I make these sandwiches in my spare time and freeze them so they're ready when needed, such as for tailgating parties when we attend Kansas State football games.
—*Donna Roberts, Manhattan, KS*

PREP: 30 min. • BAKE: 20 min.
MAKES: 4 sandwich loaves (3 pieces each)

- 1 pkg. (16 oz.) hot roll mix
- 2 lbs. reduced-fat bulk pork sausage
- 2 Tbsp. dried parsley flakes
- 2 tsp. garlic powder
- 1 tsp. onion powder
- ½ tsp. dried oregano
- 2 cups shredded part-skim mozzarella cheese
- ½ cup grated Parmesan cheese
- 1 large egg
- 1 Tbsp. water

1. Preheat oven to 350°. Prepare roll mix dough according to package directions.
2. Meanwhile, in a large skillet, cook the sausage over medium heat 8-10 minutes or until no longer pink, breaking into crumbles; drain. Stir in seasonings.
3. Divide dough into 4 portions. On a lightly floured surface, roll each into a 14x8-in. rectangle. Top each with 1¼ cups sausage mixture to within 1 in. of edges; sprinkle with ½ cup mozzarella cheese and 2 Tbsp. Parmesan cheese. Roll up jelly-roll style, starting with a long side; pinch seams and ends to seal.
4. Transfer to greased baking sheets, seam side down. In a small bowl, whisk the egg with water; brush over loaves. Bake 20-25 minutes or until golden brown and heated through. Cool for 5 minutes before slicing.

Freeze option: Cool cooked sandwiches 1 hour on wire racks. Cut each sandwich into thirds; wrap each securely in foil. Freeze until serving. To reheat in oven, place wrapped frozen sandwiches on a baking sheet. Heat in a preheated 375° oven for 20-25 minutes or until heated through.

1 piece: 432 cal., 25g fat (10g sat. fat), 103mg chol., 926mg sod., 27g carb. (5g sugars, 1g fiber), 24g pro.

SAUSAGE-STUFFED
SHELLS

CHINESE BARBECUED RIBS

One bite of these tender and flavorful ribs and you'll understand why this is the most-requested recipe from friends and family. I developed it based on a recipe from my father-in-law, adding my own variations over the years.
—*Roxanne Chan, Albany, CA*

- -

PREP: 15 min. • **BAKE:** 1½ hours
MAKES: 8 servings

- ½ cup char siu sauce
- ¼ cup rice vinegar
- ¼ cup sherry or reduced-sodium chicken broth
- ¼ cup reduced-sodium soy sauce
- ¼ cup oyster sauce
- ¼ cup hoisin sauce
- 4 garlic cloves, minced
- 2 tsp. Chinese five-spice powder
- 2 tsp. minced fresh gingerroot
- 4 lbs. pork spareribs
  Thinly sliced green onions, optional

1. Preheat oven to 350°. In a small bowl, combine the first 9 ingredients. Reserve half of the sauce for basting.
2. Place the ribs, with bone side down, in a shallow roasting pan lined with foil. Spoon remaining sauce over ribs. Cover and bake 1 hour; drain.
3. Bake, uncovered, until ribs are tender, basting occasionally with reserved sauce, 30-40 minutes. Cut into serving-sized pieces. If desired, sprinkle with green onions.
Note: Char siu sauce is a Chinese barbecue sauce. Look for it in the Asian foods section of your grocery store.
5 oz. cooked beef: 536 cal., 33g fat (12g sat. fat), 129mg chol., 1920mg sod., 23g carb. (18g sugars, 0 fiber), 32g pro.

HAM LOAF

I copied this recipe exactly the way Grandma had written it in her cookbook. The only difference today is that I can't get a home-smoked ham like those Grandpa used to cure in his smokehouse. But that never matters to the hungry folks at the dinner table—Grandma's recipe is a winner every time!
—*Esther Mishler, Hollsopple, PA*

- -

PREP: 15 min. • **BAKE:** 70 min.
MAKES: 8 servings

- 2 large eggs
- 1 cup 2% milk
- 1 cup dry bread crumbs
- ¼ tsp. pepper
- 1½ lb. ground fully cooked ham
- ½ lb. ground pork

GLAZE

- ⅓ cup packed brown sugar
- ¼ cup cider vinegar
- ½ tsp. ground mustard
- 2 Tbsp. water

1. Preheat oven to 350°. In a large bowl, beat eggs; add milk, bread crumbs and pepper. Add the ham and pork; mix lightly but thoroughly. Transfer to a 9x5-in. loaf pan. Bake for 30 minutes.
2. Meanwhile, combine glaze ingredients; spoon over loaf. Bake about 40 minutes longer or until a thermometer inserted in the loaf reads 145°, basting occasionally with glaze.
1 piece: 393 cal., 23g fat (8g sat. fat), 115mg chol., 1241mg sod., 21g carb. (11g sugars, 1g fiber), 25g pro.

HAM LOAF

MAPLE-GLAZED PORK MEDALLIONS

My sister shared this recipe with me, and it has become a favorite with family and friends. Sweet maple with salty bacon is a delicious taste combination with the pork.
—*Bonnie De Jong, Holland, MI*

PREP: 20 min. • **BAKE:** 45 min.
MAKES: 6 servings

1 cup maple syrup
2 green onions, chopped
3 Tbsp. thawed orange juice concentrate
3 Tbsp. ketchup
2 Tbsp. soy sauce
1 Tbsp. Dijon mustard
1 Tbsp. Worcestershire sauce
1 garlic clove, minced
½ tsp. curry powder
12 bacon strips
1 boneless pork loin roast (2 lbs.), cut into 6 slices
¼ cup packed brown sugar

1. Preheat oven to 325°. In small bowl, whisk the first 9 ingredients; set aside. In a large skillet, cook bacon over medium heat until partially cooked but not crisp. Remove to paper towels to drain.
2. Wrap 2 strips of bacon around sides of each pork slice; secure with toothpicks. Place in a greased 13x9-in. baking dish. Pour the syrup mixture over top. Bake, covered, 35 minutes. Uncover; sprinkle with brown sugar. Bake 10-15 minutes longer or until thermometer inserted in pork reads 145°. Discard toothpicks before serving. If desired, thicken the cooking juices; serve with pork.
1 serving: 473 cal., 13g fat (5g sat. fat), 92mg chol., 834mg sod., 51g carb. (46g sugars, 0 fiber), 36g pro.

TEST KITCHEN TIP

Remember the maple mixture the next time you're looking for a tasty glaze for baked ham.

❄️
ROCK & RYE
PORK ROAST SANDWICHES

Detroit's Faygo Rock & Rye soda (pop as we call it in Michigan) gives these pork roast sandwiches such a unique flavor with notes of vanilla and cherry. These sandwiches are a hit at summer picnics and Faygo pop brings back fond childhood memories.
—*Jennifer Gilbert, Brighton, MI*

PREP: 20 min. • **COOK:** 2 hours 5 min.
MAKES: 8 servings

½ tsp. garlic salt
½ tsp. paprika
½ tsp. pepper
1 boneless pork shoulder butt roast (1 to 2 lbs.)
4 cups Faygo Rock & Rye soda or cherry vanilla cream soda
1 cup ketchup
3 Tbsp. steak sauce
2 Tbsp. liquid smoke
1 Tbsp. light brown sugar
1 Tbsp. cider vinegar
8 hamburger buns, split

1. Preheat oven to 300°. Combine garlic salt, paprika and pepper; rub over roast. Place in an ovenproof Dutch oven; add soda. Bake, covered, until pork is tender, 2-2¼ hours.
2. Remove roast; shred with 2 forks. Skim the fat from cooking juices. Return 1 cup juices to Dutch oven. Add ketchup, steak sauce, liquid smoke, brown sugar and vinegar. Bring to a boil; cook for 5 minutes. Return meat to pan; heat through. Adjust with additional cooking juices as desired. Serve on hamburger buns.
Freeze option: Freeze cooled meat mixture and juices in freezer containers. To use, partially thaw in refrigerator overnight. Heat through in a saucepan, stirring occasionally; add water if necessary.
1 sandwich: 273 cal., 7g fat (2g sat. fat), 34mg chol., 864mg sod., 37g carb. (17g sugars, 1g fiber), 14g pro.

**SLICED HAM WITH
ROASTED VEGETABLES**

SLICED HAM WITH ROASTED VEGETABLES

To prepare this colorful, zesty oven meal, I shop in my backyard for the fresh garden vegetables and oranges (we have our own tree!) that spark the ham's hearty flavor. It's my family's favorite main dish.
—*Margaret Pache, Mesa, AZ*

PREP: 10 min. • **BAKE:** 35 min.
MAKES: 6 servings

      Cooking spray
  6   medium potatoes, peeled and cubed
  5   medium carrots, sliced
  1   medium turnip, peeled and cubed
  1   large onion, cut into thin wedges
  6   slices (4 to 6 oz. each) fully cooked ham, halved
  ¼   cup thawed orange juice concentrate
  2   Tbsp. brown sugar
  1   tsp. prepared horseradish
  1   tsp. grated orange zest
      Coarsely ground pepper

1. Grease two 15x10x1-in. baking pans with cooking spray. Add potatoes, carrots, turnip and onion; generously coat with cooking spray. Bake, uncovered, at 425° until tender, 25-30 minutes.
2. Arrange ham slices over vegetables. In a bowl, combine concentrate, brown sugar, horseradish and orange zest. Spoon over ham and vegetables. Bake until the ham is heated through, about 10 minutes longer. Sprinkle with pepper.
1 serving: 375 cal., 5g fat (1g sat. fat), 71mg chol., 1179mg sod., 55g carb. (15g sugars, 7g fiber), 31g pro.

SAVORY STUFFED PORK CHOPS

SAVORY STUFFED PORK CHOPS

Who would ever guess stuffed chops could be so simple? Baby spinach and stuffing mix are the secrets to this elegant recipe. I appreciate the 10-minute prep time!
—*Rebecca Nossaman, Hurricane, WV*

PREP: 10 min. • **BAKE:** 35 min.
MAKES: 8 servings

  8   boneless pork loin chops (1 in. thick and 8 oz. each)
  1   small onion, chopped
  ½   cup butter, cubed
  5   cups fresh baby spinach
  1   pkg. (6 oz.) sage stuffing mix
  1½   cups sour cream
  ½   tsp. rubbed sage
  ½   tsp. lemon-pepper seasoning

1. Using a sharp knife, cut a pocket in each pork chop. In a large skillet, saute onion in butter until tender. Add spinach; cook until wilted. Stir in the stuffing mix, sour cream and sage.

2. Fill each chop with about ⅓ cup of the stuffing mixture; secure with toothpicks if necessary. Place on a greased 15x10x1-in. baking pan. Sprinkle with lemon pepper.
3. Bake the chops, uncovered, at 350° 35-40 minutes or until a thermometer reads 160°. Discard toothpicks.
1 serving: 320 cal., 21g fat (13g sat. fat), 74mg chol., 535mg sod., 18g carb. (4g sugars, 1g fiber), 11g pro.

TEST KITCHEN TIP

Baby spinach comes from the smallest leaves of flat-leaf spinach. At only 7 calories per cup, it packs a healthy dose of vitamins A and C plus folate, iron and calcium.

TUSCAN PARMESAN PORK CHOPS

These pork chops are all dressed up! First they're bathed in a zesty marinade, then they're coated with crunchy nuts and cheese for a special main dish with mass appeal.
—*Jeanne Holt, St. Paul, MN*

PREP: 10 min. + marinating
BAKE: 15 min. • **MAKES:** 4 servings

- ¾ cup zesty Italian salad dressing
- 2 Tbsp. Dijon mustard
- 4 bone-in pork loin chops (7 oz. each)
- ½ tsp. salt
- ¼ tsp. pepper
- ⅔ cup shredded Parmesan cheese
- ½ cup finely chopped hazelnuts

1. In a large shallow dish, combine the salad dressing and mustard. Add pork and turn to coat. Refrigerate, covered, 4 hours or overnight.
2. Preheat oven to 400°. Drain pork, discarding marinade. Sprinkle with salt and pepper.
3. In a shallow bowl, combine cheese and hazelnuts; coat chops with mixture. Place in a greased 15x10x1-in. baking pan. Bake until a thermometer inserted in center reads 145°, 14-18 minutes. Let stand 5 minutes before serving.

1 serving: 462 cal., 32g fat (9g sat. fat), 104mg chol., 935mg sod., 4g carb. (1g sugars, 1g fiber), 37g pro.

"Beautiful and tasty. I used a thicker pork chop and they took about 30-35 minutes to bake. But the crust was a beautiful golden brown, so it didn't hurt the dish."
—AUG-95, TASTEOFHOME.COM

MOTHER'S HAM CASSEROLE

MOTHER'S HAM CASSEROLE

One of my mother's favorite dishes, this ham casserole recipe always brings back fond memories of her when I prepare it. It's a terrific use of leftover ham from a holiday dinner.
—*Linda Childers, Murfreesboro, TN*

PREP: 35 min. • **BAKE:** 25 min.
MAKES: 6 servings

- 2 cups cubed peeled potatoes
- 1 large carrot, sliced
- 2 celery ribs, chopped
- 3 cups water
- 2 cups cubed fully cooked ham
- 2 Tbsp. chopped green pepper
- 2 tsp. finely chopped onion
- 7 Tbsp. butter, divided
- 3 Tbsp. all-purpose flour
- 1½ cups 2% milk
- ¾ tsp. salt
- ⅛ tsp. pepper
- 1 cup shredded cheddar cheese
- ½ cup soft bread crumbs

1. Preheat the oven to 375°. In a saucepan, bring the potatoes, carrot, celery and water to a boil. Reduce heat; cover and cook until tender, about 15 minutes. Drain.
2. In a large skillet, saute the ham, green pepper and onion in 3 Tbsp. butter until tender. Add the potato mixture. Transfer to a greased 1½-qt. baking dish.
3. In a large saucepan, melt the remaining 4 Tbsp. butter; stir in flour until smooth. Gradually whisk in milk, salt and pepper. Bring to a boil; cook and stir for 2 minutes or until thickened. Reduce the heat; add cheese and stir until melted.
4. Pour over ham mixture. Sprinkle with bread crumbs. Bake until heated through, 25-30 minutes.

Note: To make soft bread crumbs, tear bread into pieces and place in a food processor or blender. Cover and pulse until crumbs form. One slice of bread yields ½ to ¾ cup crumbs.

1 cup: 360 cal., 23g fat (14g sat. tat), 87mg chol., 1157mg sod., 21g carb. (5g sugars, 2g fiber), 18g pro.

❄ CAMPFIRE CASSEROLE

With three different meats and four kinds of beans, this casserole really satisfies. I often serve it with cheese-topped corn bread for a complete meal.
—Flo Rahn, Hillsboro, KS

PREP: 15 min. • **BAKE:** 1 hour
MAKES: 7 servings

- ⅓ cup packed brown sugar
- ½ cup ketchup
- 1 tsp. ground mustard
- ½ cup barbecue sauce
- ⅓ cup sugar
- ½ tsp. chili powder
- ½ tsp. salt
- ¼ tsp. pepper
- ½ lb. ground beef, cooked and drained
- ½ lb. bacon, cooked and crumbled
- ½ lb. fully cooked bratwurst links, cut into 1-in. slices
- 1 can (16 oz.) kidney beans, rinsed and drained
- 1 can (16 oz.) pork and beans
- 1 can (16 oz.) chili beans, undrained
- 1 can (15¼ oz.) lima beans, rinsed and drained

1. Preheat oven to 350°. In a large bowl, combine the first 8 ingredients. Add beef, bacon and bratwurst. Stir in beans. Pour into a greased 2-qt. baking dish.
2. Bake, uncovered, until heated through, about 1 hour.
Freeze option: Freeze cooled casserole in freezer containers. To use, partially thaw in refrigerator overnight. Heat through in a saucepan, stirring occasionally; add water or broth if necessary.
1 cup: 565 cal., 18g fat (6g sat. fat), 52mg chol., 1748mg sod., 77g carb. (37g sugars, 14g fiber), 26g pro.

APRICOT-FILLED PORK TENDERLOIN

This flavorful main course is a great company offering. The tenderloin tastes wonderful and looks so pretty when it's sliced to reveal a golden apricot center. In the decades I've been using this recipe, it has never failed me.
—Jo Ann Hettel, Bushnell, FL

PREP: 10 min. + marinating
BAKE: 30 min. + standing
MAKES: 6 servings

- 2 pork tenderloins (1 lb. each)
- 1 pkg. (6 oz.) dried apricots

MARINADE

- ⅓ cup sweet-and-sour salad dressing
- ¼ cup packed brown sugar
- 3 Tbsp. teriyaki sauce
- 2 Tbsp. ketchup
- 1 tsp. Dijon mustard
- 1 onion slice, separated into rings
- 1 garlic clove, minced
- 2 tsp. minced fresh gingerroot
- ¼ tsp. pepper
- ⅛ tsp. pumpkin pie spice

1. Make a lengthwise cut three-quarters of the way through each tenderloin; pound to flatten evenly. Set aside 3 apricots for marinade. Stuff remaining apricots into pork to within ½ in. of ends; secure with toothpicks or kitchen string.
2. In a blender, combine the remaining ingredients and reserved apricots. Cover and process until smooth; set aside ⅓ cup. Pour the remaining marinade into a bowl or shallow dish; add the tenderloins and turn to coat. Refrigerate for at least 2 hours, turning meat often. Preheat oven to 400°.
3. Drain pork, discarding marinade. Place tenderloins in a greased 13x9-in. baking dish. Drizzle with the reserved marinade. Bake, uncovered, 30-35 minutes or until a thermometer reads 145°. Let stand for 10 minutes before slicing.
4 oz. cooked pork: 291 cal., 5g fat (2g sat. fat), 85mg chol., 428mg sod., 29g carb. (26g sugars, 2g fiber), 32g pro.

CAMPFIRE CASSEROLE

Fish & Seafood

SHEET-PAN SHRIMP FAJITAS

I love easy, weeknight dinners like this. This dinner comes together quickly and is customizable with your favorite toppings.
—*Carla Hubl, Hastings, NE*

PREP: 30 min. • **COOK:** 20 min.
MAKES: 6 servings

1½ lbs. uncooked shrimp (31-40 per lb.), peeled and deveined
1 each medium green, sweet red and yellow peppers, cut into ½-in. strips
1 sweet onion, cut into ½-in. strips
2 garlic cloves, minced
2 Tbsp. olive oil
2 tsp. chili powder
1 tsp. ground cumin
¾ tsp. salt
12 corn tortillas (6 in.), warmed
   Optional: Lime wedges, crema, fresh cilantro and sliced avocado

1. Preheat oven to 425°. In a large bowl, combine the shrimp, peppers, onion and garlic. Drizzle with olive oil; sprinkle with the chili powder, cumin and salt. Toss to coat. Spread evenly between 2 greased 15x10x1-in. baking pans.
2. Roast 10 minutes, rotating pans halfway through cooking. Remove pans from oven; preheat broiler.
3. Broil shrimp mixture, 1 pan at a time, 3-4 in. from heat until vegetables are lightly browned and shrimp turn pink, 4-5 minutes. Serve in tortillas with toppings as desired.

2 fajitas: 280 cal., 8g fat (1g sat. fat), 138mg chol., 484mg sod., 31g carb. (5g sugars, 5g fiber), 22g pro. **Diabetic exchanges:** 3 lean meat, 1½ starch, 1 vegetable, 1 fat.

SHEET-PAN SHRIMP FAJITAS

**SHRIMP DE JONGHE
TRIANGLES**

SHRIMP DE JONGHE TRIANGLES

Shrimp De Jonghe was invented in Chicago. It is usually baked and served in a casserole dish, but my version is a handheld. The shrimp filling is perfect with the crunchy pastry dough.
—*Arlene Erlbach, Morton Grove, IL*

PREP: 30 min. • BAKE: 20 min.
MAKES: 4 servings

- 5 Tbsp. butter, divided
- ½ cup panko bread crumbs
- 1 tsp. garlic powder, divided
- 1 lb. uncooked shrimp (31-40 per lb.), peeled and deveined, tails removed
- ⅔ cup spreadable garlic and herb cream cheese, divided
- ½ cup sherry or chicken broth
- ¼ cup minced fresh parsley
- ½ tsp. dried tarragon
- ⅛ tsp. ground nutmeg
- 1 sheet frozen puff pastry, thawed
- 1 large egg, room temperature, beaten
  Lemon wedges, optional

1. Preheat oven to 400°. In a large skillet, melt 2 Tbsp. butter over medium heat. Add bread crumbs and ¼ tsp. garlic powder. Cook and stir until toasted, 3-4 minutes. Transfer to a small bowl; wipe pan clean.
2. In the same skillet, melt remaining 3 Tbsp. butter over medium heat. Add shrimp and remaining ¾ tsp. garlic powder; cook and stir until shrimp turn pink, 6-8 minutes. Reduce heat to low; stir in ⅓ cup cream cheese, sherry, parsley, tarragon and nutmeg until combined. Remove from the heat.
3. On a lightly floured surface, unfold the puff pastry. Roll into a 12-in. square. Cut into four 6-in. squares. Spread remaining ⅓ cup cream cheese over the squares to within ½ in. of the edges. Using a slotted spoon, place about ½ cup shrimp mixture on 1 side of each square. Fold the dough over filling. Press edges with a fork to seal. Brush beaten egg over tops. Prick tops with a fork. Sprinkle with reserved crumb mixture, pressing lightly to adhere. Place on a parchment-lined baking sheet. Bake until golden brown, 20-25 minutes. If desired, serve with lemon wedges.
1 serving: 616 cal., 37g fat (15g sat. fat), 208mg chol., 586mg sod., 43g carb. (2g sugars, 5g fiber), 26g pro.

TEST KITCHEN TIP
The triangles can be cut in half to make smaller portions to serve as an appetizer.

DIJON-CRUSTED FISH

CILANTRO-TOPPED SALMON

This has been a favorite with everyone who has tried it. A tongue-tingling cilantro-lime sauce compliments tender salmon fillets in the pleasing entree.
—*Nancy Culbert, Whitehorn, CA*

- -

TAKES: 30 min. • **MAKES:** 6 servings

- 1½ lbs. salmon fillets
- ¼ cup lime juice divided
- ½ cup minced fresh cilantro
- 3 Tbsp. thinly sliced green onions
- 1 Tbsp. finely chopped jalapeno pepper
- 1 Tbsp. olive oil
- ¼ tsp. salt
- ⅛ tsp. pepper
  Optional: lime wedge, sliced jalapeno and cilantro sprigs

1. Preheat oven to 350°. Place salmon skin side down in a 13-in. x 9-in. baking dish coated with cooking spray. Drizzle with 1½ tsp. lime juice.
2. In a small bowl, combine cilantro, onions, jalapeno, oil, salt, pepper and remaining lime juice. Spread over the salmon. Bake, uncovered, until fish just begins to flakes easily with a fork, 20-25 minutes. If desired, serve with lime wedges, sliced jalapeno and cilantro sprigs.
Note: Wear disposable gloves when cutting hot peppers; the oils can burn skin. Avoid touching your face.
3 oz. cooked salmon: 232 cal., 15g fat (3g sat. fat), 67mg chol., 166mg sod., 1g carb. (0 sugars, 0 fiber), 23g pro. **Diabetic exchanges:** 3 lean meat, 1 fat.

DIJON-CRUSTED FISH

Dijon mustard, Parmesan cheese and a hint of horseradish give this toasty fish lots of flavor. The preparation is super easy, and it takes just 5 to 7 minutes to get four delicious servings ready for the oven.
—*Scott Schmidtke, Chicago, IL*

- -

TAKES: 25 min. • **MAKES:** 4 servings

- 3 Tbsp. reduced-fat mayonnaise
- 1 Tbsp. lemon juice
- 2 tsp. Dijon mustard
- 1 tsp. prepared horseradish
- 2 Tbsp. grated Parmesan cheese, divided
- 4 tilapia fillets (5 oz. each)
- ¼ cup dry bread crumbs
- 2 tsp. butter, melted

1. Preheat the oven to 425°. Mix the first 4 ingredients and 1 Tbsp. cheese. Place tilapia on a baking sheet coated with cooking spray; spread evenly with mayonnaise mixture.
2. Toss bread crumbs with melted butter and the remaining cheese; sprinkle over fillets. Bake until fish just begins to flake easily with a fork, 12-15 minutes.
1 fillet: 214 cal., 8g fat (3g sat. fat), 80mg chol., 292mg sod., 7g carb. (1g sugars, 1g fiber), 28g pro. **Diabetic exchanges:** 4 lean meat, 1½ fat, ½ starch.

TEST KITCHEN TIP
Tilapia is low in calories, rich in high-quality proteins and a good source of many B vitamins.

CILANTRO-TOPPED
SALMON

SHRIMP IN CREAM SAUCE

My family enjoys this shrimp dish on Christmas Eve. I serve it over golden egg noodles.
—*Jane Birch, Edison, NJ*

TAKES: 30 min. • **MAKES:** 8 servings

- 2 Tbsp. butter, melted
- ⅓ cup all-purpose flour
- 1½ cups chicken broth
- 4 garlic cloves, minced
- 1 cup heavy whipping cream
- ½ cup minced fresh parsley
- 2 tsp. paprika
  Salt and pepper to taste
- 2 lbs. large uncooked shrimp, peeled and deveined
  Hot cooked noodles or rice

1. Preheat the oven to 400°. In a small saucepan, melt butter; stir in the flour until smooth. Gradually add broth and garlic. Bring to a boil; cook and stir until thickened, 2 minutes. Remove from the heat. Stir in the cream, parsley, paprika, salt and pepper.

2. Butterfly shrimp, by cutting lengthwise almost in half, but leaving shrimp attached at opposite side. Spread to butterfly. Place cut side down in a greased 13-in. x 9-in. baking dish. Pour the cream sauce over shrimp. Bake, uncovered, until shrimp turn pink, 15-18 minutes. Serve with noodles or rice.

1 serving: 240 cal., 15g fat (9g sat. fat), 216mg chol., 410mg sod., 6g carb. (1g sugars, 0 fiber), 20g pro.

ALMOND-TOPPED FISH

A co-worker gave me this recipe, but I didn't try it until recently. What a mistake it was to wait! It's easier than dipping, coating and frying—and the flavor is outstanding. Once you have tried this tender fish, you'll never go back to fried.
—*Heidi Kirsch, Waterloo, IA*

TAKES: 30 min. • **MAKES:** 4 servings

- 1 Tbsp. butter
- 1 small onion, thinly sliced
- 4 cod or haddock fillets (6 oz. each)
- 1 tsp. seasoned salt
- ½ tsp. dill weed
- ¼ tsp. pepper
- ¼ cup grated Parmesan cheese
- ¼ cup reduced-fat mayonnaise
- 1 Tbsp. minced fresh parsley
- 1 Tbsp. lemon juice
- 2 Tbsp. sliced almonds, toasted

1. Place butter in a 13x9-in. baking dish; heat in a 400° oven until melted. Spread butter over bottom of dish; cover with the sliced onion.

2. Arrange the fish over onion; sprinkle with salt, dill and pepper. Combine the Parmesan cheese, mayonnaise, parsley and lemon juice; spread over fish.

3. Bake, uncovered, at 400° until fish flakes easily with a fork, 18-20 minutes. Sprinkle with almonds.

1 fillet: 220 cal., 9g fat (2g sat. fat), 74mg chol., 658mg sod., 5g carb. (2g sugars, 1g fiber), 29g pro. **Diabetic exchanges:** 4 lean meat, 2 fat.

SHRIMP IN CREAM SAUCE

ROASTED FISH
WITH LIGHT
HERB SAUCE

CRAB-STUFFED CATFISH

My family was not big on fish...until I
made this dish. I stuff catfish fillets with
a delicious mixture of crabmeat, cheese,
seasoned bread crumbs and mayonnaise.
—*Joy McConaghy, Moline, IL*

PREP: 10 min. • **BAKE:** 25 min.
MAKES: 2 servings

- 1   **can (6 oz.) crabmeat, drained, flaked and cartilage removed or 1 cup imitation crabmeat, flaked**
- 3   **Tbsp. seasoned bread crumbs**
- 2   **Tbsp. shredded Monterey Jack cheese**
- 2   **Tbsp. butter, melted**
- 1½ **tsp. mayonnaise**
- ⅛   **tsp. salt, optional**
- ⅛   **tsp. pepper**
      Dash cayenne pepper
- 2   **catfish or whitefish fillets (6 oz. each)**
- ⅛   **tsp. paprika**

Preheat oven to 425°. In a bowl, combine
the first 8 ingredients. Cut each fillet
in half widthwise; place 2 halves in a
greased 8-in. square baking dish. Press
crab mixture onto fillets; top with the
remaining halves. Sprinkle with paprika.
Bake, uncovered, until fish just begins to
flake easily with a fork, 22-26 minutes.
1 serving: 437 cal., 23g fat (8g sat. fat),
182mg chol., 611mg sod., 8g carb.
(0 sugars, 0 fiber), 48g pro.

*"This is wonderful. I use cheddar or
mozzarella cheese because I always
have them in the fridge. It's rich and
filling—add sauteed spinach and a
salad and you're done!"*
—BROWNS19FAN, TASTEOFHOME.COM

ROASTED FISH WITH LIGHT HERB SAUCE

An easy sauce with the flavors of Provence
makes fish fillets into a meal worthy of
company. I like to add steamed rice and
sautèed spinach to complete the plate.
The recipe works with many types of fish
such as cod, flounder, sole, trout, tilapia
or catfish.
—*Suzanne Banfield, Basking Ridge, NJ*

TAKES: 25 min. • **MAKES:** 4 servings

- 4   **haddock fillets (6 oz. each)**
- 2   **tsp. olive oil**
- ½   **tsp. salt**
- ½   **tsp. pepper**
- 1   **shallot, thinly sliced**
- ½   **tsp. herbes de Provence or dried rosemary, crushed**
- 1   **Tbsp. butter**
- ¼   **cup marinade for chicken**
- 2   **Tbsp. half-and-half cream**

1. Place fillets in a greased 15x10x1-in.
baking pan. Brush with oil; sprinkle with
salt and pepper. Bake at 450° until fish
flakes easily with a fork, 14-18 minutes.
2. Meanwhile, in a small saucepan over
medium heat, cook and stir shallot and
herbes de Provence in butter until shallot
is tender. Stir in marinade for chicken;
cook and stir for 1 minute. Add cream;
cook and stir 1 minute longer. Spoon
over fish.
Note: Look for herbes de Provence in the
spice aisle. This recipe was tested with
Lea & Perrins Marinade for Chicken.
1 serving: 222 cal., 7g fat (3g sat. fat),
109mg chol., 726mg sod., 5g carb. (3g
sugars, 0 fiber), 33g pro. **Diabetic
exchanges:** 4 lean meat, 1 fat.

MOROCCAN
SALMON

MOROCCAN SALMON

If you're trying to add more fish to your diet, here's a simple recipe for baked salmon. Here, salmon is topped with sauteed onion, tomatoes, golden raisins and spices, transforming an ordinary weeknight meal into a culinary adventure.
—Taste of Home *Test Kitchen*

- -

PREP: 15 min. • **BAKE:** 25 min.
MAKES: 4 servings

    2   cups sliced onions, separated
        into rings
    1   Tbsp. canola oil
    4   garlic cloves, minced
    2   cups sliced plum tomatoes
    ¼   cup golden raisins
    ½   tsp. salt
    ½   tsp. ground cumin
    ½   tsp. ground turmeric
    ⅛   tsp. ground cinnamon
    4   salmon fillets (4 oz. each)
        Hot cooked couscous, optional

1. Preheat the oven to 375°. In a large nonstick skillet, saute the onions in oil until tender, 5 minutes. Add the garlic; cook 1 minute longer. Add tomatoes, raisins and seasonings; cook and stir 5 minutes longer.
2. Place salmon in a 13-in. x 9-in. baking dish coated with cooking spray. Top with onion mixture.
3. Cover and bake just until fish begins to flake easily with a fork, 25-30 minutes. If desired, serve with couscous.
1 serving: 311 cal., 16g fat (3g sat. fat), 67mg chol., 374mg sod., 17g carb. (12g sugars, 3g fiber), 24g pro.

DID YOU KNOW?

You can tell whether salmon is wild-caught or farm-raised depending on its appearance. Wild-caught is more lean, red in color and has thin stripes of fat, while farm-raised is thicker, orange in color and has large stripes of fat.

KATHY'S SMOKED SALMON PIZZA

KATHY'S SMOKED SALMON PIZZA

This is great for a light supper. It's easy, too, so put away that frozen pizza!
—*Kathy Petty, Portland, OR*

- -

TAKES: 25 min. • **MAKES:** 8 servings

    1   prebaked 12-in. thin pizza crust
    ½   cup ranch salad dressing
    4   slices provolone cheese, cut in half
    6   slices tomato
    1   pkg. (3 oz.) smoked salmon or lox
    ½   cup crumbled feta cheese
        Chopped chives, optional

1. Preheat oven to 425°. Place crust on an ungreased 14-in. pizza pan. Spread with ranch dressing; top with provolone cheese. Arrange tomato and salmon over provolone; sprinkle with feta cheese.
2. Bake until the cheese is melted and golden, 15-20 minutes. If desired, top with chopped chives.
1 piece: 231 cal., 12g fat (4g sat. fat), 19mg chol., 584mg sod., 20g carb. (2g sugars, 1g fiber), 10g pro.

BAKED CREOLE SHRIMP

A friend shared this recipe for freshly-caught shrimp. Here in the South, we bake the shrimp unpeeled.
—*Brenda Cox, Reidsville, NC*

- -

PREP: 20 min. • **BAKE:** 15 min.
MAKES: 6 servings

    2½ lbs. uncooked medium shrimp,
        peeled and deveined
    1   cup butter, cubed
    2   medium lemons, thinly sliced
    3   Tbsp. Worcestershire sauce
    4½ tsp. Creole seasoning
    3   tsp. pepper
    1½ tsp. minced chives
    1½ tsp. cider vinegar
    ½   tsp. salt
    ½   tsp. dried rosemary, crushed
    ½   tsp. hot pepper sauce

1. Preheat oven to 400°. Place shrimp in a 3-qt. baking dish. In a small saucepan, bring remaining ingredients to a boil over medium heat. Pour over the shrimp.
2. Bake, uncovered, until the shrimp turn pink, 15-20 minutes. Serve with a slotted spoon.
1 serving: 424 cal., 32g fat (19g sat. fat), 362mg chol., 1412mg sod., 4g carb. (0 sugars, 1g fiber), 30g pro.

TUNA SPAGHETTI PIE

I'm a real pasta fan and I like fish as well, so I decided to combine the two. When my granddaughters are over, I make this dish in tart tins, so each girl can have her own pie. That works for both pint-size and senior-size appetites.
—*Ruth Lee, Troy, ON*

- -

PREP: 30 min. • **BAKE:** 35 min.
MAKES: 6 servings

- 4 oz. uncooked spaghetti, broken into 2-in. pieces
- ¼ cup grated Parmesan cheese
- 1 large egg, lightly beaten
- 1 tsp. butter
- 1 garlic clove, minced
- ¼ tsp. salt
- ⅛ tsp. pepper

FILLING

- 1 Tbsp. finely chopped onion
- 1 tsp. butter, melted
- 1 Tbsp. all-purpose flour
- ½ tsp. salt
- ¼ tsp. celery salt
- ¼ tsp. garlic and herb seasoning
- ⅛ tsp. pepper
- ¼ cup milk
- ¼ cup sour cream
- 1 large egg, lightly beaten
- 1 can (6 oz.) tuna, drained and flaked
- ¼ cup grated Parmesan cheese, divided
- 1 small tomato, thinly sliced
  Minced fresh parsley

1. Cook spaghetti according to package directions. Preheat oven to 350°.
2. In a large bowl, combine the spaghetti, Parmesan, egg, butter, garlic, salt and pepper. Press onto bottom and up side of a greased 9-in. pie plate.
3. In a large skillet, saute onion in butter until tender. Remove from the heat. Stir in the flour and seasonings until blended.
4. In a small bowl, beat together the milk, sour cream and egg. Stir into the onion mixture until blended. Fold in the tuna; spoon into crust. Sprinkle half of the Parmesan over pie. Arrange tomato slices over cheese; sprinkle with the remaining Parmesan.
5. Bake until crust is golden and filling is puffy, 35-40 minutes. Sprinkle with the parsley. Let stand for 5-10 minutes before cutting.

1 piece: 216 cal., 9g fat (5g sat. fat), 99mg chol., 636mg sod., 17g carb. (2g sugars, 1g fiber), 16g pro.

RED SNAPPER WITH ORANGE SAUCE

A tangy orange sauce, seasoned with garlic and ginger, really brings out the best in these red snapper fillets.
—*Barbara Nowakowski, Mesa, AZ*

- -

TAKES: 30 min. • **MAKES:** 6 servings

- 2 lbs. red snapper fillets
- ¼ tsp. salt
- ⅛ tsp. pepper
- 2 garlic cloves, minced
- 1 Tbsp. butter
- 3 Tbsp. orange juice
- 1 tsp. grated orange zest

ORANGE SAUCE

- 1 garlic clove, peeled
- 2 Tbsp. butter
- 3 Tbsp. orange juice
- ⅛ tsp. ground ginger
- 2 Tbsp. minced fresh parsley

1. Preheat oven to 400°. Place the fish in a single layer in a 13x9-in. baking dish coated with cooking spray; sprinkle with salt and pepper. In a small saucepan over medium heat, cook the garlic in butter for 1 minute; pour over fish. Drizzle with the orange juice; sprinkle with orange zest. Bake, uncovered, until fish just begins to flake easily with a fork, 10-15 minutes.

2. In a small saucepan over medium heat, cook garlic in butter until golden brown, 2-3 minutes. Discard garlic. Stir orange juice and ginger into butter; heat through. Cut fish into serving-size pieces; top with orange sauce and parsley.

1 serving: 206 cal., 8g fat (4g sat. fat), 68mg chol., 204mg sod., 2g carb. (1g sugars, 0 fiber), 30g pro. **Diabetic exchanges:** 4½ lean meat, meat, 1 fat.

HADDOCK EN PAPILLOTE

This is a terrific dish for entertaining. It's easy to prepare, yet impressive. You can even assemble the bundles earlier in the day and then pop them in the oven 15 minutes before dinner.
—*Amanda Singleton, Kingsport, TN*

- -

TAKES: 30 min. • **MAKES:** 4 servings

- 1½ lbs. haddock or cod fillets, cut into 4 portions
- 4 Tbsp. dry white wine
- 2 tsp. snipped fresh dill or 1 tsp. dill weed
- 1 tsp. grated lemon zest
- ½ cup julienned carrot
- ½ cup julienned zucchini
- 4 Tbsp. slivered almonds, toasted
- 4 Tbsp. butter

1. Preheat oven to 375°. Place each fillet portion on a piece of parchment or heavy-duty foil (about 12 in. square). Drizzle fillets with wine; sprinkle with dill and lemon zest. Top with carrot, zucchini and almonds; dot with butter. Fold foil or parchment around fish, sealing tightly.
2. Place packets on a baking sheet. Bake until fish just begins to flake easily with a fork, 10-12 minutes. Open foil carefully to allow steam to escape.

1 packet: 311 cal., 16g fat (8g sat. fat), 129mg chol., 219mg sod., 4g carb. (2g sugars, 1g fiber), 34g pro.

TEST KITCHEN TIP

Looking for a knockout grilled supper? Make the fish in foil packets and toss on the grill for about 10 minutes. Any meaty fish will work nicely. Cod is a good substitute for the haddock.

**HADDOCK
EN PAPILLOTE**

❄ AVOCADO CRAB CAKES

I created this recipe because I like the pairing of crab and avocado; plus I wanted a baked rather than fried crab cake. These come out crisp and golden with great flavor. It's almost impossible to tell that they aren't fried.
—Virginia Anthony, Jacksonville, FL

PREP: 40 min. • **BAKE:** 10 min.
MAKES: 4 servings

- 1 medium ripe avocado, peeled and finely chopped
- 1 Tbsp. lemon juice
- 1 cup cornflake crumbs, divided
- 1 large egg, beaten
- 2 Tbsp. finely chopped onion
- 2 Tbsp. reduced-fat mayonnaise
- 1 Tbsp. Dijon mustard
- 1½ tsp. snipped fresh dill or ½ tsp. dill weed
- 1 tsp. seafood seasoning
- ⅛ tsp. salt
- ⅛ tsp. cayenne pepper
- 3 cans (6 oz. each) lump crabmeat, drained
  Cooking spray
- 1 tsp. paprika

SAUCE
- 1 medium ripe avocado, peeled
- ¼ cup reduced-fat mayonnaise
- ¼ cup reduced-fat sour cream
- 1 Tbsp. lemon juice
- 1 tsp. snipped fresh dill or ½ tsp. dill weed
- 1 tsp. seafood seasoning
- ⅛ tsp. salt
- ⅛ tsp. cayenne pepper

1. Preheat oven to 450°. In a small bowl, combine avocado and lemon juice; toss to coat. In another small bowl, combine ¼ cup cornflake crumbs, egg, onion, mayonnaise, mustard, dill, seafood seasoning, salt and cayenne. Fold in crab and avocado mixture.
2. Place remaining ¾ cup cornflake crumbs in a shallow bowl. Drop scant ⅓ cup crab mixture into crumbs. Gently coat and shape into a ¾-in.-thick patty; place on a baking sheet. Repeat with the remaining mixture.
3. Spritz crab cakes with cooking spray; sprinkle with paprika. Bake until golden brown, 10-12 minutes.

4. For sauce, in a small bowl, mash the avocado. Stir in remaining ingredients; serve with crab cakes.
Freeze option: Freeze cooled crab cakes in freezer containers, separating layers with waxed paper. To use, reheat on a baking sheet in a preheated 325° oven until heated through.
2 crab cakes with ¼ cup sauce: 474 cal., 25g fat (4g sat. fat), 179mg chol., 1369mg sod., 32g carb. (5g sugars, 6g fiber), 32g pro.

OVER-THE-BORDER SHRIMP ENCHILADAS

These enchiladas have a bit of a kick, thanks to chili powder and green chiles, but the creamy sauce balances it all.
—Beverly O'Ferrall, Linkwood, MD

PREP: 20 min. • **BAKE:** 20 min.
MAKES: 8 servings

- 1 medium onion, chopped
- 2 Tbsp. olive oil
- ¾ lb. uncooked medium shrimp, peeled and deveined
- 1 can (4 oz.) chopped green chiles

OVER-THE-BORDER SHRIMP ENCHILADAS

- ½ tsp. chili powder
- ¼ tsp. salt
- ¼ tsp. ground cumin
- ¼ tsp. pepper
- 1 pkg. (8 oz.) cream cheese, cubed
- 8 flour tortillas (8 in.), warmed
- 1½ cups chunky salsa
- 1½ cups shredded Monterey Jack cheese

1. In a large skillet, saute onion in oil until tender. Add the shrimp, green chiles, chili powder, salt, cumin and pepper. Cook for 2-3 minutes or until shrimp turn pink. Stir in cream cheese until melted.
2. Place ⅓ cup shrimp mixture down the center of each tortilla. Roll up and place seam side down in a greased 13x9-in. baking dish. Pour the salsa over the top; sprinkle with Monterey Jack cheese. Bake, uncovered, at 350° for 20-25 minutes or until heated through.
1 enchilada: 417 cal., 23g fat (11g sat. fat), 102mg chol., 809mg sod., 32g carb. (3g sugars, 1g fiber), 19g pro.

TILAPIA FLORENTINE

Get a little more heart-healthy fish into your weekly diet with this quick and easy entree. Topped with spinach and a splash of lime, it's sure to become a favorite!
—*Melanie Bachman, Ulysses, PA*

TAKES: 30 min. • **MAKES:** 4 servings

- 1 pkg. (6 oz.) fresh baby spinach
- 6 tsp. canola oil, divided
- 4 tilapia fillets (4 oz. each)
- 2 Tbsp. lemon juice
- 2 tsp. garlic-herb seasoning blend
- 1 large egg, room temperature, lightly beaten
- ½ cup part-skim ricotta cheese
- ¼ cup grated Parmesan cheese
  Lemon wedge, optional

1. Preheat oven to 375°. In a large nonstick skillet, cook spinach in 4 tsp. oil until wilted; drain. Meanwhile, place tilapia in a greased 13-in. x 9-in. baking dish. Drizzle with the lemon juice and remaining 2 tsp. oil. Sprinkle the tilapia with seasoning blend.
2. In a small bowl, combine the egg, ricotta cheese and spinach; spoon over fillets. Sprinkle with Parmesan cheese.
3. Bake until fish just begins to flake easily with a fork, 15-20 minutes. If desired, serve with lemon wedges and additional Parmesan cheese.
1 serving: 249 cal., 13g fat (4g sat. fat), 122mg chol., 307mg sod., 4g carb. (1g sugars, 1g fiber), 29g pro.

TILAPIA FLORENTINE

TUNA NOODLE CASSEROLE

Families are sure to love the creamy texture and comforting taste of this traditional tuna casserole that goes together in a jiffy. I serve it with a green salad and warm rolls for supper.
—*Ruby Wells, Cynthiana, KY*

PREP: 20 min. • **BAKE:** 30 min.
MAKES: 4 servings

- 1 can (10¾ oz.) reduced-fat reduced-sodium condensed cream of celery soup, undiluted
- ½ cup fat-free milk
- 2 cups yolk-free noodles, cooked
- 1 cup frozen peas, thawed
- 1 can (5 oz.) light water-packed tuna, drained and flaked
- 1 jar (2 oz.) diced pimientos, drained
- 2 Tbsp. dry bread crumbs
- 1 Tbsp. butter, melted

1. Preheat oven to 400°. In a large bowl, combine soup and milk until smooth. Add the noodles, peas, tuna and pimientos; mix well.
2. Pour into a 1½-qt. baking dish coated with cooking spray. Bake, uncovered, for 25 minutes. Toss the bread crumbs and butter; sprinkle over the top. Bake until golden brown, 5 minutes longer.
1 cup: 238 cal., 5g fat (2g sat. fat), 27mg chol., 475mg sod., 32g carb. (6g sugars, 4g fiber), 15g pro. **Diabetic exchanges:** 2 starch, 2 lean meat, ½ fat.

LEMONY PARSLEY BAKED COD

If there's one thing I hate, it's overcooking a good piece of fish. The trick is to cook it at a high temperature for a short amount of time. It'll keep the fish moist and tender.
—*Sherry Day, Pinckney, MI*

TAKES: 25 min. • **MAKES:** 4 servings

3 Tbsp. minced fresh parsley
2 Tbsp. lemon juice
1 Tbsp. grated lemon zest
1 Tbsp. olive oil
2 garlic cloves, minced
¼ tsp. salt
⅛ tsp. pepper
4 cod fillets (6 oz. each)
2 green onions, chopped

Preheat the oven to 400°. In a small bowl, mix the first 7 ingredients. Place cod in an ungreased 11x7-in. baking dish; top with parsley mixture. Sprinkle with green onions. Bake, covered, until fish flakes easily with a fork 10-15 minutes.
1 fillet: 161 cal., 4g fat (1g sat. fat), 65mg chol., 95mg sod., 2g carb. (0 sugars, 1g fiber), 27g pro. **Diabetic exchanges:** 4 lean meat, ½ fat.

PISTACHIO SALMON

This simple salmon gets its crunch from a coating of crushed pistachios, panko bread crumbs and Parmesan cheese. Add steamed veggies and some rice and it's dinnertime!
—*Anthony Oraczewski, Port St. Lucie, FL*

TAKES: 25 min. • **MAKES:** 4 servings

⅓ cup pistachios, finely chopped
¼ cup panko bread crumbs
¼ cup grated Parmesan cheese
1 salmon fillet (1 lb.)
½ tsp. salt
¼ tsp. pepper

1. Preheat the oven to 400°. In a shallow bowl, toss pistachios with bread crumbs and cheese.

2. Place salmon on a greased foil-lined 15x10x1-in. pan, skin side down; sprinkle with salt and pepper. Top with pistachio mixture, pressing to adhere. Bake fish, uncovered, until it just begins to flake easily with a fork, 15-20 minutes.
3 oz. cooked fish: 269 cal., 17g fat (3g sat. fat), 61mg chol., 497mg sod., 6g carb. (1g sugars, 1g fiber), 23g pro. **Diabetic exchanges:** 3 lean meat, 1 fat, ½ starch.

TEST KITCHEN TIP
Save any leftover pistachios for snacks. A serving (about 50 nuts) packs 6 grams of protein, 3 grams of fiber and over 10 percent of the B6, thiamine, copper and phosphorous we need daily.

PISTACHIO SALMON

LEMON-PEPPER TILAPIA

SEAFOOD-STUFFED SHELLS

Even if you don't like fish, chances are you'll still love this dish.
—*Ezra Weaver, Wolcott, NY*

- -

PREP: 35 min. • **BAKE:** 30 min.
MAKES: 10 servings

30	uncooked jumbo pasta shells
½	lb. bay scallops
2	tsp. butter
2	large eggs
2	cups cream-style cottage cheese
1	carton (15 oz.) ricotta cheese
½	tsp. ground nutmeg
¼	tsp. pepper
1	can (6 oz.) lump crabmeat, drained
¾	lb. cooked small shrimp, peeled and deveined
1	jar (15 oz.) Alfredo sauce

1. Cook pasta shells according to package directions. Preheat oven to 350°.
2. Meanwhile, in a small skillet over medium heat, cook scallops in butter until opaque, 1-2 minutes. Transfer to a large bowl.
3. Place 1 egg and half the cottage cheese, ricotta, nutmeg and pepper in a blender; cover and process until smooth. Add to scallops. Repeat with remaining egg, cottage cheese, ricotta, nutmeg and pepper. Add to scallops. Stir in the crab and shrimp.
4. Stuff cooked pasta shells with the seafood mixture. Place in a greased 13x9-in. baking dish; top with Alfredo sauce. Cover and bake until bubbly, 30-35 minutes.

3 stuffed shells: 356 cal., 13g fat (8g sat. fat), 150mg chol., 641mg sod., 29g carb. (4g sugars, 1g fiber), 30g pro.

"These tasted great! Remember to cook shells in plenty of water to avoid sticking together."
—SKYWAITRESS, TASTEOFHOME.COM

🍎 LEMON-PEPPER TILAPIA

I usually have the ingredients on hand for this lemony dish that's ready in a jiff. I use tilapia, but this method peps up any white fish.
—*Jill Thomas, Washington, IN*

- -

TAKES: 20 min. • **MAKES:** 6 servings

6	tilapia fillets (6 oz. each)
2	Tbsp. butter
2	tsp. grated lemon zest
1	Tbsp. lemon juice
1	tsp. garlic salt
1	tsp. paprika
½	tsp. freshly ground pepper
¼	cup minced fresh parsley

1. Preheat oven to 425°. Place tilapia in a 15x10x1-in. baking pan. In a microwave, melt butter; stir in lemon zest and juice. Drizzle over fish; sprinkle with garlic salt, paprika and pepper.
2. Bake, uncovered, until fish just begins to flake easily with a fork, 10-12 minutes. Sprinkle with parsley.

1 fillet: 177 cal., 5g fat (3g sat. fat), 93mg chol., 254mg sod., 1g carb. (0 sugars, 0 fiber), 32g pro. **Diabetic exchanges:** 5 lean meat, 1 fat.

Bonus:
Vegetarian Mains

**TOMATO
BAGUETTE PIZZA**

TOMATO BAGUETTE PIZZA

When my tomatoes ripen all at once, I use them up in simple recipes like this one. Cheesy baguette pizzas, served with a salad, are ideal for lunch—and they make standout appetizers, too.
—*Lorraine Caland, Shuniah, ON*

PREP: 25 min. • **BAKE:** 10 min.
MAKES: 6 servings

  2 **tsp. olive oil**
  8 **oz. sliced fresh mushrooms**
  2 **medium onions, halved and sliced**
  2 **garlic cloves, minced**
  ½ **tsp. Italian seasoning**
  ¼ **tsp. salt**
     Dash pepper
  1 **French bread baguette (10½ oz.), halved lengthwise**
1½ **cups shredded part-skim mozzarella cheese**
  ¾ **cup thinly sliced fresh basil leaves, divided**
  3 **medium tomatoes, sliced**

1. Preheat oven to 400°. In a large skillet, heat oil over medium-high heat; saute the mushrooms and onions until tender. Add the garlic and seasonings; cook and stir 1 minute.
2. Place the baguette halves on a baking sheet, cut side up; sprinkle with half the cheese and ½ cup basil . Top with the mushroom mixture, the tomatoes and remaining cheese.
3. Bake for 10-15 minutes or until cheese is melted. Sprinkle with the remaining basil. Cut each half into 3 portions.
1 piece: 260 cal., 7g fat (4g sat. fat), 18mg chol., 614mg sod., 36g carb. (5g sugars, 3g fiber), 13g pro. **Diabetic exchanges:** 2 starch, 1 vegetable, 1 medium-fat meat.

CARIBBEAN POTATO SOUP

CONTEST-WINNING BLACK BEAN SOUP

Fill your tummy without expanding your waistline when you dig into a bowl of this soup. If you want to add meat, use lean beef or chicken to pack in extra protein.
—*Angee Owens, Lufkin, TX*

PREP: 20 min. • **COOK:** 25 min.
MAKES: 8 servings (2 qt.)

- 3 cans (15 oz. each) black beans, rinsed and drained, divided
- 3 celery ribs with leaves, chopped
- 1 large onion, chopped
- 1 medium sweet red pepper, chopped
- 1 jalapeno pepper, seeded and chopped
- 2 Tbsp. olive oil
- 4 garlic cloves, minced
- 2 cans (14½ oz. each) reduced-sodium vegetable broth
- 1 can (14½ oz.) diced tomatoes with green peppers and onions, undrained
- 3 tsp. ground cumin
- 1½ tsp. ground coriander
- 1 tsp. Louisiana-style hot sauce
- ¼ tsp. pepper
- 1 bay leaf
- 1 tsp. lime juice
- ½ cup reduced-fat sour cream
- ¼ cup chopped green onions

1. In a small bowl, mash 1 can black beans; set aside. In a large saucepan, saute the celery, onion, red pepper and jalapeno in oil until tender. Add garlic; cook 1 minute longer.
2. Stir in the broth, tomatoes, cumin, coriander, hot sauce, pepper, bay leaf, mashed black beans and remaining whole beans. Bring to a boil. Reduce heat; cover and simmer for 15 minutes.
3. Discard bay leaf. Stir in lime juice. Garnish each serving with 1 Tbsp. sour cream and 1½ tsp. green onion.
Note: Wear disposable gloves when cutting hot peppers; the oils can burn skin. Avoid touching your face.
1 cup: 222 cal., 5g fat (1g sat. fat), 5mg chol., 779mg sod., 32g carb. (7g sugars, 9g fiber), 11g pro.

❄

CARIBBEAN POTATO SOUP

An interesting blend of veggies that includes okra, kale and black-eyed peas goes into this bright and hearty soup. No kale on hand? Use spinach instead.
—*Crystal Jo Bruns, Iliff, CO*

TAKES: 30 min.
MAKES: 6 servings (2¼ qt.)

- 2 medium onions, chopped
- 2 tsp. canola oil
- 3 garlic cloves, minced
- 2 tsp. minced fresh gingerroot
- 2 tsp. ground coriander
- 1 tsp. ground turmeric
- ½ tsp. dried thyme
- ¼ tsp. ground allspice
- 5 cups vegetable broth
- 2 cups cubed peeled sweet potato
- 3 cups chopped fresh kale
- 1 cup frozen sliced okra
- 1 cup coconut milk
- 1 cup canned diced tomatoes, drained
- 1 cup canned black-eyed peas, rinsed and drained
- 2 Tbsp. lime juice

1. In a Dutch oven, saute onions in oil until tender. Add the garlic, ginger and spices; cook 1 minute longer.
2. Stir in the broth and potato. Bring to a boil. Reduce the heat; cover and simmer for 5 minutes. Stir in kale and okra. Return to a boil; cover and simmer 10 minutes longer or until potato is tender. Add milk, tomatoes, peas and juice; heat through.
Freeze option: Freeze the cooled soup in freezer containers. To use, partially thaw in refrigerator overnight. Heat through in a saucepan, stirring occasionally; add broth or water if necessary.
1½ cups: 213 cal., 10g fat (7g sat. fat), 0 chol., 954mg sod., 28g carb. (9g sugars, 6g fiber), 5g pro.

GENERAL TSO'S
CAULIFLOWER

ASPARAGUS TOFU STIR-FRY

With its flavorful ginger sauce and fresh vegetables, this tasty dish is a favorite. I get rave reviews every time I serve it to family and friends. I like that it doesn't bother my husband's food allergies.
—*Phyllis Smith, Chimacum, WA*

PREP: 15 min. • **COOK:** 20 min.
MAKES: 4 servings

- 1 Tbsp. cornstarch
- ½ tsp. sugar
- 1¼ cups vegetable broth
- 4 tsp. reduced-sodium soy sauce
- 2 tsp. minced fresh gingerroot, divided
- 3 tsp. canola oil, divided
- 1 lb. fresh asparagus, trimmed and cut into 1-in. pieces
- 1 medium yellow summer squash, halved and sliced
- 2 green onions, thinly sliced
- 1 pkg. (14 oz.) extra-firm tofu, drained and cut into ½-in. cubes
- ¼ tsp. salt
- ¼ tsp. pepper
- 2 cups hot cooked brown rice
- 2 Tbsp. sliced almonds, toasted

1. In a small bowl, combine cornstarch, sugar, broth and soy sauce until smooth; set aside.
2. In a large nonstick skillet or wok, stir-fry 1 tsp. ginger in 1 tsp. oil for 1 minute. Add the asparagus; stir-fry for 2 minutes. Add squash; stir-fry 2 minutes longer. Add the onions; stir-fry 1 minute longer or until vegetables are crisp-tender. Remove and keep warm.
3. In same pan, stir-fry tofu, salt, pepper and the remaining ginger in remaining oil for 7-9 minutes or until lightly browned. Remove and keep warm.
4. Stir cornstarch mixture; add to the pan. Bring to a boil; cook and stir for 2 minutes or until thickened. Add asparagus mixture and tofu; heat through. Serve with the rice; sprinkle with almonds.
1 cup: 278 cal., 11g fat (1g sat. fat), 0 chol., 682mg sod., 34g carb. (4g sugars, 4g fiber), 14g pro. **Diabetic exchanges:** 2 starch, 1 vegetable, 1 lean meat, 1 fat.

GENERAL TSO'S CAULIFLOWER

Cauliflower florets are deep-fried to a crispy golden brown, then coated in a sauce with just the right amount of kick. This is a fun alternative to the classic chicken dish.
—*Nick Iverson, Denver, CO*

PREP: 25 min. • **COOK:** 20 min.
MAKES: 4 servings

Oil for deep-fat frying
- ½ cup all-purpose flour
- ½ cup cornstarch
- 1 tsp. salt
- 1 tsp. baking powder
- ¾ cup club soda
- 1 medium head cauliflower, cut into 1-in. florets (about 6 cups)

SAUCE
- ¼ cup orange juice
- 3 Tbsp. sugar
- 3 Tbsp. soy sauce
- 3 Tbsp. vegetable broth
- 2 Tbsp. rice vinegar
- 2 tsp. sesame oil
- 2 tsp. cornstarch
- 2 Tbsp. canola oil
- 2 to 6 dried pasilla or other hot chiles, chopped
- 3 green onions, white part minced, green part thinly sliced
- 3 garlic cloves, minced
- 1 tsp. grated fresh gingerroot
- ½ tsp. grated orange zest
- 4 cups hot cooked rice

1. In an electric skillet or deep fryer, heat oil to 375°. Combine flour, cornstarch, salt and baking powder. Stir in club soda just until blended (the batter will be thin). Dip florets, a few at a time, into batter and fry until tender and coating is light brown, 8-10 minutes. Drain on paper towels.
2. For the sauce, in a small bowl, whisk together the first 6 ingredients; whisk in cornstarch until smooth.
3. In a large saucepan, heat canola oil over medium-high heat. Add chiles; cook and stir until fragrant, 1-2 minutes. Add white part of onions, garlic, ginger and orange zest; cook until fragrant, about 1 minute. Stir the soy sauce mixture; add to the saucepan. Bring to a boil; cook and stir until thickened, 2-4 minutes.
4. Add cauliflower to sauce; toss to coat. Serve with rice; sprinkle with thinly sliced green onions.
1 cup with 1 cup rice: 584 cal., 17g fat (2g sat. fat), 0 chol., 1628mg sod., 97g carb. (17g sugars, 5g fiber), 11g pro.

ASPARAGUS TOFU
STIR-FRY

DILLY CHICKPEA SALAD SANDWICHES

This chickpea salad is super flavorful and contains less fat and cholesterol than chicken salad. These make delightful picnic sandwiches.
—*Deanna Wolfe, Muskegon, MI*

TAKES: 15 min. • **MAKES:** 6 servings

- 1 can (15 oz.) chickpeas or garbanzo beans, rinsed and drained
- ½ cup finely chopped onion
- ½ cup finely chopped celery
- ½ cup reduced-fat mayonnaise or vegan mayonnaise
- 3 Tbsp. honey mustard or Dijon mustard
- 2 Tbsp. snipped fresh dill
- 1 Tbsp. red wine vinegar
- ¼ tsp. salt
- ¼ tsp. paprika
- ¼ tsp. pepper
- 12 slices multigrain bread
  Optional toppings: Romaine leaves, tomato slices, dill pickle slices and sweet red pepper rings

Place chickpeas in a large bowl; mash to desired consistency. Stir in onion, celery, mayonnaise, mustard, dill, vinegar, salt, paprika and pepper. Spread over 6 bread slices; layer with toppings of your choice and remaining bread.
1 sandwich: 295 cal., 11g fat (2g sat. fat), 7mg chol., 586mg sod., 41g carb. (9g sugars, 7g fiber), 10g pro.

COOL BEANS SALAD

This protein-filled dish could be served as a colorful side dish or a meatless main entree. When you make it, you'll want to double the recipe because it will be gone in a flash! Basmati rice adds unique flavor, and the dressing gives it a bit of a tang.
—*Janelle Lee, Appleton, WI*

TAKES: 20 min. • **MAKES:** 6 servings

- ½ cup olive oil
- ¼ cup red wine vinegar
- 1 Tbsp. sugar
- 1 garlic clove, minced
- 1 tsp. salt
- 1 tsp. ground cumin
- 1 tsp. chili powder
- ¼ tsp. pepper
- 3 cups cooked basmati rice
- 1 can (16 oz.) kidney beans, rinsed and drained
- 1 can (15 oz.) black beans, rinsed and drained
- 1½ cups frozen corn, thawed
- 4 green onions, sliced
- 1 small sweet red pepper, chopped
- ¼ cup minced fresh cilantro

In a large bowl, whisk first 8 ingredients. Add the remaining ingredients; toss to coat. Chill until serving.
1⅓ cups: 440 cal., 19g fat (3g sat. fat), 0 chol., 659mg sod., 58g carb. (5g sugars, 8g fiber), 12g pro.

TEST KITCHEN TIP

Giving this salad some time to soak in the blissful dressing makes a huge flavor difference. The longer it sits, the better it tastes. Just give it a quick stir before serving.

COOL BEANS SALAD

EGGPLANT ROLL-UPS

We love these easy Italian eggplant roll-ups stuffed with creamy ricotta and spinach. The fact that they are vegetarian is a bonus, especially when you're cooking for people following different diets.
—*Laura Haugen, Portland, OR*

PREP: 50 min. • **BAKE:** 20 min.
MAKES: 6 servings

- 2 medium eggplants (about 2½ lbs.), divided
  Cooking spray
- ½ tsp. salt
- 3 cups fresh spinach leaves

SAUCE
- 1 Tbsp. olive oil
- 2 garlic cloves, minced
- 1 can (14½ oz.) diced tomatoes
- 1 can (15 oz.) tomato puree
- 3 Tbsp. minced fresh basil or 3 tsp. dried basil
- 2 tsp. sugar
- 1 tsp. dried oregano
- ¼ tsp. salt
- ¼ tsp. pepper

FILLING
- 1 carton (15 oz.) reduced-fat ricotta cheese
- ¼ cup grated Parmesan cheese
- ½ tsp. dried oregano
- ¼ tsp. pepper
  Dash ground nutmeg

TOPPING
- ¼ cup grated Parmesan cheese
- 3 Tbsp. panko bread crumbs
  Minced fresh parsley, optional

1. Preheat oven to 400°. Cut the eggplants lengthwise into eighteen ¼-in.-thick slices, reserving leftover pieces. Line 2 baking sheets with foil. Coat both sides of the eggplant slices with cooking spray; place in a single layer on prepared pans. Sprinkle the eggplant with ½ tsp. salt. Bake until just pliable (do not let soften completely), 10-12 minutes; cool slightly.
2. Meanwhile, in a large saucepan, bring ½ in. of water to a boil. Add spinach; cover and boil 2-3 minutes or until wilted. Drain spinach and squeeze dry. Chop spinach and set aside.
3. For sauce, finely chop leftover eggplant pieces to measure 1 cup (discard the remaining or save for another use). In a large saucepan, heat oil over medium heat. Add the chopped eggplant; cook and stir until tender. Add garlic; cook 1 minute longer. Stir in tomatoes, tomato puree, basil, sugar, oregano, salt and pepper. Bring to a boil. Reduce heat; simmer, uncovered, 8-10 minutes or until the flavors are blended.
4. Spread 1 cup sauce into a 13x9-in. baking dish coated with cooking spray. In a bowl, combine filling ingredients and spinach. Place 1 rounded Tbsp. of filling on the wide end of each eggplant slice; carefully roll up. Place roll-ups in baking dish over the sauce, seam side down. Top with 1½ cups sauce. In a small bowl, mix Parmesan cheese and bread crumbs; sprinkle over the top. Bake until heated through and bubbly, 20-25 minutes. Serve with the remaining sauce and, if desired, sprinkle with parsley.
3 roll-ups: 257 cal., 10g fat (3g sat. fat), 23mg chol., 652mg sod., 28g carb. (14g sugars, 8g fiber), 12g pro. **Diabetic exchanges:** 2 starch, 2 medium-fat meat, ½ fat.

EGGPLANT
ROLL-UPS

VEGETABLE PAD THAI

VEGETABLE PAD THAI

Classic flavors of Thailand abound in this fragrant and flavorful dish featuring peanuts, tofu and noodles. Tofu gives the entree its satisfying protein.
—*Sara Landry, Brookline, MA*

- -

PREP: 25 min. • **COOK:** 15 min.
MAKES: 6 servings

- 1   pkg. (12 oz.) whole wheat fettuccine
- ¼   cup rice vinegar
- 3   Tbsp. reduced-sodium soy sauce
- 2   Tbsp. brown sugar
- 2   Tbsp. fish sauce or additional reduced-sodium soy sauce
- 1   Tbsp. lime juice
      Dash Louisiana-style hot sauce
- 3   tsp. canola oil, divided
- 1   pkg. (12 oz.) extra-firm tofu, drained and cut into ½-in. cubes
- 2   medium carrots, grated
- 2   cups fresh snow peas
- 3   garlic cloves, minced
- 2   large eggs, lightly beaten
- 2   cups bean sprouts
- 3   green onions, chopped
- ½   cup minced fresh cilantro
- ¼   cup unsalted peanuts, chopped

1. Cook fettuccine according to package directions. Meanwhile, in a small bowl, combine vinegar, soy sauce, brown sugar, fish sauce, lime juice and hot sauce until smooth; set aside.
2. In a large skillet or wok heat 2 tsp. oil over medium-high heat. Add tofu; cook and stir until golden brown, 4-6 minutes. Remove and keep warm. Cook and stir the carrots and snow peas in remaining 1 tsp. oil until crisp-tender, 3-5 minutes. Add garlic; cook 1 minute longer. Add eggs; cook and stir until set.
3. Drain pasta; add to vegetable mixture. Stir vinegar mixture and add to the skillet. Bring to a boil. Add the tofu, bean sprouts and onions; heat through. Sprinkle with cilantro and peanuts.
1⅓ cups: 404 cal., 11g fat (2g sat. fat), 62mg chol., 951mg sod., 59g carb. (13g sugars, 9g fiber), 20g pro.

GRILLED EGGPLANT
PANINI WITH BASIL AIOLI

GRILLED EGGPLANT PANINI WITH BASIL AIOLI

I love being able to use the bounty of fresh vegetables and herbs from my garden for summer meals. This sandwich is loaded with veggies and has such a satisfying crunch. The melty provolone finishes things off perfectly.
—*Joseph A. Sciascia, San Mateo, CA*

- -

PREP: 25 min. • **GRILL:** 20 min.
MAKES: 4 servings

- ¾   cup mayonnaise
- ⅓   cup chopped fresh basil
- 3   Tbsp. grated Parmesan cheese
- 2   Tbsp. minced fresh chives
- 1   Tbsp. lemon juice
- 2   garlic cloves, minced
- ½   tsp. salt
- ½   tsp. pepper
- 1   large eggplant, cut into 8 slices
- 2   large sweet red peppers, cut into large pieces
- 2   Tbsp. olive oil
- 4   ciabatta rolls, split
- 8   slices provolone cheese

1. For aioli, place the first 8 ingredients in a blender; cover and process until smooth.
2. Brush the vegetables with oil. Place in broiling pan and broil in oven 3-4 in. from heat, or grill, covered, over medium heat until tender, 4-5 minutes per side. Chop the peppers when cool enough to handle.
3. Spread the cut sides of each roll with 2 Tbsp. aioli; top each with 2 slices of cheese. Layer bottoms with the eggplant and peppers. Replace tops.
4. In a panini press, grill sandwiches until the cheese is melted, 5-7 minutes. Serve remaining aioli with sandwiches or save for another use.
1 sandwich: 732 cal., 38g fat (11g sat. fat), 33mg chol., 1116mg sod., 83g carb. (12g sugars, 9g fiber), 23g pro.

TEST KITCHEN TIP
Try cooking these sandwiches on an outdoor grill! Just wrap individually in foil, then cook for 2-3 minutes on each side.

HERBED ARTICHOKE CHEESE TORTELLINI

Vegetarians as well as meat-and-potato lovers both rave about this flavor-packed meatless recipe with tomatoes, black olives and artichoke hearts tossed with tender cheese tortellini.
—*Karen Anzelc, Peoria, AZ*

TAKES: 30 min. • **MAKES:** 8 servings

- 2 cans (14½ oz. each) Italian diced tomatoes
- 2 jars (6½ oz. each) marinated quartered artichoke hearts
- ½ cup olive oil
- 2 medium onions, chopped
- ½ cup minced fresh parsley
- 2 to 4 Tbsp. minced fresh basil or 2 to 4 tsp. dried basil
- ½ tsp. dried oregano
- 2 garlic cloves, minced
- ⅛ tsp. crushed red pepper flakes
- 2 pkg. (9 oz. each) refrigerated cheese tortellini
- 1 can (2¼ oz.) sliced ripe olives, drained
- ½ tsp. salt
- ¼ cup shredded Parmesan cheese

1. Drain tomatoes, reserving ⅔ cup juice. Drain artichoke hearts, reserving ¾ cup marinade; chop artichokes.
2. In a Dutch oven, heat oil over medium-high heat. Add the onions, herbs, garlic and pepper flakes; cook and stir until onion is tender, 4-5 minutes. Stir in the tomatoes and reserved tomato juice and artichoke marinade; bring to a boil. Reduce the heat; simmer, uncovered, for 10-12 minutes or until slightly thickened. Meanwhile, cook tortellini according to package directions.
3. Drain the tortellini; add to the tomato mixture. Gently stir in olives, salt and artichoke hearts; heat through. Sprinkle with cheese.
1¼ cups: 474 cal., 28g fat (7g sat. fat), 29mg chol., 975mg sod., 45g carb. (12g sugars, 3g fiber), 11g pro.

🍎 CREAMY LENTILS WITH KALE ARTICHOKE SAUTE

I've been trying to eat more meatless meals, so I experimented with this hearty saute and served it over brown rice. It was so good that even those who aren't big fans of kale gobbled it up.
—*Teri Rasey, Cadillac, MI*

TAKES: 30 min. • **MAKES:** 4 servings

- ½ cup dried red lentils, rinsed and sorted
- ¼ tsp. dried oregano
- ⅛ tsp. pepper
- 1¼ cups vegetable broth
- ¼ tsp. sea salt, divided
- 1 Tbsp. olive oil or grapeseed oil
- 16 cups chopped fresh kale (about 12 oz.)
- 1 can (14 oz.) water-packed artichoke hearts, drained and chopped
- 3 garlic cloves, minced
- ½ tsp. Italian seasoning
- 2 Tbsp. grated Romano cheese
- 2 cups hot cooked brown or basmati rice

1. Place the first 4 ingredients and ⅛ tsp. salt in a small saucepan; bring to a boil. Reduce heat; simmer, covered, until lentils are tender and liquid is almost absorbed, 12-15 minutes. Remove from heat.
2. In a 6-qt. stockpot, heat oil over medium heat. Add kale and remaining salt; cook, covered, until kale is wilted, 4-5 minutes, stirring occasionally. Add artichoke hearts, garlic and Italian seasoning; cook and stir 3 minutes. Remove from the heat; stir in the Romano cheese.
3. Serve lentils and kale mixture over rice.
1 serving: 321 cal., 6g fat (2g sat. fat), 1mg chol., 661mg sod., 53g carb. (1g sugars, 5g fiber), 15g pro.

DID YOU KNOW?

Of all varieties, red lentils cook the fastest, mainly because they're split during processing. Since they're split, red lentils break down while cooking and don't hold their shape like brown lentils. Don't be surprised by the soft texture of this dish.

CREAMY LENTILS WITH KALE ARTICHOKE SAUTE

GREAT GRAIN
BURGERS

GREAT GRAIN BURGERS

I've experimented with many combinations of ingredients to make a good meatless burger and this is our favorite. The patties cook up golden brown and crispy.
—*Pat Whitaker, Alsea, OR*

PREP: 45 min. + chilling • **COOK:** 30 min.
MAKES: 12 servings

- ½ cup uncooked brown rice
- ½ cup uncooked bulgur
- 1 Tbsp. salt-free seasoning blend
- ¼ tsp. poultry seasoning
- 2 cups water
- ¼ cup egg substitute
- ½ cup fat-free cottage cheese
- 2 cups finely chopped fresh mushrooms
- ¾ cup old-fashioned oats
- ⅓ cup finely chopped onion
- 2 Tbsp. minced fresh parsley
- 1 tsp. salt
- ½ tsp. dried basil
- ⅛ tsp. celery seed
- 1 cup shredded part-skim mozzarella cheese
- ¼ cup shredded reduced-fat cheddar cheese
- 3 tsp. canola oil, divided
- 12 sandwich rolls
  Optional toppings: Watercress and tomato, red onion and avocado slices

1. Place the first 5 ingredients in a large saucepan; bring to a boil. Reduce heat; simmer, covered, until the rice is tender, about 30 minutes. Remove to a bowl; cool slightly. Refrigerate, covered, until cold.
2. Place the egg substitute and cottage cheese in a blender; cover and process until smooth. Transfer to a large bowl. Stir in mushrooms, oats, onion, parsley and seasonings. Add mozzarella cheese, cheddar cheese and rice mixture; mix well. Refrigerate, covered, 2 hours or overnight before shaping.
3. Shape ½ cupfuls of mixture into patties, pressing to adhere. In a large nonstick skillet, heat 1 tsp. oil over medium heat; cook 4 patties until lightly browned, about 5 minutes per side. Repeat with remaining patties and oil. Serve on sandwich rolls with toppings as desired.
1 burger: 335 cal., 9g fat (3g sat. fat), 8mg chol., 701mg sod., 51g carb. (6g sugars, 3g fiber), 14g pro.

POLENTA CHILI CASSEROLE

This delicious vegetarian bake combines spicy chili, mixed veggies and homemade polenta. It's so hearty that no one seems to miss the meat.
—*Dan Kelmenson, West Bloomfield, MI*

PREP: 20 min. • **BAKE:** 35 min. + standing
MAKES: 8 servings

- 4 cups water
- ½ tsp. salt
- 1¼ cups yellow cornmeal
- 2 cups shredded cheddar cheese, divided
- 3 cans (15 oz. each) vegetarian chili with beans
- 1 pkg. (16 oz.) frozen mixed vegetables, thawed and well drained

1. Preheat oven to 350°. In a large heavy saucepan, bring the water and salt to a boil. Reduce heat to a gentle boil; slowly whisk in cornmeal. Cook and stir with a wooden spoon until polenta is thickened and pulls away cleanly from side of pan, 15-20 minutes.

2. Remove from the heat. Stir in ¼ cup cheddar cheese until melted.

3. Spread polenta into a 13x9-in. baking dish coated with cooking spray. Bake, uncovered, 20 minutes. Meanwhile, heat chili according to package directions.

4. Spread the vegetables over the polenta; top with chili. Sprinkle with the remaining cheese. Bake 12-15 minutes longer or until the cheese is melted. Let stand for 10 minutes before serving.

1 serving: 297 cal., 7g fat (4g sat. fat), 20mg chol., 556mg sod., 43g carb. (7g sugars, 12g fiber), 19g pro.

"Add a dollop of sour cream on top of this to make it extra yummy! A wonderful meal!"
—JAKNEE, TASTEOFHOME.COM

CUMIN QUINOA PATTIES (photo caption)

CUMIN QUINOA PATTIES

These easy-to-make veggie patties pack an amazing taste, and the crunch from the addition of quinoa makes the texture to die for. Pan-frying them brings the crunch to the next level. The mixture can be made ahead of time and it freezes very well. Enjoy!
—*Beth Klein, Arlington, VA*

TAKES: 30 min.
MAKES: 4 servings

- 1 cup water
- ½ cup quinoa, rinsed
- 1 medium carrot, cut into 1-in. pieces
- 1 cup canned cannellini beans, rinsed and drained
- ¼ cup panko bread crumbs
- 3 green onions, chopped
- 1 large egg, lightly beaten
- 3 tsp. ground cumin
- ¼ tsp. salt
- ⅛ tsp. pepper
- 2 Tbsp. olive oil
  Optional: Sour cream, salsa and minced fresh cilantro

1. In a small saucepan, bring water to a boil. Add the quinoa. Reduce the heat; simmer, covered, until liquid is absorbed, 12-15 minutes. Remove from heat; fluff with a fork.

2. Meanwhile, place the carrot in a food processor; pulse until coarsely chopped. Add the beans; process until chopped. Transfer mixture to a large bowl. Mix in the cooked quinoa, bread crumbs, green onions, egg and seasonings. Shape the mixture into 8 patties.

3. In a skillet, heat oil over medium heat. Add patties; cook until a thermometer reads 160°, 3-4 minutes on each side, turning carefully. If desired, serve with sour cream, salsa and cilantro.

Freeze option: Freeze cooled quinoa patties in freezer containers, separating layers with waxed paper. To use, reheat patties on a baking sheet in a preheated 325° oven until heated through.

2 patties: 235 cal., 10g fat (1g sat. fat), 47mg chol., 273mg sod., 28g carb. (2g sugars, 5g fiber), 8g pro. **Diabetic exchanges:** 2 starch, 1½ fat, 1 lean meat.

POLENTA
CHILI CASSEROLE

GARDEN VEGETABLE GNOCCHI

When we go meatless, we toss gnocchi (my husband's favorite) with veggies and a dab of prepared pesto. I use zucchini, too.
—*Elisabeth Larsen, Pleasant Grove, UT*

TAKES: 30 min. • **MAKES:** 4 servings

- 2 medium yellow summer squash, sliced
- 1 medium sweet red pepper, chopped
- 8 oz. sliced fresh mushrooms
- 1 Tbsp. olive oil
- ¼ tsp. salt
- ¼ tsp. pepper
- 1 pkg. (16 oz.) potato gnocchi
- ½ cup Alfredo sauce
- ¼ cup prepared pesto
  Chopped fresh basil, optional

1. Preheat oven to 450°. In a greased 15x10x1-in. baking pan, toss squash, pepper and mushrooms with oil, salt and pepper. Roast for 18-22 minutes or until tender, stirring once.
2. Meanwhile, in a large saucepan, cook gnocchi according to package directions. Drain and return to pan.
3. Stir in the roasted vegetables, Alfredo sauce and pesto. If desired, sprinkle with chopped fresh basil.
1½ cups: 402 cal., 14g fat (4g sat. fat), 17mg chol., 955mg sod., 57g carb. (12g sugars, 5g fiber), 13g pro.

BLACK BEAN & RICE ENCHILADAS

I love Mexican food, but I'm always looking for ways to make it a little more healthy. I modified a dish that I have enjoyed in restaurants to suit my taste and lifestyle.
—*Christie Ladd, Mechanicsburg, PA*

PREP: 40 min. • **BAKE:** 30 min.
MAKES: 8 servings

- 1 Tbsp. olive oil
- 1 green pepper, chopped
- 1 medium onion, chopped
- 3 garlic cloves, minced
- 1 can (15 oz.) black beans, rinsed and drained
- 1 can (14½ oz.) diced tomatoes and green chiles
- ¼ cup picante sauce
- 1 Tbsp. chili powder
- 1 tsp. ground cumin
- ¼ tsp. crushed red pepper flakes
- 2 cups cooked brown rice
- 8 flour tortillas (6 in.), warmed
- 1 cup salsa
- 1 cup shredded reduced-fat cheddar cheese
- 3 Tbsp. chopped fresh cilantro leaves
  Optional: Sliced red onion and jalapeno peppers

1. Preheat the oven to 350°. In a nonstick skillet, heat oil over medium heat. Add the green pepper, onion and garlic; saute until tender. Add the next 6 ingredients; bring to a boil. Reduce heat; simmer, uncovered, until heated through. Add the rice; cook 5 minutes longer.
2. Spoon a rounded ½ cup of rice mixture down center of each tortilla. Fold sides over filling and roll up. Place seam side down in a 13x9-in. baking dish coated with cooking spray. Spoon the remaining rice mixture along sides of dish. Top tortillas with salsa. Bake, covered, for 25 minutes. Uncover; sprinkle with cheese. Bake until the cheese is melted, 2-3 minutes longer. Sprinkle with the cilantro and, if desired, onions and jalapenos.
Freeze option: Cover and freeze unbaked enchiladas. To use, partially thaw in the refrigerator overnight. Remove 30 minutes before baking; top with salsa. Preheat oven to 350°. Cover enchiladas with foil; bake until heated through. Sprinkle with cheese. Bake 30-35 minutes or until the cheese is melted. Serve as directed.
1 enchilada: 279 cal., 8g fat (2g sat. fat), 10mg chol., 807mg sod., 39g carb. (4g sugars, 5g fiber), 11g pro. **Diabetic exchanges:** 2½ starch, 1 vegetable, 1 lean meat.

LENTIL LOAF

This lentil loaf is so flavorful, you won't miss the meat. And it's packed with fiber and nutrients. Serve it alongside mashed cauliflower for a complete meal.
—*Tracy Fleming, Phoenix, AZ*

- -

PREP: 35 min. • **BAKE:** 45 min. + standing
MAKES: 6 servings

¾ cup brown lentils, rinsed
1 can (14½ oz.) vegetable broth
1 Tbsp. olive oil
1¾ cups shredded carrots
1 cup finely chopped onion
1 cup chopped fresh mushrooms
2 Tbsp. minced fresh basil or 2 tsp. dried basil
1 Tbsp. minced fresh parsley
½ cup cooked brown rice

1 cup shredded part-skim mozzarella cheese
½ cup cooked brown rice
1 large egg
1 large egg white
½ tsp. salt
½ tsp. garlic powder
¼ tsp. pepper
2 Tbsp. tomato paste
2 Tbsp. water

1. Place the lentils and broth in a small saucepan; bring to a boil. Reduce the heat; simmer, covered, until tender, about 30 minutes.
2. Preheat oven to 350°. Line a 9x5-in. loaf pan with parchment, letting ends extend up sides. Coat paper with cooking spray.
3. In a skillet, heat oil over medium heat; saute carrots, onion and mushrooms until tender, about 10 minutes. Stir in herbs. Transfer to a large bowl; cool slightly.
4. Add the rice, cheese, egg, egg white, seasonings and lentils to vegetables; mix well. Transfer to prepared loaf pan. Mix tomato paste and water; spread over loaf.
5. Bake until a thermometer inserted into the center reads 160°, 45-50 minutes. Let stand 10 minutes before slicing.
1 piece: 213 cal., 5g fat (3g sat. fat), 43mg chol., 580mg sod., 29g carb. (5g sugars, 5g fiber), 14g pro. **Diabetic exchanges:** 2 lean meat, 1½ starch, 1 vegetable, ½ fat.

TEST KITCHEN TIP

A good ol' box grater works great for shredding carrots. You need about 4 medium-sized carrots to yield 2 cups shredded.

LENTIL
LOAF

REFRIED BEAN TOSTADAS

REFRIED BEAN TOSTADAS

Your family won't miss the meat in these tasty tostadas topped with refried beans, corn, zucchini and salsa.
—Taste of Home *Test Kitchen*

- -

TAKES: 30 min. • **MAKES:** 6 tostadas

- 6 flour tortillas (8 in.)
- ½ lb. sliced fresh mushrooms
- 1 cup diced zucchini
- 2 Tbsp. canola oil
- 1 jar (16 oz.) chunky salsa
- 1 can (7 oz.) white or shoepeg corn, drained
- 1 can (16 oz.) vegetarian refried beans, warmed
- 1½ cups shredded lettuce
- 1½ cups shredded cheddar cheese
- 2 medium ripe avocados, peeled and sliced
- 1½ cups chopped tomatoes
- 6 Tbsp. sour cream

1. In an ungreased skillet, cook tortillas for 1-2 minutes on each side or until lightly browned. Remove and set aside.
2. In the same skillet, saute mushrooms and zucchini in oil until crisp-tender. Add salsa and corn; cook for 2-3 minutes or until heated through.
3. Spread refried beans over each tortilla; top with lettuce, salsa mixture, cheese, avocados, tomatoes and sour cream.

1 tostada: 588 cal., 31g fat (10g sat. fat), 40mg chol., 1250mg sod., 60g carb. (9g sugars, 12g fiber), 19g pro.

"Delicious! This recipe was fantastic, and my family liked it better than the traditional tostadas with beef or chicken on them. I'm vegan, so I used vegan cheese and left out the sour cream. I also added some chopped onion to the mushroom and zucchini. I will be making this recipe over and over again."
—SERENEPHOENIX, TASTEOFHOME.COM

GREEK SALAD RAVIOLI

🍎 ❄
GREEK SALAD RAVIOLI

Turn the fresh flavors of a Greek salad into a warm dish for cold winter nights. I like to make a large batch and freeze it.
—*Carla Mendres, Winnipeg, MB*

- -

PREP: 45 min. • **COOK:** 5 min./batch
MAKES: 8 servings

- 10 oz. (about 12 cups) fresh baby spinach
- ½ cup finely chopped roasted sweet red peppers
- ½ cup pitted and finely chopped ripe olives
- ½ cup crumbled feta cheese
- 3 Tbsp. snipped fresh dill
- 2 to 3 tsp. dried oregano
- 2 Tbsp. butter
- 3 Tbsp. all-purpose flour
- 2 cups whole milk
- 96 pot sticker or gyoza wrappers
  Additional snipped fresh dill, optional
  Sauce of your choice

1. In a large skillet over medium heat, cook and stir spinach in batches until wilted, 3-4 minutes. Drain on paper towels. In a bowl, combine spinach with next 5 ingredients.
2. In a small saucepan, melt butter over medium heat. Stir in flour until smooth; gradually whisk in milk. Bring to a boil, stirring constantly, until sauce thickens and coats a spoon, 2-3 minutes. Stir into spinach mixture.
3. Place 1 Tbsp. spinach mixture in center of a pot sticker wrapper. (Cover remaining wrappers with a damp paper towel until ready to use.) Moisten wrapper edges with water, and place another wrapper on top. Press the edges to seal. Repeat with the remaining wrappers.
4. Fill a Dutch oven two-thirds full with water; bring to a boil. Reduce the heat; drop ravioli in batches into simmering water until cooked through, 3-4 minutes. If desired, sprinkle with additional dill. Serve with sauce of your choice.

Freeze option: Cover and freeze uncooked ravioli on waxed paper-lined baking sheets until firm. Transfer to freezer containers; return to freezer. To use, cook as directed, increasing time to 6 minutes.

Note: Wonton wrappers may be substituted for the pot sticker or gyoza wrappers. Stack 2 or 3 wonton wrappers on a work surface; cut into circles with a 3½-in. biscuit or round cookie cutter. Fill and wrap as directed.

6 ravioli: 283 cal., 8g fat (4g sat. fat), 22mg chol., 442mg sod., 44g carb. (4g sugars, 2g fiber), 10g pro. **Diabetic exchanges:** 3 starch, 1 high-fat meat, 1 fat.

MEDITERRANEAN CHICKPEAS

Add this to your meatless Monday lineup.
It's great with feta cheese on top.
—*Elaine Ober, Brookline, MA*

TAKES: 25 min. • **MAKES:** 4 servings

- 1 cup water
- ¾ cup uncooked whole wheat couscous
- 1 Tbsp. olive oil
- 1 medium onion, chopped
- 2 garlic cloves, minced
- 1 can (15 oz.) chickpeas or garbanzo beans, rinsed and drained
- 1 can (14½ oz.) no-salt-added stewed tomatoes, cut up
- 1 can (14 oz.) water-packed artichoke hearts, rinsed, drained and chopped
- ½ cup pitted Greek olives, coarsely chopped
- 1 Tbsp. lemon juice
- ½ tsp. dried oregano
- Dash pepper
- Dash cayenne pepper

1. In a small saucepan, bring water to a boil. Stir in couscous. Remove from heat; let stand, covered, 5-10 minutes or until water is absorbed. Fluff with a fork.
2. Meanwhile, in a large nonstick skillet, heat oil over medium-high heat. Add onion; cook and stir until tender. Add garlic; cook 1 minute longer. Sir in the remaining ingredients; heat through, stirring occasionally. Serve with couscous.
1 cup chickpea mixture with ⅔ cup couscous: 340 cal., 10g fat (1g sat. fat), 0 chol., 677mg sod., 51g carb. (9g sugars, 9g fiber), 11g pro.

SPICY BREAKFAST PIZZA

SPICY BREAKFAST PIZZA

Eggs and hash browns have extra pizazz when they're served up on a pizza pan. My family requests this fun breakfast often and it's a snap to make with prebaked crust. I adjust the heat index of the toppings to suit the taste buds of my diners.
—*Christy Hinrichs, Parkville, MO*

TAKES: 30 min. • **MAKES:** 6 servings

- 2 cups frozen shredded hash brown potatoes
- ¼ tsp. ground cumin
- ¼ tsp. chili powder
- 2 Tbsp. canola oil, divided
- 4 large eggs
- 2 Tbsp. 2% milk
- ¼ tsp. salt
- 2 green onions, chopped
- 2 Tbsp. diced sweet red pepper
- 1 Tbsp. finely chopped jalapeno pepper
- 1 garlic clove, minced
- 1 prebaked 12-in. thin pizza crust
- ½ cup salsa
- ¾ cup shredded cheddar cheese

1. Preheat the oven to 375°. In a large nonstick skillet, cook the hash browns, cumin and chili powder in 1 Tbsp. oil over medium heat until golden. Remove and keep warm.
2. In a small bowl, beat the eggs, milk and salt; set aside. In the same skillet, saute onions, peppers and garlic in remaining 1 Tbsp. oil until tender. Add egg mixture. Cook and stir over medium heat until almost set. Remove from the heat.
3. Place crust on an ungreased round 14-in. cast-iron griddle or pizza pan. Spread salsa over crust. Top with the egg mixture. Sprinkle with hash browns and cheese. Bake until cheese is melted, 8-10 minutes.
Note: Wear disposable gloves when cutting hot peppers; the oils can burn skin. Avoid touching your face.
1 piece: 320 cal., 16g fat (5g sat. fat), 138mg chol., 605mg sod., 31g carb. (2g sugars, 1g fiber), 13g pro.

MUSHROOM & BROWN RICE HASH WITH POACHED EGGS

I made my mother's famous roast beef hash healthier by using cremini mushrooms instead of beef, and brown rice instead of potatoes. It's ideal for a light main dish.

—*Lily Julow, Lawrenceville, GA*

- -

TAKES: 30 min. • **MAKES:** 4 servings

- 2 Tbsp. olive oil
- 1 lb. sliced baby portobello mushrooms
- ½ cup chopped sweet onion
- 1 pkg. (8.8 oz.) ready-to-serve brown rice
- 1 large carrot, grated
- 2 green onions, thinly sliced
- ½ tsp. salt
- ¼ tsp. pepper
- ¼ tsp. caraway seeds
- 4 large eggs, cold

1. In a large skillet, heat oil over medium-high heat; saute mushrooms until lightly browned, 5-7 minutes. Add sweet onion; cook 1 minute. Add rice and carrot; cook and stir until the vegetables are tender, 4-5 minutes. Stir in green onions, salt, pepper and caraway seeds; heat through.

2. Meanwhile, place 2-3 in. water in a large saucepan or skillet with high sides. Bring to a boil; adjust heat to maintain a gentle simmer. Break cold eggs, 1 at a time, into a small bowl; holding the bowl close to surface of water, slip each egg into water.

3. Cook, uncovered, until the whites are completely set and yolks begin to thicken but are not hard, 3-5 minutes. Using a slotted spoon, lift the eggs out of water. Serve over rice mixture.

1 serving: 282 cal., 13g fat (3g sat. fat), 186mg chol., 393mg sod., 26g carb. (4g sugars, 3g fiber), 13g pro. **Diabetic exchanges:** 1½ starch, 1½ fat, 1 medium-fat meat.

TEST KITCHEN TIP

This is a great recipe for when you need to use up leftover rice, quinoa or roasted potatoes. You'll need about 2 cups in place of the package of ready-to-serve rice.

MUSHROOM & BROWN RICE HASH WITH POACHED EGGS

Recipe Index